ANNUAL EDITIONS

Marketing 11/12

Thirty-Fourth Edition

EDITOR

John E. Richardson
Pepperdine University

Dr. John E. Richardson is Professor of Marketing in The George L. Graziadio School of Business and Management at Pepperdine University. He is president of his own consulting firm and has consulted with organizations such as Bell and Howell, Dayton-Hudson, Epson, and the U.S. Navy, as well as with various service, nonprofit, and franchise organizations. Dr. Richardson is a member of the American Marketing Association, the American Management Association, the Society for Business Ethics, and Beta Gamma Sigma honorary business fraternity.

The McGraw-Hill Companies

ANNUAL EDITIONS: MARKETING, THIRTY-FOURTH EDITION

Published by McGraw-Hill, a business unit of The McGraw-Hill Companies, Inc., 1221 Avenue of the Americas, New York, NY 10020.
Annual Editions is published by the **Contemporary Learning Series** group within the McGraw-Hill Higher Education division.

1 2 3 4 5 6 7 8 9 0 QDB/QDB 1 0 9 8 7 6 5 4 3 2 1

ISBN 978-0-07-352864-9
MHID 0-07-352864-1
ISSN 0730-2606 (print)
ISSN 2159-0621 (online)

Managing Editor: *Larry Loeppke*
Developmental Editor: *Dave Welsh*
Permissions Supervisor: *Lenny J. Behnke*
Marketing Specialist: *Alice Link*
Project Manager: *Robin A. Reed*
Design Coordinator: *Margarite Reynolds*
Cover Graphics: *Kristine Jubeck*
Buyer: *Susan K. Culbertson*
Media Project Manager: *Sridevi Palani*

Compositor: Laserwords Private Limited
Cover images: © PhotoAlto (inset); Royalty-Free/CORBIS (background)

www.mhhe.com

Editors/Academic Advisory Board

Members of the Academic Advisory Board are instrumental in the final selection of articles for each edition of ANNUAL EDITIONS. Their review of articles for content, level, and appropriateness provides critical direction to the editors and staff. We think that you will find their careful consideration well reflected in this volume.

ANNUAL EDITIONS: Marketing 11/12

34th Edition

EDITOR

John E. Richardson
Pepperdine University

ACADEMIC ADVISORY BOARD MEMBERS

Preface

In publishing ANNUAL EDITIONS we recognize the enormous role played by the magazines, newspapers, and journals of the public press in providing current, first-rate educational information in a broad spectrum of interest areas. Many of these articles are appropriate for students, researchers, and professionals seeking accurate, current material to help bridge the gap between principles and theories and the real world. These articles, however, become more useful for study when those of lasting value are carefully collected, organized, indexed, and reproduced in a low-cost format, which provides easy and permanent access when the material is needed. That is the role played by ANNUAL EDITIONS.

The new millennium should prove to be an exciting and challenging time for the American business community. Recent dramatic social, economic, and technological changes have become an important part of the present marketplace. These changes—accompanied by increasing domestic and foreign competition—are leading a wide array of companies and industries toward the realization that better marketing must become a top priority now to assure their future success.

How does the marketing manager respond to this growing challenge? How does the marketing student apply marketing theory to the real-world practice? Many reach for the *Wall Street Journal, BusinessWeek, Fortune,* and other well-known sources of business information. There, specific industry and company strategies are discussed and analyzed, marketing principles are often reaffirmed by real occurrences, and textbook theories are supported or challenged by current events.

The articles reprinted in this edition of *Annual Editions: Marketing 11/12* have been carefully chosen from numerous public press sources to provide current information on marketing in the world today. Within these pages you will find articles that address marketing theory and application in a wide range of industries. In addition, the selections reveal how several firms interpret and utilize marketing principles in their daily operations and corporate planning.

The volume contains a number of features designed to make it useful for marketing students, researchers, and professionals. These include the *Topic Guide* to locate articles on specific marketing subjects; *Internet References* pages; the *Table of Contents* abstracts, which summarize each article and highlights key concepts; and a *Glossary* of key marketing terms. And new to this edition are Critical Thinking study questions after each article to help students better understand what they have read.

The articles are organized into four units. Selections that focus on similar issues are concentrated into subsections within the broader units. Each unit is preceded by a list of unit selections, as well as a list of key points to consider that focus on major themes running throughout the selections, web links that provide extra support for the unit's data, and an overview that provides background for informed reading of the articles and emphasizes critical issues.

This is the thirty-fourth edition of *Annual Editions: Marketing.* Since its first edition in the mid-1970s, the efforts of many individuals have contributed toward its success. We think this is by far the most useful collection of material available for the marketing student. We are anxious to know what you think. What are your opinions? What are your recommendations? Please take a moment to complete and return the *Article Rating Form* on the last page of this volume. Any book can be improved and this one will continue to be, annually.

John E. Richardson

John E. Richardson
Editor

Contents

UNIT 1
Marketing in the 2000s and Beyond

The concepts in bold italics are developed in the article. For further expansion, please refer to the Topic Guide.

UNIT 2
Research, Markets, and Consumer Behavior

The concepts in bold italics are developed in the article. For further expansion, please refer to the Topic Guide.

UNIT 3
Developing and Implementing Marketing Strategies

The concepts in bold italics are developed in the article. For further expansion, please refer to the Topic Guide.

UNIT 4
Global Marketing

The concepts in bold italics are developed in the article. For further expansion, please refer to the Topic Guide.

Correlation Guide

The *Annual Editions* series provides students with convenient, inexpensive access to current, carefully selected articles from the public press. **Annual Editions: Marketing 11/12** is an easy-to-use reader that presents articles on important topics such as *the future of marketing, developing marketing strategies,* and many more. For more information on *Annual Editions* and other *McGraw-Hill Contemporary Learning Series* titles, visit www.mhhe.com/cls.

This convenient guide matches the units in **Annual Editions: Marketing 11/12** with the corresponding chapters in three of our best-selling McGraw-Hill Marketing textbooks by Kerin et al. and Grewal/Levy.

Annual Editions: Marketing 11/12	Marketing: The Core, 4/e by Kerin et al.	Marketing, 10/e by Kerin et al.	Marketing, 3/e by Grewal/Levy
Unit 1: Marketing in the 2000s and Beyond	**Chapter 3:** Scanning the Marketing Environment **Chapter 4:** Ethical and Social Responsibility in Marketing	**Chapter 3:** Scanning the Marketing Environment **Chapter 4:** Ethical and Social Responsibility in Marketing	**Chapter 3:** Marketing Ethics **Chapter 12:** Services: The Intangible Product
Unit 2: Research, Markets, and Consumer Behavior	**Chapter 1:** Creating Customer Relationships and Value through Marketing **Chapter 5:** Understanding Consumer Behavior **Chapter 8:** Marketing Research: From Customer Insights to Actions	**Chapter 1:** Creating Customer Relationships and Value through Marketing **Chapter 5:** Understanding Consumer Behavior **Chapter 8:** Marketing Research: From Customer Insights to Actions	**Chapter 4:** Analyzing the Marketing Environment **Chapter 5:** Consumer Behavior **Chapter 9:** Marketing Research and Information Systems
Unit 3: Developing and Implementing Marketing Strategies	**Chapter 2:** Developing Successful Marketing and Organizational Strategies **Chapter 3:** Scanning the Marketing Environment **Chapter 6:** Understanding Organizations as Customers **Chapter 9:** Market Segmentation, Targeting, and Positioning **Chapter 12:** Pricing Products and Services **Chapter 13:** Managing Marketing Channels and Supply Chains **Chapter 14:** Retailing and Wholesaling **Chapter 15:** Integrated Marketing Communications and Direct Marketing **Chapter 16:** Advertising, Sales Promotion, and Public Relations **Chapter 17:** Personal Selling and Sales Management **Chapter 18:** Implementing Interactive and Multichannel Marketing	**Chapter 2:** Developing Successful Marketing and Organizational Strategies **Chapter 3:** Scanning the Marketing Environment **Chapter 6:** Understanding Organizations as Customers **Chapter 13:** Building the Price Foundation **Chapter 14:** Arriving at the Final Price **Chapter 15:** Managing Marketing Channels and Wholesaling **Chapter 16:** Customer-Driven Supply Chain and Logistics Management **Chapter 17:** Retailing **Chapter 18:** Integrated Marketing Communications and Direct Marketing **Chapter 19:** Advertising, Sales Promotion, and Public Relations **Chapter 21:** Implementing Interactive and Multichannel Marketing **Chapter 22:** Pulling It All Together: The Strategic Marketing Process	**Chapter 2:** Developing Marketing Strategies and a Marketing Plan **Chapter 6:** Business-to-Business Marketing **Chapter 8:** Segmentation, Targeting, and Positioning **Chapter 10:** Product, Branding, and Package Decisions **Chapter 11:** Developing New Products **Chapter 13:** Pricing Concepts for Establishing Value **Chapter 14:** Strategic Pricing Methods **Chapter 15:** Supply Chain Management **Chapter 16:** Retailing and Multi-Channel Marketing **Chapter 17:** Integrated Marketing Communications **Chapter 18:** Advertising and Sales Promotions
Unit 4: Global Marketing	**Chapter 7:** Understanding and Reaching Global Consumers and Markets	**Chapter 7:** Understanding and Reaching Global Consumers and Markets	**Chapter 7:** Global Marketing

Topic Guide

This topic guide suggests how the selections in this book relate to the subjects covered in your course. You may want to use the topics listed on these pages to search the Web more easily.

On the following pages a number of websites have been gathered specifically for this book. They are arranged to reflect the units of this Annual Editions reader. You can link to these sites by going to www.mhhe.com/cls.

All the articles that relate to each topic are listed below the bold-faced term.

Internet References

The following Internet sites have been selected to support the articles found in this reader. These sites were available at the time of publication. However, because websites often change their structure and content, the information listed may no longer be available. We invite you to visit www.mhhe.com/cls for easy access to these sites.

Annual Editions: Marketing 11/12

General Sources

Baruch College BusinessWeek—Harris Poll Demographics
www.businessweek.com/1997/18/b352511.htm

The Baruch College–Harris poll commissioned by *BusinessWeek* is used at this site to show interested businesses that are on the Net in the United States.

General Social Survey
(webapp.icpsr.umich.edu/cocoon/ICPSR-SERIES/00028.xml

The GSS (see DPLS Archive: http://DPLS.DACC.WISC.EDU/SAF/) is an almost annual personal interview survey of U.S. households that began in 1972. More than 35,000 respondents have answered 2,500 questions. It covers a broad range of variables, many of which relate to microeconomic issues.

BestOfAdvertising.net
www.bestofadvertising.net

This is a complete list of sites that include information on marketing research, marketing on the Internet, demographic sources, and organizations and associations. The site also features current books on the subject of marketing.

STAT-USA/Internet Site Economic, Trade, Business Information
www.stat-usa.gov

This site, from the U.S. Department of Commerce, contains Daily Economic News, Frequently Requested Statistical Releases, Information on Export and International Trade, Domestic Economic News and Statistical Series, and Databases.

U.S. Census Bureau Home Page
www.census.gov

This is a major source of social, demographic, and economic information, such as income/employment data and the latest indicators, income distribution, and poverty data.

UNIT 1: Marketing in the 2000s and Beyond

American Marketing Association Code of Ethics
www.marketingpower.com

At this American Marketing Association site, use the search mechanism to access the organization's Code of Ethics for marketers.

Futures Research Quarterly
www.wfs.org/frq.htm

Published by the World Future Society, this publication describes future research that encompasses both an evolving philosophy and a range of techniques, with the aim of assisting decision makers in all fields to understand better the potential consequences of decisions by developing images of alternative futures. From this page explore the current and back issues and What's Coming Up!

Center for Innovation in Product Development (CIPD)
web.mit.edu/cipd/research/prdctdevelop.htm

CIPD is one of the National Science Foundation's engineering research centers. It shares the goal of future product development with academia, industry, and government.

UNIT 2: Research, Markets, and Consumer Behavior

Canadian Innovation Centre
www.innovationcentre.ca

The Canadian Innovation Centre has developed a unique mix of innovation services that can help a company from idea to market launch. Their services are based on the review of 12,000 new product ideas through their technology and market assessment programs over the past 20 years.

BizMiner—Industry Analysis and Trends
www.bizminer.com/market_research.asp

The importance of using market research databases and pinpointing local and national trends, including details of industry and small business startups, is emphasized by this site of the Brandow Company that offers samples of market research profiles.

Small Business Center—Articles & Insights
www.bcentral.com/articles/krotz/123.asp

This article discusses five market intelligence blunders made by the giant retailer K-Mart. "There were warning signs that K-Mart management mishandled, downplayed or just plain ignored," Joanna L. Krotz says.

Maritz Marketing Research
www.maritzresearch.com

Maritz Marketing Research Inc. (MMRI) specializes in custom-designed research studies that link the consumer to the marketer through information. Go to Maritz Loyalty Marketing in the Maritz Companies menu to find resources to identify, retain, and grow your most valuable customers. Also visit Maritz Research for polls, stats, and archived research reports.

USADATA
www.usadata.com

This leading provider of marketing, company, advertising, and consumer behavior data offers national and local data covering the top 60 U.S. markets.

WWW Virtual Library: Demography & Population Studies
http://demography.anu.edu.au/VirtualLibrary

More than 150 links can be found at this major resource to keep track of information of value to researchers in the fields of demography and population studies.

UNIT 3: Developing and Implementing Marketing Strategies

American Marketing Association Homepage
www.marketingpower.com

This site of the American Marketing Association is geared to managers, educators, researchers, students, and global electronic members. It contains a search mechanism, definitions of marketing and market research, and links.

Internet References

Consumer Buying Behavior

www.courses.psu.edu/mktg/mktg220_rso3/sls_cons.htm

The Center for Academic Computing at Penn State posts this course data that includes a review of consumer buying behaviors; group, environment, and internal influences; problem-solving; and post-purchasing behavior.

UNIT 4: Global Marketing

International Trade Administration

www.ita.doc.gov

The U.S. Department of Commerce is dedicated to helping U.S. businesses compete in the global marketplace, and at this site it offers assistance through many web links under such headings as Trade Statistics, Cross-Cutting Programs, Regions and Countries, and Import Administration.

World Chambers Network

www.worldchambers.net

International trade at work is viewable at this site. For example, click on Global Business eXchange (GBX) for a list of active business opportunities worldwide or to submit your new business opportunity for validation.

World Trade Center Association OnLine

http://iserve.wtca.org

Data on world trade is available at this site that features information, services, a virtual trade fair, an exporter's encyclopedia, trade opportunities, and a resource center.

UNIT 1

Marketing in the 2000s and Beyond

Unit Selections

1. **Hot Stuff: Make These Top Trends Part of Your Marketing Mix,** Gwen Moran
2. **Evolve,** Chris Penttila
3. **The Unmarketables,** Piet Levy, John N. Frank, and Allison Enright
4. **Six Strategies for Successful Niche Marketing,** Eric K. Clemons, Paul F. Nunes, and Matt Reilly
5. **The Secrets of Marketing in a Web 2.0 World,** Salvatore Parise, Patricia J. Guinan, and Bruce D. Weinberg
6. **The Branding Sweet Spot,** Kevin Lane Keller and Frederick E. Webster, Jr.
7. **Putting Customers First: Nine Surefire Ways to Increase Brand Loyalty,** Kyle LaMalfa
8. **Making the Most of Customer Complaints,** Stefan Michel, David Bowen, and Robert Johnston
9. **When Service Means Survival,** Jena McGregor
10. **Become the Main Attraction,** Piet Levy
11. **Beyond Products,** Stephen W. Brown, Anders Gustafsson, and Lars Witell
12. **Imaginative Service,** Chip R. Bell and John R. Patterson
13. **Service with a Style,** Kitty Bean Yancey
14. **Marketers, Come on Down!,** Allison Enright and Elisabeth A. Sullivan
15. **Honest Innovation,** Calvin L. Hodock
16. **Trust in the Marketplace,** John E. Richardson and Linnea Bernard McCord
17. **Green Fallout,** Jason Daley

Learning Outcomes

- Dramatic changes are occurring in the marketing of products and services. What social and economic trends do you believe are most significant today, and how do you think these will affect marketing in the future?
- Theodore Levitt suggests that as times change, the marketing concept must be reinterpreted. Given the varied perspectives of the other articles in this unit, what do you think this reinterpretation will entail?
- In the present competitive business arena, is it possible for marketers to behave ethically in the environment and both survive and prosper? What suggestions can you give that could be incorporated into the marketing strategy for firms that want to be both ethical and successful?

Student Website

www.mhhe.com/cls

Internet References

American Marketing Association Code of Ethics
www.marketingpower.com

Futures Research Quarterly
www.wfs.org/frq.htm

Center for Innovation in Product Development (CIPD)
www.web.mit.edu/cipd/research/prdctdevelop.htm

"If we want to know what a business is we must start with its purpose. . . . There is only one valid definition of business purpose: to create a customer. What business thinks it produces is not of first importance—especially not to the future of the business or to its success. What the customer thinks he is buying, what he considers 'value' is decisive—it determines what a business is, what it produces, and whether it will prosper."

—Peter Drucker,
The Practice of Management

When Peter Drucker penned these words in 1954, American industry was just awakening to the realization that marketing would play an important role in the future success of businesses. The ensuing years have seen an increasing number of firms in highly competitive areas—particularly in the consumer goods industry—adopt a more sophisticated customer orientation and an integrated marketing focus.

The dramatic economic and social changes of the last decade have stirred companies in an even broader range of industries—from banking and air travel to communications—to the realization that marketing will provide them with their cutting edge. Demographic and lifestyle changes have splintered mass, homogeneous markets into many markets, each with different needs and interests. Deregulation has made once-protected industries vulnerable to the vagaries of competition. Vast and rapid technological changes are making an increasing number of products and services obsolete. Intense international competition, rapid expansion of the Internet-based economy, and the growth of truly global markets have many firms looking well beyond their national boundaries.

Indeed, it appears that during the new millennium marketing will take on a unique significance—and not just within the industrial sector. Social institutions of all kinds, which had thought themselves exempt from the pressures of the marketplace, are also beginning to recognize the need for marketing in the management of their affairs. Colleges and universities, charities, museums, symphony orchestras, and even hospitals are beginning to give attention the marketing concept—to provide what the consumer wants to buy.

The selections in this unit are grouped into four areas. Their purposes are to provide current perspectives on marketing, discuss differing views of the marketing concept, analyze the use of marketing by social institutions and nonprofit organizations, and examine the ethical and social responsibilities of marketing.

The articles in the first subsection provide significant clues about salient approaches and issues that marketers need to address in the future in order to create, promote, and sell their products and services in ways that meet the expectation of consumers.

The selections that address the marketing concept include "Putting Customers First," which suggests nine ways to increase customers' brand loyalty. The next two articles in this subsection reflect the importance of companies focusing on customer satisfaction and customer service. The last article in this subsection, "Become the Main Attraction," gives some practical suggestions for successful event marketing.

© Randy Allbritton/Getty Images

In the *Services and Social Marketing* subsection, the first article discusses why some manufacturers are branching out into the service business. The second article discloses the importance of delivering unique value and faster service to meet and exceed customer expectations. "Service with a Style" shows how Ritz-Carlton Chicago personifies service in its treatment of customers. The final article in this subsection reveals how six marketers have positioned their companies' services to respond to consumers' changing behaviors.

In the final subsection, *Marketing Ethics and Social Responsibility,* a careful look is taken at the strategic process and practice of incorporating ethics and social responsibility into the marketplace. "Honest Innovation" reveals that ethical issues in new product development could be hampering innovation growth. "Trust in the Marketplace" discusses the importance of gaining and maintaining customers' trust. The last article in this subsection, "Green Fallout," reflects that green marketing claims are now undergoing much closer scrutiny than in the past.

Hot Stuff

Make These Top Trends Part of Your Marketing Mix

GWEN MORAN

Still using the same marketing tactics you were using five years ago? Those won't work with today's shifting demographics and preferences. The U.S. population is older, more multicultural, more time-pressed and more jaded toward overt sales pitches than ever before. And your marketing strategy should be built accordingly.

So what's working? After consulting over a dozen experts in the field, we've uncovered the following hot trends in marketing.

Market on the Move

According to the Mobile Marketing Association, by 2008, 89 percent of brands will use text and multimedia messaging to reach their audiences, with nearly one-third planning to spend more than 10 percent of their marketing budgets on advertising in the medium. As phones with video capability become more prevalent, expect more rich media marketing options. Plus, now that mobile phone service providers are dipping their toes into the credit card pool—soon your phone or PDA may make plastic obsolete—customers will be relying on these devices more than ever.

"There are some low-cost mobile marketing onramps for small businesses," says Kim Bayne, author of *Marketing Without Wires.* "Businesses can implement opt-in text messaging services and coupons with their loyal customers. We've already seen local restaurants send the day's specials to nearby lunch patrons. The cost is fairly low, and it can be done from a PC, without involving a pricey service provider."

Go Online

"Think globally, act locally" is now the mantra for entrepreneurs advertising online. Online ad spending is up as much as 33 percent over last year, says David J. Moore, chairman and CEO of digital marketing firm 24/7 Real Media Inc. in New York City. Earlier this year, Google announced a new local advertising program linked to its map service and AdWords program, allowing businesses to drive some of Google's traffic to their brick-and-mortar locations.

"[Entrepreneurs] should pay attention to any targeting that allows them to increase advertising efficiency by reaching users in their particular geographic area," says Moore. Online ads are also migrating to podcasts and blogs, where advertisers can reach very specific niche audiences. And with increased access to broadband and the falling cost of video production, Moore foresees a rise in online video ads for businesses as well.

Court the Boom

A baby boomer turns 50 every 7 seconds—joining a population segment that will grow by 25 percent in the next decade while other segments remain flat.

Matt Thornhill, founder of consulting firm The Boomer Project, which helps businesses reach adults born between 1946 and 1964, says it's time for marketers to recalibrate their thinking about marketing to older adults. Boomers are a dynamic group that's much more open to new experiences and brands than previous generations of older adults have been.

Stephanie Lakhani found that to be true at her upscale Breathe Wellness Spas (www.breathetoheal.com) in Boise, Idaho. Catering primarily to boomers, the two spas bring in about $1.2 million per year. She says boomers are an excellent target, with disposable income and a tendency to refer business. "They expect perfect service," says Lakhani, 35, who adds, "They tend to travel and buy in groups, so giving them an incentive to refer a friend in the form of an upgrade or a thank you [gesture] works very well. They are also very responsive to direct mail."

Thornhill adds that marketers should target boomers by what they're doing instead of how old they are. "Boomers are living such cyclical lives. In their 40s or 50s, they could be going back to college, be empty nesters or be married a second time and raising a young family," he explains. "You wouldn't sell the same vacation package to all these people. So pick the lifestyle segment you're targeting, and focus on that."

Sindicate Simply

For something that's named Really Simple Syndication, few tools are more misunderstood or misused than RSS. Provided by such companies as Bloglines (www.bloglines.com) and NewsGator (www.newsgator.com), RSS lets you send and receive information without using e-mail. Instead, the information is sent directly to a subscriber, who receives it through an RSS reader. With browsers like Internet Explorer integrating such readers, we'll be seeing more information feeds. That could be a good thing—or not—depending on whether businesses use them properly.

"You don't need to blog to offer an RSS feed," says online marketing consultant Debbie Weil, author of *The Corporate Blogging Book.* "But you should have a blogging mind-set. Show the reader what's in it for them. Write clear and interesting headlines. There's a bit of an art to writing RSS [content]." She adds that you should break up your feeds by audience—customers, investors, media and the like—just as you would any other message distribution.

Jim Edwards, 38, uses a blog and RSS to promote his business, Guaranteed Response Marketing. "Whenever I publish an article, either through my blog [www.igottatellyou.com/blog] or through another site's RSS feeder, I expect to get 100 to 300 references back to me in a week," says Edwards, whose $2 million Lightfoot, Virginia, business provides electronic tutorials and publications. "It's a quick way to get links back to you, as well as to get on sites that people are actively looking at."

Use Social Networks

Customers are making friends online through social networking sites like MySpace.com. The massive site—boasting millions of users, all segmented by age, geography and interests—offers an unbridled opportunity for marketers, according to Libby Pigg, senior account manager at Edelman Interactive in New York City.

"You [can] launch a profile for your business and give it a personality," says Pigg, who has launched MySpace marketing campaigns for major consumer products companies. "It's similar to a dating site, where you tell people a bit about yourself. Then, you use the search function to find the group you want to target—maybe single people in New York [City] between 24 and 30—and contact them to become your 'friends.'"

A MySpace profile helped Taylor Bond generate interest in Egismoz.com, the electronics division of his $20 million retail company, Children's Orchard, in Ann Arbor, Michigan. Earlier this year, Bond sent invitations to some of the site's young, tech-savvy users. The key to maintaining their interest, he says, is to provide fresh content and special offers.

"We're seeing more people come into the store saying that they saw us on MySpace," says Bond, 44. "We're definitely seeing more traffic and feedback on the profile, and we're getting some incredible feedback about what's hot and what people want, so it's good for market research, too." Opportunities also exist on other networking sites like Friendster.com, LinkedIn .com, and even niche sites like Adholes.com, which focuses on the advertising community.

Advertise in Unusual Places

From valet tickets and hubcaps to T-shirts emblazoned with video displays, advertising is popping up in new places. A March survey of marketing executives by Blackfriars Communications entitled "Marketing 2006: 2006's Timid Start" found that business spending on traditional advertising continued its decline, and spending on nontraditional marketing methods—from online promotions to buzz marketing—rose 12 percent since late 2005.

Scott Montgomery, principal and creative director of Bradley and Montgomery, an advertising and branding firm in Indianapolis, says the shift in ad spending will continue as advertisers look to make their ad dollars more effective.

Make It Stick

Tap these marketing trends to get into customers' hearts and minds.

- **Multicultural Market:** By 2010, the buying power of American blacks and Hispanics is expected to exceed the gross domestic product of Canada, according to the Selig Center for Economic Growth at the University of Georgia in Athens. Make sure you're not overlooking this market. Rochelle Newman-Carrasco, CEO of Enlace Communications, a Los Angeles multicultural marketing firm, advises companies not only to translate materials when appropriate, but also to be conscious of cultural images: "In lifestyle shots, go beyond multicultural casting. Show scenes where the clothing, food and other backgrounds reflect different cultures."
- **Experiential Marketing:** Kathy Sherbrooke, president of Circles, an experiential marketing firm in Boston, says businesses must figure out the key messages of their brand and find ways for their staffs and locations to reflect that image—young and trendy, sophisticated and elegant, and so on. "Create an environment that's consistent with your brand," she says. She points to Apple Computer's retail stores, where clerks use handheld checkout machines and pull product bags out of their back pockets to reinforce the ease-of-use and streamlined processes for which Apple is known.
- **Customer Evangelism:** From hiring word-of-mouth marketing companies to creating incentives for customer referrals, businesses are placing more importance on customer evangelism, says Andrew Pierce, senior partner at New York City branding firm Prophet. "Companies need to be customer-centric for this to happen," he explains. "If you're not finding ways to increase value and inspire loyalty, it won't work."

At the simplest level, Pierce advises using customer testimonials to add credibility to marketing efforts, including webinars where customers talk about your company. More extreme examples include buzz marketing campaigns where happy customers talk up the product, or inviting customers to trade shows or other events where they can show their enthusiasm in person.

Montgomery and his team were the first to develop advertising programs on electrical outlets in airports. Reasoning that business travelers—one of the holy grail audiences marketers love—power up portable technology while waiting for their planes, it seemed a natural place to reach them.

"Smart marketers are looking [for] places where people are engaged," says Montgomery. "You have to target your message in a way that makes sense for [how] people behave."

Premium-ize Your Brand

Brands like Coach and Grey Goose vodka have mastered the art of taking everyday items and introducing luxe versions at much higher price points. Now, growing businesses are also going upscale with their products or services.

Andrew Rohm, professor of marketing at Northeastern University's College of Business Administration in Boston, says smaller businesses can often "trickle up" more easily than large brands, which may find that customers are resistant to accepting their more expensive offerings. "A small brand can reinvent itself without having to swim upstream against its image," says Rohm.

To posh up your product, he advises the same best practices as with any new offering: Do your research, and make sure there's a market for the product or service before you make your brand go bling.

Blog On

With the blogosphere more than 43.1 million blogs strong, according to blog search engine Technorati, it appears everyone and his grandmother are blogging. Robert Scoble, technical evangelist at Microsoft and author of *Naked Conversations: How Blogs Are Changing the Way That Businesses Talk With Customers,* believes blogs are important for businesses that want direct customer feedback. And development blogs, where businesses get direct input about products and services from readers, will soon become even more important, he says.

Scoble predicts a rise in regional blogs linked to Google's new local advertising program and Mapquest.com for quick access to directions, giving people more insight into the local businesses they want to frequent. He also says we'll see more video blogs, which won't replace text blogs but will more effectively communicate with some audiences. "If I'm trying to explain to you what [video game] Halo 2 is, I can write 10,000 words and I'm not going to get it right, but you can see a 2-minute video and you'll understand," he says.

Take these trends into consideration as you plan for the coming year. Not every idea may apply to your company, but most are market forces you can't afford to ignore.

Critical Thinking

1. Discuss some recent shifts in the demographic and socio-cultural environments in the United State.
2. Explain how technology impacts marketing strategies and decisions, namely promotional tactics.

Gwen Moran is Entrepreneur's "Retail Register" and "Quick Pick" columnist.

Evolve

The old business methods won't work anymore. It's time to evolve.

CHRIS PENTTILA

For companies feeling their way through the worst recession since the 1930s, it's easiest to stay focused on next quarter's numbers, improving operations and lowering costs where possible. Just stick with the playbook and keep your head down, and things will be fine, right?

Wrong. This recession is different from other recessions in its scope and depth, and the worst thing you can do is more of the same. Staying the course with your current business model "might let you survive a little bit longer, but you're not going to create that competitive advantage necessary for the long term," says Scott Anthony, president of Innosight, an innovation consulting firm, and author of next month's new book *The Silver Lining: An Innovation Playbook for Uncertain Times.*

You've got to change your game. But how can you do it? Here are seven ways to be a game changer right now:

Get comfortable with chaos. Globalization and technology are leading to constant economic turbulence. Being a game changer begins with a recognition of this new normality, says John A. Caslione, founder of GCS Business Capital, an M&A advisory company with offices worldwide, and co-author of *Chaotics: The Business of Managing and Marketing in the Age of Turbulence.* "[There's] going to be continuous turbulence punctuated by spurts of prosperity and downturns," he explains. "Understand that you're not going to be able to count on uninterrupted periods of prosperity."

Reassess your customers' values. This recession is changing people's mind-sets, not just their spending habits. It's still too early to tell what long-term impact this recession will have on customer behavior, but a more cautious, anxiety-ridden consumer has arisen in the short term. People are reevaluating their values and their purchases. How have your customers' values changed in the past six months, and how have their needs changed? The answers could spark new product and service ideas aimed at value-conscious consumers. Your company's closeness to customers is a huge advantage, so talk to them or work up a simple survey. Says Caslione, "You've got to be talking to your customers more than ever before to be able to understand how their needs are changing."

The Dos and Don'ts of Game Changing

Do

- Look at your business through the lens of another industry to find new ways to operate. If you're in manufacturing, how would you operate as a retailer, or vice versa?
- Talk to your customers about what they need today. This will help you find new competitive advantages.
- Get employees on the front lines talking about how customer mind-sets have changed and how the company can better reach consumers.
- Reexamine your business model for products, processes, promotions and so on that are no longer effective.
- Constantly look for ways to add value to your company, product or service. This doesn't have to be expensive. A retailer, for example, might set up a small play area with secondhand toys to keep kids busy while parents shop. It's the small things that can boost a revenue line.

Don't

- Stay the course. Realize the economy has changed and your company must change with it.
- Stop marketing your product or service. You need to actually communicate with customers now more than ever.
- Assume your suppliers, vendors and distributors are doing fine. Go see them in person. Check in with their suppliers, too.
- Get complacent if margins are still good because rapid industry transformations rise to the surface in tough times. The newspaper industry, for example, saw trouble coming for years, but healthy sales kept it from making necessary changes.
- Stop being creative. Aim for discipline in your core business balanced with a willingness to try new things and create new markets.

Understand that a good product always sells. A startling number of companies and game-changing products were actually launched in very tough times. Campbell's Soup was introduced in the 1890s. IBM launched its personal computer in 1981. The first iPod came out in late 2001. These periods were economic low points and seemingly not the time to launch new products. Marketing research company Nielsen found customers' willingness to purchase innovative products in good times and bad times has stayed remarkably constant over the past 30 years. "Just because times get tough," says Anthony, "doesn't mean people aren't willing to pay for things that help them solve problems."

Think new markets, not just cost cutting. Trimming costs where you can (renegotiating prices with suppliers and distributors and lowering your overhead) is very important, but don't stop there. Game changers see levers they can pull (e.g., affordability, convenience, accessibility, location and cost) that change a market or create an entirely new one. When MinuteClinic, a timesaving one-stop shop for simple ailments, launched in 2000 inside select CVS pharmacies, its model changed the game-and consumers responded.

View scarcity as a good thing. When sales are good, there's no urgency or any real need to be innovative. Feeling like your back is against the wall actually forces you to try new things. Now's the time to ramp up a few low-cost experiments and reexamine your entire business model for weaknesses in light of the economy. What have you got to lose? Welcome the challenge.

Stop defending the status quo. An idea sounds great—until you realize the operating margin or some other metric will be lower than expected. Microsoft had all the tools to create Google's search advertising business but abandoned the idea when search produced a paltry (by Microsoft standards) $1 million in sales during its first few months. By the time Microsoft finally recognized the importance of search, Google had a commanding lead in the market. Bending a little bit could pay off big time.

Serve the customers you hate. Every company has customers it sees as undesirable from a cost or profit perspective. Consider Netflix, which started out with a traditional pay-per-rental model in which customers paid late fees. In early 2000, 45-employee Netflix switched to a subscription model without late fees, a move that appealed particularly to customers who have trouble returning movies on time. Today, Netflix has around 250 employees and its business model is thriving in the recession. "It's not just the customers you've learned to love but, in fact, customers you've learned to hate and figuring out ways to innovate to make them great customers," Anthony says.

Every game has winners and losers. Which side will you be on? "Continue to dream, continue to experiment, continue to think differently," Anthony says. "But you've got to prove your dream more quickly than you ever did before." Now hurry—your customers are waiting.

Critical Thinking

1. In your perspective, what recent economic forces require companies to transform their business approach?
2. List and summarize the seven changes that the authors of the article recommend businesses make.

Chris Penttila is a freelance journalist in the Chapel Hill, North Carolina, area.

The Unmarketables

Tough times call for new marketing strategies and tactics. Here are five approaches that these practitioners hope will revitalize their images and put them on the road to business recovery.

PIET LEVY, JOHN N. FRANK, AND ALLISON ENRIGHT

Brands, products and business segments have their ups and downs. The downs challenge marketers to find new approaches to revitalize and rejuvenate images to reconnect with key audiences.

This feature looks at a cross-section of businesses and products that are down for a variety of reasons. Some, like restaurants, financial services companies, and business travel and meeting resources, have been pushed out of favor because of the recession. Others, like U.S. auto makers GM and Chrysler, need to battle the negatives that come with filing for bankruptcy protection. And another, high fructose corn syrup, faces image and health issues.

The first lesson for any brand, company or business segment facing similar challenges is that adversity means it's time to find new approaches for marketing, says brand guru David Aaker, vice chairman of Prophet, a San Francisco-based branding and marketing consultancy.

"I just don't think you can do business as usual and continue to spend money the way you've been spending money; you just need to be really creative," he counsels. Look to connect with your key audiences in new ways, with approaches that help you stand out dramatically from competitors, he says. You'll find more advice from Aaker, who also is *Marketing News*' newest columnist, throughout this piece. Look for his first *Marketing News* column in our Aug. 30 issue.

Restaurants: Value Tops the Menu

When your stomach's growling but your wallet's whimpering, a restaurant meal isn't as appetizing as it may have been in better times.

As a result, restaurant chains are hurting. Fine dining and casual dining sales likely will drop 10 to 15% and 5 to 8% respectively this year, says Darren Tristano, executive vice president of Chicago-based food industry consulting firm Technomic Inc.

Trying to do better than those predictions, many restaurant groups are stressing value and unique experiences in their marketing efforts.

Denny's Corp., for example, grabbed attention with its Grand Slam giveaway advertised during the Super Bowl. It gave away nearly 2 million free meals on Feb. 3, introducing consumers to its recently revamped menu in the process. It also provided incentives for return trips, says Mark Chmiel, executive vice president and chief marketing and innovation officer for the Spartanburg, S.C.-based company. Sales dropped in the first quarter but beat analyst expectations. In a statement, Denny's CEO Nelson Marchioli said the promotion was an "overwhelming success" and that the company "made significant progress on our primary goal of improving sales and guest traffic trends." Denny's continues to offer free meals through Twitter.

Besides value, Denny's is targeting niche audiences with new items and campaigns. Health nuts finally have some Denny's options, including chicken sausage and granola, which debuted in June. The company also has been stepping up early morning, young adult business with a funky social media campaign involving emerging rock bands and a talking unicorn.

Like Denny's, The Cheesecake Factory Inc., based in Calabasas Hills, Calif., had better than expected sales in the first quarter. Mark Mears, the company's senior vice president and CMO, says one reason for that is the chain's "Small Plates & Snacks" menu, nationally released in March. Meanwhile, the 200-item main menu trumpets variety and sharable meals as value options, Mears says.

Cheesecake Factory's "Share the Love" and "Share the Celebration" campaigns offered dine-again incentives during select weeks; the former touted a design-a-cheesecake feature online, and the latter encouraged fans to post descriptions of events they celebrated at Cheesecake Factory for entry into a sweepstakes.

At the higher end of the dining price chain, Morton's Restaurant Group Inc. in Chicago experienced a 24.1% decrease in comparable restaurant revenues in the first quarter of its fiscal 2009 because of cutbacks in business-related dining.

Aaker Advice
Restaurants

Find True Points of Difference

"You really need to help generate really different ideas that will break out of the clutter. You always need to find new things, but these days [it's] the only way."

Aaker Advice
Financial Services

Target Consumer Education

"If they really want to educate, the problem becomes how do you do it effectively? You need to segment the population. You need to target people."

It's trying to turn things around with value messaging driven by social media. Morton's blog recently featured recipes for meals and details on a new Morton's cookbook being promoted on a national tour at Morton outlets. Roger J. Drake, the company's chief communications officer, says the book pushes brand awareness and the book events drive restaurant traffic.

The company's biggest social media success has been through Twitter, with 1,424 followers as of late June. Twitter was exclusively used to promote a networking event at the new Bar 1221 inside a Chicago Morton's restaurant; Drake says sales were so successful that the strategy will be used at other locations.

Morton's Facebook page showcases other events like an absinthe tasting experience and price promotions such as a $99.99 deal for a pair of three-course steak and seafood dinners.

Value messaging, to many consumers, equals lower prices. So offering value through too many price promotions carries its own problems for when the economy improves. "It's not something you want consumers to get used to," Technomic's Tristano says. "It's hard to go back to the regular price points."

The Problem	Consumers are less likely to eat out in a bad economy.
The Fix	Create value messaging via price promotions, lower-cost menus and new food offerings.
Potential Pitfall	Consumers will continue to demand lower prices even in a healthier economy.

Financial Services: Listen to Customers

Financial services firms have seen better days.

"Banking as a business and bankers in a generic sense have been getting bashed pretty badly," acknowledges long-time banking consultant Bert Ely, founder of Ely & Co. in Alexandria, Va.

Indeed, the credit card corner of the banking world became one of the first hit with new legislation this year when Congress passed a bill restricting a wide range of card issuer practices.

In the face of such negative perceptions, credit card companies are stressing their core brand values in marketing. They're also talking about responsible borrowing and financial education. Banks are trying a variety of approaches, including changing their names and their product offerings in response to consumer input.

Credit card companies such as Discover Financial Services "face a major challenge to their business models because now they have to invest an enormous amount of money changing all their systems to conform with new rules," Ely says. They need to do that while cutting overall spending in response to shareholder concerns. This recession is the first in which the major credit card companies—Discover, MasterCard and Visa—all are publicly traded companies. "The fact that they're public could change marketing spending. . . . You have to meet investor expectations," says Michael Kon, a senior analyst who follows credit cards at Morning-star Inc. in Chicago. Visa cut spending on marketing, advertising, sales and promotions by 8.8% in the first quarter of 2009 compared with the same period in 2008; MasterCard cut such spending 35%, Discover 21% and American Express Co. 42%, Kon notes.

Harit Talwar, CMO at Riverwoods, Ill.-based Discover, says he's using more online tools in his marketing mix and working to better integrate all his marketing efforts. Messaging stresses what he calls Discover's core brand mission, which is "helping consumers spend smarter, manage debt better, save more," he says. Discover in February introduced its Paydown Planner, Purchase Planner and Spend Analyzer on its Web site, three financial management tools that speak to its core mission, he says.

At rival MasterCard Worldwide, "we focus on what the Priceless campaign [MasterCard's ongoing advertising effort] has always been about; [it's] not about conspicuous consumption, it's about things that matter most," says Chris Jogis, vice president of U.S. consumer marketing for the Purchase, N.Y. company.

MasterCard's digital efforts center on financial education and the utility of using MasterCard. An iPhone application, for example, helps people find the nearest MasterCard-accepting ATM.

In an effort to get a more up-to-the-minute read on consumer sentiment, MasterCard has stepped up the frequency of economic focus groups to ask consumers how they're feeling financially.

Asking consumers what they want led to new products and a new name at what was known as GMAC Bank, an online banking operation owned by General Motors' financing arm, GMAC.

The newly named Ally kicked off its marketing campaign May 15, offering consumer-requested products like no withdrawal penalty CDs and less legalese in describing its offerings, notes Vinoo Vijay, product, brand and marketing executive at Ally. "Consumers are going to demand that banks do better by them, recession or not," Vijay says.

The Problem	Counter negative consumer and legislator perceptions.
The Fix	Stress responsible borrowing and spending, and offer financial education.
Potential Pitfall	Consumers will see new financial education efforts as disingenuous.

Business Travel: Go to Washington

As they boarded their luxury corporate jets last fall to testify before Congress about their incredibly, painfully red financial statements, the heads of GM, Ford and Chrysler probably couldn't fathom the storm they were flying into. Nor, perhaps, could the meeting planners for AIG, who hosted a $440,000 corporate retreat at a California luxury resort in September, less than a week after accepting $85 billion in bailout funds from taxpayers. Certainly, a large part of their collective actions were rooted in habit and pre-planning—albeit executed in a state of economic tone-deafness.

The resulting press coverage and 'can-you-believe-it' water cooler conversations produced a devastating effect on the related industries—private jet travel and the meeting planning and hotel industries—by default.

Faced with the enormous challenge of changing consumer sentiment and revving up business, the two industries quickly created separate integrated marketing efforts that shared similar messaging and intent. The National Business Aviation Association (NBAA) and the General Aviation Manufacturers Association jointly created "No Plane No Gain," while the U.S. Travel Association (USTA) tried to shore up its interests via a "Meetings Mean Business" campaign, coordinated with eight other travel-oriented association groups. The messages for both stressed the impact the negativity and related business losses had on front-line employment among employees serving these industries and the businesspeople that benefit from using those services. Both made a strong effort to change the tenor of statements coming from influential voices on Capitol Hill.

"We watched [the Meetings Mean Business] campaign with great interest because there is so much commonality there. . . . For us, it's 'how did you get there?' In [USTA's] case, it's 'where did you go?' " says Dan Hubbard, vice president of communications for NBAA and the in-house manager of the No Plane No Gain campaign in Washington, D.C.

"The tenor of the conversation had neglected a lot of facts. . . . [The campaign] helped frame it in the right terms, to help politicians understand that when you make off-the-cuff comments, you are putting people out of a job," says Chris Gaia, vice president of marketing for meetings, events and travel incentive planner Maritz Travel in St. Louis.

Maritz Travel's leadership worked with USTA to develop the Meetings Mean Business effort. Gaia estimates that Maritz Travel saw a 30% decline in the November time frame from 2007 to 2008. "A large portion of that was driven by [clients] not wanting to be targets of the media. They didn't want to get called out for excesses. There were genuine economic problems [and adding the] political thing was icing on the cake," he says.

> ### Aaker Advice
> ### Business Travel
>
> **Stress the Business Value of Conferences**
>
> "Make sure people remember why they're doing these things—the importance of building the team."

Both marketing efforts included intense communication efforts in the Washington area—No Plane No Gain included ad buys on local cable and in *Roll Call, Politico, USA Today* and *The Wall Street Journal*—and culminated in separate meetings at the White House with President Obama.

Business is trickling back at Maritz Travel, Gaia says. "In the last 60 days, we've had clients who cancelled stuff scheduled two years out come back and say: 'We need to add a short-term incentive sprint. We need to do a CEO roadshow to increase communication,' " he says.

At NBAA, Hubbard is optimistic that the efforts are taking hold. "A lot of that has come together in recent weeks and we're hopeful. It seems to have had a helpful impact."

The Problem	Condemned by the excesses of a few, the private aviation and corporate travel and meetings industries are hit hard by the economy.
The Fix	Industry groups installed intensive marketing initiatives to challenge and correct the public comments made by influencers.

See more, www.NoPlaneNoGain.com and www.MeetingsMeanBusiness.com

Bankrupt Automakers: Come Back, Shoppers

To say that U.S. automakers are facing marketing challenges this year is a bit akin to saying the crew of the Titanic had some problems with ice—the scale involved dwarfs anything Detroit has faced before.

"This is not an auto recession, it's an auto depression. The challenge everyone is facing is just staying alive," says David Cole, chairman of the nonprofit Center for Automotive Research, an Ann Arbor, Mich.-based auto think tank. U.S. car and light truck sales had been between 16.5 million and 17 million units annually two years ago. They fell to 13.5 million in 2008 and this year have been hovering around the 9 to 10 million annual rate.

The market dive drove Chrysler and General Motors into bankruptcy court by the start of June.

The marketing battle for each company has become a two-front war. Each needs to convince consumers it will still be in business once the recession ends. They also need to get reluctant buyers back into showrooms.

Aaker Advice
U.S. Automakers

Regain Consumer Trust

"You need a branded program that packages the logic of why [consumers] should trust you and why it's going to be OK. Just to run ads that say 'we're trustworthy' [is] a complete waste of time. There needs to be substance."

Chrysler addressed the first challenge with an advertising campaign starting May 3 that included print ads in 50 large U.S. newspapers, including the *New York Times, Wall Street Journal* and *USA Today.* "The tagline is, 'We're building a new car company, come see what we're building for you,' " says Jodi Tinson, Chrysler's manager of marketing communications.

"The whole purpose of the campaign is to let people know, yes, we're still out there for you."

The "We Build" campaign also includes five TV ads, two discussing restructuring and three featuring Chrysler, Dodge and Jeep products. The product ads focus on various Chrysler products in efforts to distinguish them from the competition. The Auburn Hills, Mich.-based automaker continues to work with its ad agency of record, BBDO, on the campaign, which also will have some online elements, Tinson says.

General Motors has joined industry efforts to assure people they won't get stuck with a new car and no regular paycheck. It's offering a payment protection plan to pay up to $500 a month for nine months to any buyer who loses a job, explains John M. McDonald, GM's manager for pricing incentives and market trends. It's also touting a vehicle protection plan that addresses trade-in values by offering buyers up to $5,000 if they trade in a GM car in the next two-and-a-half years and find the trade-in value has fallen below the amount of their auto loan.

For its Cadillac and Hummer lines, marketing has focused on letting people know financing is available, McDonald says. GM partnered with credit unions earlier this year to get discounted financing for credit union members buying GM products.

Cole thinks automakers should be touting the fact that the deals being offered now won't last once the economy revives. "One of the things that gets Americans to move is a deal or the potential loss of a deal," he says.

McDonald agrees that deal messaging will help with anyone already thinking about buying, but adds that "the issue right now is getting people into the marketplace."

The Problem	Convince consumers the companies won't go out of business; get consumers into a buying mood again.
The Fix	Stress corporate staying power, product attributes and financial concerns.
Potential Pitfall	Only those already thinking about a purchase will care; the rest will stay on the sidelines.

Aaker Advice
HFCS

Combat Rumors with Facts

"Find out what the facts are [about HFCS] and find a way to communicate them."

Corn Syrup: Sticky Sweet Truths

Give me your gut reaction: Is high fructose corn syrup (HFCS) good or bad?

It is generally agreed that most consumers' first reactions fall somewhere on the scale from negative to neutral. And that's meant marketing troubles for the HFCS business. Indeed, 67% of consumers indicated they were trying to consume less HFCS last year, up from 60% in 2007 and 54% in 2006, found the Washington-based International Food Information Council's 2008 Food & Health Survey.

Turning negative perceptions around has become a major industry challenge. The marketing response from the Washington-based Corn Refiners Association (CRA), which represents the largest corn refiners in the United States including Archer Daniels Midland and Corn Products International, has been a consumer education campaign begun in June 2008. The Sweet Surprise integrated campaign produced with agency DDB Chicago presents the scientific data about HFCS via TV ads, print and online elements, and includes a PR media outreach effort coordinated by Weber Shandwick. The CRA won't disclose spending, but industry estimates put the campaign in the $20-$30 million range.

"The reason [for the campaign] is to correct the significant misinformation being given to consumers about our corn sweetener," says Audrae Erickson, the president of the CRA. "Most of that information was misleading and completely inaccurate. Our goal is to ensure that consumers have the facts [and] that they understand that these two sweeteners [sugar and HFCS] are essentially the same."

HFCS is a corn-derived sweetener that is nearly identical in chemical composition to sugar. It has the same calorie count per gram and numerous scientific studies have indicated that the human body processes the product the same way. And government subsidies made to U.S. corn farmers also makes it a cheaper ingredient for food and beverage makers to use than sugar, which is why it appears in food and beverage products that formerly contained natural sugar.

Since the ingredient is found in few products produced outside the United States—it is cheaper to use sugar elsewhere—and frequent news headlines at home alert us that we are turning into a nation of chunks, some health and dietary groups assert that a connection can be made between our obesity problem and the growth of HFCS consumption during the past 30 years. Those headlines appear to be having an impact on consumer consumption patterns.

The per capita delivery of HFCS for food and beverage use declined 16.4% from 1999 (HFCS's peak year) to 2008, according to U.S. Department of Agriculture statistics. Worried about a consumer backlash, food and beverage marketers have begun to try to distinguish their products as containing no HFCS; 146 products carried the claim in 2007, up from just six products in 2003, according to London-based Datamonitor.

The Sweet Surprise campaign's target market is mothers, says Don Hoffman, executive vice president and managing director of accounts with DDB Chicago. "The tone of the communications is simple and straightforward. It is targeted to women as decision makers and good communicators. . . . [Women] find the right facts and disseminate the right facts," he says.

Early returns are limited, but Erickson says the campaign is helping. "We have been very successful in making a difference in correcting the record. But based on the stories that continue, there is more work to be done to ensure that consumers get the truth."

The Problem High fructose corn syrup is getting a bad rep in the media and among consumers.

The Fix The Corn Refiners Association launched an integrated media blitz to disseminate scientifically backed facts about the ingredient. For more, see www.SweetSurprise.com.

Trivia The average U.S. consumer consumed 40.1 pounds of HFCS and 44.2 pounds of refined sugar in 2007, according to the U.S.D.A. Economic Research Service.

Critical Thinking

1. Describe the effects of the current economic recession on various industries and sectors.
2. Explain how technology impacts marketing strategies and decisions, namely promotional tactics.

Six Strategies for Successful Niche Marketing

How to win big by thinking small.

Eric K. Clemons, Paul F. Nunes, and Matt Reilly

There's been a lot of buzz about the long-tail phenomenon—the strategy of selling smaller quantities of a wider range of goods that are designed to resonate with consumers' preferences and earn higher margins. And a quick scan of everyday products seems to confirm the long tail's merit: Where once we wore jeans from Levi, Wrangler or Lee, we now have scores of options from design houses. If you're looking for a nutrition bar, there's one exactly right for you, whether you're a triathlete, a dieter or a weight lifter. Hundreds of brewers offer thousands of craft beers suited to every conceivable taste.

It's not surprising that so many companies have embraced this strategy. It allows them to avoid the intense competition found in mass markets. Look at the sales growth that has taken place in low-volume, high-margin products such as super-premium ice cream, noncarbonated beverages, heritage meats and heirloom vegetables.

But the case for the long tail has frequently been overstated. This strategy can be expensive to implement, and it doesn't work for all products or all categories. It's surely better to produce a blockbuster film, for instance, than a smattering of low-volume art films.

In other words, simply avoiding the clutter of mass markets isn't enough. Companies need to stake out unique market *sweet spots,* those areas that resonate so strongly with target consumers that they are willing to pay a premium price, which offsets the higher production and distribution costs associated with niche offerings. We call this approach resonance marketing.

The vast amount of information available on the Internet has made this kind of niche marketing more important than ever and easier to do. More important because all that information encourages comparison shopping, putting tremendous downward pressure on prices and profits in highly competitive mass markets. And easier because it eliminates much of consumers' uncertainty about new

Questions to Ask Yourself

1. As part of a strategy of selling a wider range of high-margin goods, are you being careful to distinguish potential future market sweet spots from valueless niches that produce needless complexity?
2. Are you listening carefully to what consumers are saying online about your products, not just to you but also to each other, and are you reacting quickly to make improvements that address any negative comments?
3. Are you standardizing design components as much as possible to limit the costs of producing an extensive product line?
4. Are you aggressively keeping inventory and distribution costs down with strategies that allow you to configure finished products quickly when orders arrive, swap inventory among outlets or share distribution with other producers?
5. Are you continually reviewing your product portfolio to weed out those products that aren't contributing to profits, while being careful not to dump products that aren't big sellers but still contribute to the portfolio's overall profitability?

If you answered no to any of these questions, you're not getting the most out of what we call resonance marketing—selling a variety of precisely targeted goods designed to resonate with consumers. Following the steps in this article will help you manage the complexity of this strategy and reap superior profitability.

For Further Reading

These related articles from MIT Sloan Management Review can be accessed online

From Niches to Riches: Anatomy of the Long Tail

Erik Brynjolfsson, Yu "Jeffrey" Hu and Michael D. Smith (Summer 2006)

The Internet marketplace allows companies to produce and sell a far wider range of products than ever before. This profoundly changes both consumer behavior and business strategy.

Harnessing the Power of the Oh-So-Social Web

Josh Bernoff and Charlene Li (Spring 2008)

People are connecting with one another in increasing numbers, thanks to blogs, social networking sites and countless communities across the Web. Some companies are learning to turn this growing groundswell to their advantage.

Cracking the Code of Mass Customization

Fabrizio Salvador, Pablo Martin de Holan and Frank Piller (Spring 2009)

Most companies can benefit from mass customization, yet few do. The key is to think of it as a process for aligning a business with its customers' needs.

niche products, since they can easily find reviews, ratings and comments on everything that hits the market. For decades consumer uncertainty blocked the launch of new offerings that were too focused to be supported by national ad campaigns; today's empowered consumer is truly listening to word-of-mouth.

Finding sweet spots in the market is especially important in these tough economic times, when so many consumers are strapped for cash. Many shoppers will compromise whenever possible by looking for cheaper alternatives to the things they usually buy—but keep buying products that don't have any direct substitutes.

With the right approach, resonance marketing can fulfill its promise. We have found that six marketing principles, taken together, will allow a company to manage the complexity of this strategy and reap superior profitability.

Target Carefully

Sweet-spot offerings aren't better than other products in any absolute sense; they simply have to be different from existing options and better for their target consumers. They have to resonate powerfully with them.

But that's not as easy as it might sound. Finding profitable new niches requires a set of skills different from those needed to build market share or to create variations of an existing product—you're looking for places where no offerings exist, not one where consumers are complaining about existing choices.

Consider the success of Toyota Motor Corp.'s Lexus line of luxury cars. Toyota's research indicated there was an untapped market in the U.S. for Mercedes-quality luxury cars at a lower price, rather than superior quality at a comparable price. The Lexus line was designed to offer quality at a price that indicated the owners could afford whatever they wanted but also were smart enough to get it at a great price. The brand fulfilled an unmet need in the market and enjoyed immediate success.

Simply identifying gaps in the market isn't enough, though. Plenty of unique consumer products have failed to capture the imagination of shoppers. There's no guaranteed way to avoid such failures, but extensive research is essential. Often an ethnologist can help. Many companies use these analysts to explore why consumers buy what they do and what they would buy if it were available.

Listen to Your Customers. Really Listen.

Traditional advertising campaigns don't make sense for most niche markets; they're too expensive and too difficult to target precisely enough. Indeed, there are entire product categories, including nutrition bars and craft beers, where most products are never advertised. Their producers have learned how to work with consumer-generated content online—reviews, ratings or just chatter about a product. They don't just listen when customers talk to them; they listen just as carefully when customers talk about them.

The beauty of consumer-generated content is that companies get immediate and continuous feedback about their products. The key here is to listen closely and react quickly. Marketing executives should watch for the first online comments about their wares with the same excitement and apprehension as Broadway producers waiting for opening-night reviews. Consumers will make it clear right away what they like about the product and what they don't.

Harsh reviews can have devastating consequences. We analyzed two years of data on hotel bookings and found that the length, specificity and detail of negative online reviews are the best predictors of a hotel's inability to sell itself online.

So what do you do if the product you so carefully crafted to appeal to a particular market segment is trashed by those very consumers? Fix it immediately.

If defects pointed out by consumers are fixed quickly, more-favorable comments will emerge just as quickly. But companies should never assume that they've gotten it right and can stop listening. Continuous monitoring of online comments will alert executives to any new issues that arise, any improvements consumers might like to see as they become more familiar with the product, and even the emergence of any competitors or alternatives that might siphon off buyers.

Some traditional marketing still has its place, and indeed has become more powerful thanks to the way word-of-mouth spreads so quickly over the Internet. Companies can generate positive buzz for niche products with events like the Great American Beer Festival that small, specialty brewers attend every year. The brewers make sure to attract both professional critics and passionate amateur bloggers alike.

Moreover, craft brewers have learned to work together to make these events successful; they understand that at this point in their industry's development, their greatest danger comes not from each other but from consumer acceptance of mass-produced, generic beers.

Control Production Costs

Selling a large number of narrowly targeted products may sound like a production nightmare, but it doesn't have to be. There are several ways to maintain economies of scale over a broad range of product offerings.

Variety and standardization can coexist. For instance, Callaway Golf Co. offers buyers of its drivers multiple options for a club's head, loft angle and shaft—several hundred different combinations in all. But the company doesn't manufacture every variety separately. Any configuration of the various components can be readily assembled, since the interconnections are standardized.

Manufacturing processes can also be standardized to a large extent. While pumpkin spice ice cream appeals to a very different group of consumers than vanilla does, the manufacturing process is nearly identical for both flavors and any others. Brewing involves cold-fermenting lagers in one set of tanks and warm-fermenting ales in another, but the two varieties share many other processes: mashing grains, adding hops, bottling.

It also pays for a company to have a high-volume product in its portfolio that will keep its manufacturing equipment and employees from sitting idle for stretches of time. The relatively low volume of sales in narrowly targeted markets means production plants might not need to work to their full capacity to meet demand. A high-volume, if less profitable, product can take up the slack.

Control Distribution Costs

It's not just production costs that will determine the profitability and ultimate success of resonance offerings. Distribution costs are also important. There are ways here, too, to keep costs under control.

It can be difficult to forecast demand for products with limited sales, but that doesn't necessarily mean a company needs to stockpile high levels of inventory to keep from getting caught short. Companies that offer many varieties of a product based on different combinations of components, as Callaway does with its golf clubs, can keep inventory low by postponing final assembly until a particular product is ordered—there's no need to keep a given number of every combination in stock.

Flexible inventory allocation is another way to keep from having to stockpile goods. Auto makers, for instance, often swap needed items. If a customer in New Jersey wants a copper-colored Infiniti FX35 and his dealer has the car in silver, while a customer in Pennsylvania wants the same car in silver and his dealer has the copper, the dealers can arrange an exchange.

Shared distribution is another option worth considering. Small brewers, for instance, cut costs this way.

Selling to customers directly from a company Web site can reduce costs by eliminating intermediaries. But companies should be aware that shoppers can be less forgiving online than they are offline. A consumer who visits a store to buy a product or orders it from a catalog may be miffed if it is temporarily out of stock. But frustration may rise to the level of anger if the same consumer orders the product online and isn't notified until three days later that the item is out of stock, because of a glitch in the site's inventory software.

Some Apparent Losers Are Worth Keeping

Even with the best research and the most careful marketing, production and distribution, some products will be unprofitable or only marginally profitable. But before discontinuing a product, a company should consider the product's value in broader terms.

Some products that don't generate significant profit directly still help make a company's other products more profitable. Feeder routes on airlines transport customers to more-profitable routes, such as trans-Atlantic flights. Likewise, niche books that don't account for a significant portion of Amazon.com Inc.'s sales are valuable to the company because they contribute to its reputation as a one-stop source for any book.

Prune Your Portfolio Ruthlessly

Companies must relentlessly drop niche offerings that don't contribute to profitability directly or indirectly. The scores of flavors discontinued over the years by Ben & Jerry's Homemade Inc., remembered fondly in the "flavor graveyard" on the company's Web site, serve as a reminder to all companies that the flip side of creative expansion of a product line is eliminating those that no longer resonate with consumers. And the success of Ben & Jerry's is a reminder of the power of resonance marketing done right.

Dr. Clemons is a professor of operations and information management at the Wharton School of the University of Pennsylvania. **Mr. Nunes** is executive director of research at the Accenture Institute for High Performance and is based in Boston. **Mr. Reilly** is a senior executive in Accenture's management-consulting business, global managing director of the firm's Process and Innovation Performance practice and global co-leader of its Operational Excellence service. They can be reached at reports@wsj.com.

Article 5

The Secrets of Marketing in a Web 2.0 World

Consumers are flocking to blogs, social-networking sites and virtual worlds. And they are leaving a lot of marketers behind.

SALVATORE PARISE, PATRICIA J. GUINAN, AND BRUCE D. WEINBERG

For marketers, Web 2.0 offers a remarkable new opportunity to engage consumers.

If only they knew how to do it.

That's where this article aims to help. We interviewed more than 30 executives and managers in both large and small organizations that are at the forefront of experimenting with Web 2.0 tools. From those conversations and further research, we identified a set of emerging principles for marketing.

But first, a more basic question: What is Web 2.0, anyway? Essentially, it encompasses the set of tools that allow people to build social and business connections, share information and collaborate on projects online. That includes blogs, wikis, social-networking sites and other online communities, and virtual worlds.

Millions of people have become familiar with these tools through sites like Facebook, Wikipedia and Second Life, or by writing their own blogs. And a growing number of marketers are using Web 2.0 tools to collaborate with consumers on product development, service enhancement and promotion. But most companies still don't appear to be well versed in this area.

So here's a look at the principles we arrived at—and how marketers can use them to get the best results.

Getting Sociable

- **A New Approach:** Marketing these days is more about building a two-way relationship with consumers. Web 2.0 tools are a powerful way to do that.
- **The Pioneers:** A growing number of companies are learning how to collaborate with consumers online on product development, service enhancement and promotion.
- **The Lessons:** From these early efforts, a set of marketing principles have emerged. Among them: get consumers involved in all aspects of marketing, listen to and join the online conversation about your products outside your site, and give the consumers you work with plenty of leeway to express their opinions.

Don't just talk at consumers—work with them throughout the marketing process.

Web 2.0 tools can be used to do what traditional advertising does: persuade consumers to buy a company's products or services. An executive can write a blog, for instance, that regularly talks up the company's goods. But that kind of approach misses the point of 2.0. Instead, companies should use these tools to get the consumers *involved,* inviting them to participate in marketing-related activities from product development to feedback to customer service.

How can you do that? A leading greeting-card and gift company that we spoke with is one of many that have set up an online community—a site where it can talk to consumers and the consumers can talk to each other. The company solicits opinions on various aspects of greeting-card design and on ideas for gifts and their pricing. It also asks the consumers to talk about their lifestyles and even upload photos of themselves, so that it can better understand its market.

A marketing manager at the company says that, as a way to obtain consumer feedback and ideas for product development, the online community is much faster and cheaper than the traditional focus groups and surveys used in the past. The conversations consumers have with each other, he adds, result in "some of the most interesting insights," including gift ideas for specific occasions, such as a college graduation, and the prices consumers are willing to pay for different gifts.

Similarly, a large technology company uses several Web 2.0 tools to improve collaboration with both its business partners and consumers. Among other things, company employees have created wikis—websites that allow users to add, delete and edit content—to list answers to frequently asked questions about each product, and consumers have added significant contributions. For instance, within days of the release of a new piece of software by the company, consumers spotted a problem with it and posted a way for users to deal with it. They later proposed a way to fix the problem, which the company adopted. Having those solutions available so quickly showed customers that the company was on top of problems with its products.

Give consumers a reason to participate.

Consumers have to have some incentive to share their thoughts, opinions and experiences on a company website.

One lure is to make sure consumers can use the online community to network among themselves on topics of their own choosing. That way the site isn't all about the company, it's also about them. For instance, a toy company that created a community of hundreds of mothers to solicit their opinions and ideas on toys also enables them to write their own blogs on the site, a feature that many use to discuss family issues.

Other companies provide more-direct incentives: cash rewards or products, some of which are available only to members of the online community. Still others offer consumers peer recognition by awarding points each time they post comments, answer questions or contribute to a wiki entry. Such recognition not only encourages participation, but also has the benefit of allowing both the company and the other members of the community to identify experts on various topics.

Many companies told us that a moderator plays a critical role in keeping conversations going, highlighting information that's important to a discussion and maintaining order. That's important because consumers are likely to drift away if conversations peter out or if they feel that their voices are lost in a chaotic flood of comments. The moderator can also see to it that consumer input is seen and responded to by the right people within the company.

And, of course, it's important to make a site as easy to use as possible. For instance, there should be clear, simple instructions for consumers to set up a blog or contribute to a wiki.

Consumers tend to trust one another's opinions more than a company's marketing pitch. And there is no shortage of opinions online.

The managers we interviewed accept that this type of content is here to stay and are aware of its potential impact—positive or negative—on consumers' buying decisions. So they monitor relevant online conversations among consumers and, when appropriate, look for opportunities to inject themselves into a conversation or initiate a potential collaboration.

For example, a marketing manager of a leading consumer-electronics company monitors blogs immediately after a new-product launch in order to understand "how customers are actually reacting to the product." Other managers keep an eye on sites like Digg.com and Del.icio.us that track the most popular topics on the Web, to see if there's any buzz around their new products, and whether they should be adjusting, say, features or prices.

In one case, a company found a popular blogger who had spoken highly of the company's brand. Just prior to launching a new product, the company sent the blogger a free sample, inviting him to review it with no strings attached. The end result: The blogger wrote a favorable review and generated a flood of comments. So the company got nearly free publicity and feedback.

Resist the temptation to sell, sell, sell.

Many marketers have been trained to bludgeon consumers with advertising—to sell, sell, sell anytime and anywhere consumers can be found. In an online community, it pays to resist that temptation.

When consumers are invited to participate in online communities, they expect marketers to listen and to consider their ideas. They don't want to feel like they're simply a captive audience for advertising, and if they do they're likely to abandon the community.

The head of consumer research for a leading consumer-electronics organization created an online community of nearly 50,000 consumers to discuss product-development and marketing issues. One of the key principles of the community, she says, was "not to do anything about marketing, because we weren't about selling; we were about conversing."

In short order, community members not only identified what it was they were looking for in the company's products, but also suggested innovations to satisfy those needs. The company quickly developed prototypes based on those suggestions, and got an enthusiastic response: Community members asked when they would be able to buy the products and if they would get the first opportunity to buy them. They didn't have to be sold on anything.

Don't control, let it go.

In an online community, every company needs to find an effective balance between trying to steer the conversation about its products and allowing the conversation to flow freely. In general, though, the managers we interviewed believe that companies are better off giving consumers the opportunity to say whatever is on their minds, positive or negative. Moderators can keep things running smoothly and coherently, but they shouldn't always keep the conversation on a predetermined track. The more that consumers talk freely, the more a company can learn about how it can improve its products and its marketing.

One marketing executive recalled the first time she let an online community created for a client interact with very little control or moderation, resulting in an animated discussion about the look of the company's product. The client, with great concern, asked. "Who told them [the consumers] they could do this, that they could go this far?" Of course, when this process resulted in totally new packaging that helped boost sales, the client was ecstatic.

As another executive of a company that creates online communities for clients told us: "You have to let the members drive. When community members feel controlled, told how to respond and how to act, the community shuts down."

Find a 'marketing technopologist.'

So who should direct a company's forays into Web 2.0 marketing? A number of managers identified an ideal set of skills for an executive that go beyond those of a typical M.B.A. holder or tech expert. We coined the term *marketing technopologist* for a person who brings together strengths in marketing, technology and social interaction. A manager said, "I'd want to see someone with the usual M.B.A. consultant's background, strong interest in psychology and sociology, and good social-networking skills throughout the organization."

Foot soldiers need to be carefully selected as well. One large technology company weighs employees' proven skills to choose writers for blogs that are read by consumers. The company has long used blogs internally to help employees discuss technical issues, products, and company and industry topics. When it decided to use blogs to raise its profile online, it recruited those who had shown the most skill at blogging within the company. The company currently has about 15 employees who blog publicly, mostly on technology trends, and is recruiting more the same way. Meanwhile, the bloggers plan to meet occasionally to share the lessons learned from their experiences.

Embrace experimentation.

One Web 2.0 strategy does not fit all, and sometimes the best way to find out what's best for a given company is to try some things out and see what happens.

Blogs, wikis and online communities are among the tools that companies are most commonly using for marketing, but there are other ways to reach consumers. Some of the companies we talked with have gotten their feet wet in the online virtual world Second Life, where millions of users interact with each other through avatars. Companies can sell their goods and services and sponsor events in Second Life just as they do in the real world; one sponsored a contest for the best avatar.

Others are considering new ways to use more-familiar tools. For instance, many companies have long used instant messaging on their websites to allow shoppers to chat with customer-service representatives. One executive we spoke with said he would like to experiment with allowing consumers to chat with each other as they shop on his company's site.

Critical Thinking

1. In your perspective, why are online communities more effective than traditional methods of exploratory research such as surveys and focus groups?
2. With a small group of peers from your class, list some possible incentives for consumers to become engaged and involved in online communities.

Dr. Parise is an assistant professor of technology, operations and information management at Babson College in Wellesley, Mass. **Dr. Guinan** is an associate professor of technology, operations and information management at Babson College. **Dr. Weinberg** is chairman of the marketing department and an associate professor of marketing and e-commerce at Bentley University in Waltham, Mass. They can be reached at reports@wsj.com.

The Branding Sweet Spot

KEVIN LANE KELLER AND FREDERICK E. WEBSTER, JR.

One of the realities of modern brand marketing is that many of the decisions that marketers make with respect to their brands are seemingly characterized by conflicting goals, objectives and possible outcomes. Unfortunately, in our experience, too many marketers define their problems in "either/or" terms, creating situations where one idea, one individual or one option wins out. Opportunities are missed for finding an even better solution, a new idea that could have been discovered and developed by combining and refining conflicting points of view. As a result, resources may be squandered, consumers may be left unsatisfied or confused and the organization may find itself struggling with lingering internal conflict.

We submit that this is dangerously wrong, and there is a better way to approach such problems, one which we call "marketing balance." Achieving marketing balance requires understanding and addressing conflicting objectives and points of view, taking into account and resolving multiple interests. It is synonymous with moderation, and the opposite of self-indulgence or turbulence. It involves finding "win-wins"—the branding sweet spot—so that vulnerable extreme solutions and suboptimal compromises are avoided.

Marketing Trade-offs

Conflict and trade-offs are inherent in marketing decision making, and are the most fundamental challenge of marketing and brand management. Table 1 organizes these trade-offs or conflicts into four broad categories—strategic, tactical, financial or organizational decisions—which we briefly highlight here.

Strategy trade-offs. Marketing strategy trade-offs involve decisions related to targeting and positioning brands. Some involve trade-offs in growth strategies, such as concentrating marketing resources on expanding the brand into new product categories vs. fortifying the brand and further penetrating existing product categories. Another growth trade-off is emphasizing market retention and targeting existing customers vs. emphasizing market expansion and targeting new customers.

Whether to use funds to build and retain existing customer relationships or spend resources to develop new customers is certainly a dilemma that many firms face.

Other marketing strategy trade-offs revolve around how brands are competitively positioned in the minds of customers—such as an emphasis on brand tangibles (product performance) vs. brand intangibles (user imagery); a classic vs. contemporary image; an independent vs. universal image; and so on. Some of the product-related performance trade-offs in brand positioning are between attributes and benefits—such as price and quality, convenience and quality, variety and simplicity, strength and sophistication, performance and luxury and efficacy and mildness.

One common trade-off is whether the marketing program should stress points of difference (i.e., how the brand is unique) or points of parity (i.e., how the brand is similar), with respect to competitors' offerings. Product development decisions are often defined in terms of whether to bring the next generation of products in line with a major competitor's level of performance, or to commit more research and development funds and time to achieving a technological breakthrough.

Tactics trade-offs. Marketing tactic trade-offs involve decisions related to the design and implementation of marketing program activities. Some of the more common trade-offs evident with marketing programs are push (intermediary-directed) vs. pull (end-consumer-related) strategies or how the program is updated over time (emphasizing continuity vs. change).

A real dilemma for many companies is whether to support existing channels or to develop new ones, which usually means creating competition for the companies' traditional outlets. The problem often comes down to a stark choice: Given evolution in customer buying patterns and preferences, and significant declines in the market position of our traditional dealers, do we create a whole new system for going to market or do we re-segment the market,

Table 1 Representative Marketing Trade-offs

Strategic (Targeting and Positioning)
- Retaining vs. acquiring customers
- Brand fortification vs. brand expansion
- Brand awareness vs. brand image
- Product performance vs. user imagery
- Points of parity vs. points of difference

Tactical (Design and Implementation)
- Push vs. pull
- Continuity vs. change
- Existing vs. new channels
- Direct market coverage vs. use of middlemen
- Selling systems vs. selling components
- Creative, attention-getting ads vs. informative, product-focused ads

Financial (Allocation and Accountability)
- Short-run vs. long-run objectives
- Revenue-generating vs. brand-building activities
- Easily measurable marketing activities vs. difficult to quantify marketing activities
- Quality maximization vs. cost minimization
- Social responsibility vs. profit maximizing

Organizational (Structure, Processes, and Responsibilities)
- Central vs. local control
- Top-down vs. bottom-up brand management
- Customized vs. standardized marketing plans and programs
- Internal vs. external focus

Executive Briefing

One of the challenges in modern brand marketing is the many strategic, tactical, financial and organizational trade-offs that seem to exist. Successfully developing and implementing marketing programs and activities, to build and maintain strong brands over time, often requires that marketers overcome conflicting objectives and realities in the marketplace. Guidelines and suggestions are offered on achieving marketing balance, to hit the branding sweet spot by arriving at "win-win" decisions that successfully reconcile marketing trade-offs.

refine our strategy and strengthen our position with our traditional distribution partners?

Financial trade-offs. Marketing financial trade-offs involve decisions related to the allocation and accountability of investments in marketing program activities. In arriving at marketing investment decisions, these are some common trade-offs:

- Invest in generating revenue vs. building brand equity.
- Go for clearly measurable effects vs. "softer" effects that are more difficult to measure.
- Maximize product or service quality vs. minimizing costs.

Perhaps the most common trade-off is the tension on long-term brand-building strategies created by pressure for short-term earnings results and "making the numbers." Marketing expenditures, especially for advertising and brand development, are among the most vulnerable when management is looking for ways to improve the bottom line, because the long-term effects of most marketing expenditures are so hard to determine due to the problem of multiple causation.

Unfortunately, the paths of commerce are strewn with the debris of once-powerful brands that were milked for profit and cash, based on the mistaken belief that they were strong enough to sustain major spending cuts for improving the bottom line. As one example, Coors Brewing cut advertising spending in the 1990s for its flagship Coors beer brand—from $43 million annually to a meager $4 million. Not surprisingly, the brand's market share subsequently dropped in half.

Organization trade-offs. Finally, marketing organization trade-offs involve decisions in the structure, processes and responsibilities involved in marketing decision making. For large global organizations especially, trade-offs found in this area include centrally mandated vs. locally controlled authority and standardized vs. customized marketing approaches. As effective a marketer as Nike has been, the company has often lamented that it has not historically balanced global objectives with local realities as well as it would have liked. Walt Disney Co. has been even more blunt in its belief that it has needed to achieve more cultural relevance in its global pursuits.

In terms of brand management, trade-offs often emerge between top-down (corporate-level) vs. bottom-up (product/market level) and internal vs. external focus. Strong business-to-business brands, such as GE, often find themselves challenged with managing their corporate brand in the face of diverse business units with different competitive challenges and potentially different stages of brand development in the marketplace and in different countries.

Marketing Balance Levels

Although we discussed marketing trade-offs within our four main categories, trade-offs certainly exist across the categories too. Pressure to achieve certain earnings targets may lead to an emphasis on short-term tactical moves, for example. One response to these trade-offs is to adopt an "extreme" solution and maximize one of the two dimensions involved with the trade-off. Many management gurus advocate positions that, in effect, lead to such a singular, but clearly limited, focus. These approaches, however, obviously leave the brand vulnerable to the negative consequences of ignoring the other dimension.

The reality is that for marketing success, both dimensions in each of these different types of decision trade-offs must typically be adequately addressed. To do so involves achieving a more balanced marketing solution. Marketing balance occurs when marketers attempt to address the strategic, tactical, financial and organizational trade-offs as clearly as possible in organizing, planning and implementing their marketing programs.

There are three means or levels of achieving marketing balance—in increasing order of potential effectiveness as well as difficulty.

Alternate. The first means would be to identify and recognize the various trade-offs, but to emphasize one dimension at a time, alternating so that neither dimension is completely ignored. Although potentially effective, the downside with this approach is that the firm often experiences a "pendulum effect," as there can be a tendency to overreact to a perceived imbalance on one dimension leading to a subsequent imbalance on the other dimension. Too often, there is too much of the wrong thing at the wrong time.

Divide. The second means of achieving marketing balance would be to "split the difference" and do a little of both to "cover all the bases." The idea here is to mix and match marketing efforts, so that both dimensions are covered. For example, at one point, Dewar's Scotch ran two print ad campaigns simultaneously. "Portraits" offered descriptive "personals" type of information of young scotch drinkers in an attempt to make the brand more relevant to a younger audience. And "Authentics" focused on the heritage and quality of the scotch, appealing to an older audience that was already part of the brand franchise and presumably valued more intrinsic product qualities.

Clearly, such solutions can be expensive and difficult, as two distinct marketing programs have to be successfully designed, financed and implemented. They can also result in conflicting messages and customer confusion. Although potentially effective if properly executed, this approach may suffer if insufficient or inadequate resources are put against the two objectives, with critical mass not being achieved. Attempting to do "a little of this and a little of that" may be too wishy-washy and lack sufficient impact.

Reconcile. Finally, perhaps the best way to achieve marketing balance is by reconciling the differences and achieving a positive synergy between the two dimensions. Marketing balance in this way occurs by shrewdly addressing the decision trade-offs head-on (i.e., by resolving the conflicting dimensions in some uniquely creative manner). Hitting the branding sweet spot in this way may involve some well thought out moderation and balance throughout the marketing organization and its activities. Top marketing organizations such as Procter & Gamble (P&G), Nike, LVMH, Virgin and Toyota differ in many ways, but they share one characteristic: They have been remarkably adept at balancing trade-offs in building and managing their brands.

Achieving Marketing Balance

A two-step approach can help in achieving marketing balance: First, the extent and nature of the marketing trade-offs faced by the organization must be defined. Then, appropriate solutions must be developed to address the trade-offs as carefully and completely as possible.

To understand the nature and extent of the marketing trade-offs, some key questions must be answered: How severe are they? Are they unavoidable, inherent in the nature of the decision problem and situation? How have they been dealt with before? Of particular importance is to recognize whether the trade-offs result from internal, organizational considerations or external, structural issues inherent in the marketing environment where management has less control.

Next, marketers must develop effective means for achieving marketing balance. Given the wide range of marketing trade-offs that exists, it is perhaps no surprise that a correspondingly wide range of solutions is also typically available. We briefly outline six different options that are available to marketers to achieve marketing balance in Table 2.

Breakthrough Product or Service

One compelling way to resolve potential marketing strategy trade-offs is through product or service innovations. For example, Miller Lite became the first successful nationally marketed light beer through an innovative brewing formulation that was able to retain more of the taste profile of a full-strength regular beer, while still having a lower calorie count. Breakthrough product or service innovations

Table 2 Achieving Marketing Balance

- Breakthrough product or service innovation
- Improved business models
- Expanded or leveraged resources
- Embellished marketing
- Perceptual framing
- Creativity and inspiration

may not necessarily always require such significant initial investments. Decades later, Miller Lite was able to re-assert its straddle "Tastes Great, Less Filling" brand promise through an intensive ad campaign that focused on its low carbohydrate levels. Miller Lite had always had a performance advantage on the basis of "low carbs," but it only became a positioning advantage when the company could tap into a growing consumer health trend.

As another example, when BMW first made a strong competitive push into the U.S. market in the early 1980s, it positioned the brand as being the only automobile that offered both luxury and performance. At that time, American luxury cars were seen by many as lacking performance, and American performance cars were seen as lacking luxury. By relying on the incomparable design of their car—and to some extent their German heritage too—BMW was able to simultaneously achieve (1) a point of difference on performance and a point of parity on luxury with respect to luxury cars and (2) a point of difference on luxury and a point of parity on performance with respect to performance cars. The clever slogan, "The Ultimate Driving Machine," effectively captured the newly created umbrella category: luxury performance cars. Product differentiation can occur through technological innovation or creative repositioning.

Improved Business Models

Sometimes the solution is broader than just the product itself, and encompasses other aspects of the business. For example, P&G's switch to every-day low prices (EDLP) necessitated that the company overcome the potential trade-offs between high-quality products vs. the high costs and prices that are typically involved in delivering high levels of quality. P&G knew it could not deliver everyday low prices without having low everyday costs.

To reduce costs, P&G implemented a number of changes, simplifying the distribution chain to make restocking more efficient through continuous product replenishment. The company also scaled back its product portfolio by eliminating 25 percent of its stock-keeping units. Importantly, all of these cost-reduction changes were done without sacrificing product quality, allowing P&G to maintain much of its market leadership.

Expanded or Leveraged Resources

Another means of achieving balance and overcoming the inherent trade-offs in marketing decision making is to find ways to expand or leverage existing resources to make them more productive. For example, one approach often employed in addressing positioning trade-offs—albeit not without some investment implications—is to use ingredient brands (e.g., "Intel Inside") or a celebrity spokesperson / endorser. Ingredient brands or celebrities can reinforce a potentially weak area of a brand image. For example, General Motors used the popular appeal of golfer Tiger Woods for a number of years, to give its aging Buick brand a potentially more youthful and contemporary image.

Skillfully expanding resources is another means to adequately address more dimensions in a trade-off. For example, taking the cue from Harley-Davidson, Apple and others, many firms are attempting to build online and/or off-line brand communities. Building brand communities allows firms to tap into the passions and dedication of existing customers, reinforcing their loyalty and motivating and empowering them to serve as brand ambassadors or even brand missionaries with other consumers. In this way, existing customers help to bring new customers into the fold. Brand communities can thus be an effective means to help a firm both acquire and retain customers for its brands.

Embellished Marketing

Another potentially productive strategy is to find ways to embellish existing marketing programs to encompass a neglected or even missing dimension. In what ways can a marketing decision or action that typically emphasizes one dimension be modified or augmented to also encompass another dimension at the same time?

For example, many sales promotions emphasize price or discounts at the expense of product or service advantages, and thus the equity of the brand. Bucking that trend, however, P&G ran a clever promotion for Ivory soap that reinforced its key attribute of "floating" and its key benefit of "purity" while also providing an incentive for purchase: A select number of bars of soap were weighted such that they sank in the bathtub, giving the purchaser the right to enter a contest to win $250,000. Equity-building promotions that introduce key selling points into traditionally price-focused sales promotions are thus one way to incorporate an important but underemphasized dimension into marketing decisions.

Perceptual Framing

Trade-offs vary in terms of whether they are based in reality, reflecting inherent "laws" of the marketplace or, instead, are based on perceptions—thus reflecting the potentially biased or maybe just idiosyncratic views of the parties involved. The more the latter is the case, the more opportunities there are for marketing efforts to overcome potentially inaccurate or incorrect perceptions.

Perceptual framing can be an especially powerful way to achieve robust brand positions and, thus, marketing balance. For example, when Apple Computer Inc. launched the Macintosh, its key point of difference was "user friendly." Many consumers valued ease of use—especially those who bought personal computers for the home, but customers who bought personal computers for business applications inferred that ease of use meant that the computer must not be very powerful—a key choice consideration in that market.

Recognizing this potential problem, Apple ran a clever ad campaign with the tag line "The power to be your best," to redefine what a powerful computer meant. The message behind the ads was that because Apple was easy to use, people in fact did just that—they used them! It was a simple, but important, indication of "power." From that point of view, there was a positive, not negative, correlation between the two choice criteria.

Creativity and Inspiration

One powerful solution to reconcile conflicts in marketing decision making is to find potentially overlooked synergies. Perhaps the common denominator to all the different advocated solutions reviewed in this article is marketing creativity and the ability to address seemingly insurmountable problems through imaginative marketing solutions. Achieving marketing balance requires penetrating insights, shrewd judgments and a knack for arriving at solutions that go beyond the obvious. Creativity, the combination of previously unrelated ideas into new forms, is often the inspiration to achieve marketing balance.

For example, in the early 1990s, the California Milk Processor Board (CMPB) uncovered an insight that had been overlooked by marketers of milk all over the world. Unlike traditional and increasingly ineffective marketing campaigns that emphasized the healthful benefits of milk (e.g., how it made people look and feel good), the CMPB recognized that one powerful advantage of milk was as an indispensable companion or even "ingredient" with certain foods (e.g., cookies, cakes, etc.). With their ad agency Goodby Silverstein, the CMPB took that insight and developed the highly creative Got Milk? ad campaign that entertained and engaged consumers and sold milk in the process. The amusing and beloved ads ensured that its humor did not detract from its fundamental message: Running out of milk is a pain!

The Implications of Marketing Balance

One of the challenges in modern brand marketing is the many strategic, tactical, financial and organizational trade-offs that seem to exist. Successfully developing and implementing marketing programs and activities to build and maintain strong brands over time often requires that marketers overcome conflicting objectives and realities in the marketplace. After reviewing the nature of these trade-offs, a set of guidelines and suggestions was offered toward achieving marketing balance and hitting the branding sweet spot—by arriving at "win-win" decisions that successfully reconcile marketing trade-offs.

Marketing balance can actually be more difficult to achieve than more extreme solutions that only emphasize one option, involving greater discipline, care and thought. To use a golf analogy, the golfer with the smoothest swing is often the one who hits the ball farther and straighter. Marketing balance may not be as exciting as more radical proposed solutions, but it can actually turn out to be much more challenging and productive.

It is all about making marketing work harder, be more versatile and achieve more objectives. To realize marketing balance, it is necessary to create multiple meanings, multiple responses and multiple effects with marketing activities. Marketing balance does not imply that marketers not take chances, not do different things or not do things differently. It just emphasizes the importance of recognizing the potential downside of failing to reconcile marketing trade-offs.

That said, there certainly may be times that given extreme circumstances, dire straits or an overwhelming need to achieve one objective at all costs, radical solutions are warranted. But even in these cases, marketers would be well-served to recognize exactly the extent and nature of the decision trade-offs they face, and the consequences of ignoring other options. Radical solutions should be thoroughly vetted and contrasted to more balanced solutions that offer more robust and complete solutions.

Marketing balance implies an acceptance of the fact that marketing is multi-faceted and involves multiple objectives, markets and activities. Marketing balance recognizes the importance of avoiding over-simplification: Marketers must do many things, and do them right. Fundamentally, to achieve marketing balance and truly hit the branding sweet spot, marketers must understand and fully address important marketing trade-offs.

Critical Thinking

1. Define Marketing Balance.
2. According to the article, why is maintaining marketing balance superior to the existence of strategic, tactical, financial, and organizational trade-offs?

Kevin Lane Keller has served as brand confidant for some of the world's successful brands, including Accenture, American Express, Disney, Intel, Levi-Strauss, Procter & Gamble, Samsung and Starbucks. His textbook, *Strategic Brand Management,* is in its 3rd edition and has been adopted at top business schools and firms around the world. He may be reached at kevin.keller@dartmouth.edu **Frederick E. Webster,** Jr. is widely recognized for his extensive research, writing, teaching and consulting in the field of marketing strategy and organization. Author of 15 books and more than 75 academic and management journal articles, his executive program teaching and consulting clients have included Ford, Mobil, IBM, DuPont, Monsanto, Praxair, General Electric, ABB, Chase Manhattan, Volvo and Phillips. He may be reached at fred.webster@dartmouth.edu.

Article 7

Putting Customers First

Nine Surefire Ways to Increase Brand Loyalty

KYLE LAMALFA

"Customers first." It's the mantra of businesses everywhere. Yet the average company still loses 10% to 15% of customers each year. Most of them leave due to poor service or a disappointing product experience, yet only 4% of them will tell you about it. And once they've left, it's difficult (not to mention expensive) to get them back.

Fostering true loyalty and engagement with customers starts at a basic level, but here are nine techniques you can employ to make customer loyalty a powerful competitive advantage for your company. They can be broken down into three categories: loyalty basics (one through four), loyalty technologies (five through seven) and loyalty measurement (eight and nine).

1. Give Customers What They Expect

Knowing your customer's expectations and making sure your product or service meets them is Business 101, yet often ignored. At the basic level, business needs to be a balanced transaction where someone pays for something and expects a fair trade in return.

Expectations of product quality come from many sources, including previous quality levels set by your organization, what competitors are saying about you, and the media. Marketing and sales should work together to monitor customer expectations through feedback and surveys.

2. Go Beyond Simple Reward Programs

Points and rewards encourage repeat purchases, but don't actually build loyalty. This is demonstrated by a drop in sales when the rewards are no longer offered. True loyalty comes when customers purchase products without being bribed.

3. Turn Complaints into Opportunities

Managing questions, comments and concerns benefits your business in two important ways. First, research indicates that an upset customer whose problem is addressed with swiftness and certainty can be turned into a highly loyal customer. Second, unstructured feedback, gathered and managed appropriately, can be a rich source of ideas. To that end:

- Establish channels (electronic, phone and written) to build engagement, one customer at a time.
- Encourage customers to voice their thoughts.
- Create metrics to improve response to concerns (i.e., "time to first response," "time to resolution," etc.).
- Create metrics to measure loyalty before and after the problem.
- Use technology to help you centralize the information, create reports and structure drill-downs.

4. Build Opportunities for Repeat Business

Give your customers a chance to be loyal by offering products for repeat business. Monitor what customers request most and offer products or services that compliment other purchases. In addition, exceed expectations by driving product development to offer more value for less cost. Use technology to track, classify and categorize open-ended feedback.

5. Engage Customers in a Two-Way Dialogue

An engaged customer is more than satisfied and more than loyal. They support you during both good and bad times because they believe what you have to offer is superior to others.

Engagement takes your customer beyond passive loyalty to become an active participant and promoter of your product. Engaged customers will give you more feedback so you should be ready to handle it! All this translates into a customer who will spend more money with you over time. Accordingly:

- Listen to customer feedback from comment cards, letters, phone calls and surveys.
- Respond quickly and personally to concerns of high interest to your customers.
- Organize unstructured feedback for tracking and trending over time.
- Trust your customers to tell you what the problem is.
- Use statistical techniques to discover which action items will have the most impact on your business.

6. Survey Customers and Solicit Feedback

Actively soliciting information from a population of customers is a time-tested technique pioneered by Arthur Nielsen (creator of the Nielsen ratings) in the 1920s. Survey research can be used for problem identification or solving. Questions with simple scales such as "agree/ disagree" deliver quantitative insight for problem identification. Open-ended follow-up questions can provide rich insight for solving problems. Some tips:

- Make sure your surveys are short, bias-free and well structured.
- Use random sampling to gather feedback continuously without over-surveying.
- Create summary survey indices that can be displayed graphically and tracked over time.

7. Create a Centralized System for Managing Feedback throughout the Enterprise

Technology such as enterprise feedback management (EFM) helps to centralize surveys and customer feedback and track both qualitative and quantitative information. EFM involves more than just collecting data, though; it adopts a strategic approach to building dialogs with your customers. Follow these steps:

- Empower customers to give feedback through common advertised channels.
- Centralize reporting for proactive surveys and complaint management solutions.
- Structure quantitative feedback into a drill-down or rollup report.
- Make open-ended feedback intuitively searchable.

8. Tie Customer Loyalty and Engagement to Business Outcomes

Orienting your organization to focus on satisfaction, loyalty and engagement is no panacea. But researchers have clearly documented evidence of short-term benefits to customer/ employee retention and long-term benefits to profitability. Hence:

- Determine whether to measure your engagement outcome by satisfaction, likelihood to purchase again, likelihood to recommend, or another voice of the customer (VOC) metric.
- If necessary, create hybrid VOC measurements using more than one metric.
- Link your VOC metrics with business outcomes like shareholder returns, annual sales growth, gross margin, market share, cash flows, Tobin's Q or customer churn.
- Be aware that changes in loyalty/engagement scores generally precede changes in business outcomes.

9. Use Analysis to Predict Future Loyalty

Businesses use a variety of statistical techniques to make predictions about the potential for future events. Furthermore, predictive analytics may be used to ascertain the degree to which answers from a survey relate to particular goals (such as loyalty and engagement). Tactical knowledge of how action items impact an outcome discourages the wasting of resources on ineffective programs, and competent statistical modeling reveals which tactical options work. Consequently:

- Analyze data using a statistical technique to reveal the most important areas of focus.
- Ask your analyst about common statistical methods, including correlation and logit models.
- Recognize that the major areas of focus may change in response to changes in your economic, competitive and demographic environments.

Following these steps may not be the easiest process, but stay focused. Increasing your engagement and loyalty equals increasing profits and a competitive edge.

Critical Thinking

1. Discuss the importance of establishing two-way dialogue with customers and effectively responding to customer feedback.
2. With a small group of peers from your class, develop some ways that companies can achieve affective two-way dialogue with customers.

Kyle LaMalfa is the best practices manager and loyalty expert for Allegiance, Inc. He can be reached at kyle.lamalfa@allegiance.com. For more information about how to increase your loyalty and engagement, visit www.allegiance.com.

Making the Most of Customer Complaints

Dealing with service failures means a lot more than just fixing the immediate problem. Here's how to do it right.

STEFAN MICHEL, DAVID BOWEN, AND ROBERT JOHNSTON

Nobody's perfect. That's a fact, not an excuse.

Which is why it's crucial for companies to realize that the way they handle customer complaints is every bit as important as trying to provide great service in the first place. Because things happen.

Customers are constantly judging companies for service failures large and small, from a glitch-ridden business-software program to a hamburger served cold. They judge the company first on how it handles the problem, then on its willingness to make sure similar problems don't happen in the future. And they are far less forgiving when it comes to the latter. Fixing breakdowns in service—we call this service recovery—has enormous impact on customer satisfaction, repeat business, and, ultimately, profits and growth.

But unfortunately, most companies limit service recovery to the staff who deal directly with customers. All too often, companies have customer service sort out the immediate problem, offer an apology or some compensation, and then assume all is well. This approach is particularly damaging because it does nothing to address the underlying problem, practically guaranteeing similar failures and complaints.

What businesses should be doing is looking at service recovery as a mission that involves three stakeholders: customers who want their complaints resolved; managers in charge of the process of addressing those concerns; and the frontline employees who deal with the customers. All three need to be integrated into addressing and fixing service problems.

Tensions naturally arise in and among the groups. For example, customers can be left feeling that their problem wasn't addressed seriously, even when they've received some form of compensation. Service reps can start seeing complaining customers as the enemy, even though they point out flaws that need fixing.

Managers in charge of service recovery, meanwhile, can feel pressure to limit flows of critical customer comments, even though acting on the information will improve efficiency and profits.

However, successfully integrating these three perspectives is something that fewer than 8% of the 60 organizations in our study did well.

Based on our research and our own years of work in service management, here is a look at the three stakeholders in service recovery, focusing on their different perspectives and the tensions that arise among them. We then make recommendations on how to address these tensions and integrate the aims of all three to achieve better—if not perfect—service.

The Customer

Fairness is typically the biggest concern of customers who have lodged a service complaint. Because a service failure implies unfair treatment of the customer, service recovery has to reestablish justice from the customer's perspective.

Say a bank customer requests a deposit receipt from an ATM but the machine fails to print one. The customer becomes worried and goes to one of the bank tellers. The teller checks the account, and assures the customer that there is no problem, that the deposit was made. But if the teller only focuses on the fact that the account was credited, he or she has ignored what in the customer's view was the most severe and critical aspect of the service failure: the worry initially felt, and the extra time it took to verify the deposit.

Customers often want to know—within a reasonable time—not only that their problem has been resolved, but how the failure occurred and what the company is doing to make sure it doesn't happen again.

A customer's faith can be restored using this kind of approach—once. We have even noted something referred to as a "recovery paradox," in which customers can be more delighted by a skillful service recovery than they are by service that was failure-free to start with.

But there is a flip side to this as well: Customers have more tolerance for poor service than for poor service recovery. And if a customer experiences a second failure of the same service, there is no recovery strategy that can work well. In all likelihood, that customer will be lost forever.

Our research suggests that after a failed service recovery, what annoys—and even angers—customers is not that they weren't satisfied, but that they believe the system remains unchanged and likely to fail again.

The Manager

The chief aim of managers in service recovery is to help the company learn from service failures so it doesn't repeat them. Learning from failures is more important than simply fixing problems for individual customers, because process improvements increase overall customer satisfaction and thus have a direct impact on the bottom line.

But companies generally obtain and study only a fraction of the service-failure data that could be gathered from customers, employees and managers. Even when managers agree that customer feedback is essential, there is often poor information flow between the division that collects and deals with customer problems and the rest of the organization.

In some cases, one study revealed, the more negative feedback a customer-service department collects, the more isolated that department becomes, because it doesn't want to be seen by the company at large as a source of friction. Some companies even create specialist units that can soak up customer complaints and problems with no expectation of feeding this information back to the organization. Others actually impede service recovery by rewarding low complaint rates, and then assuming that a decline in the number of reports indicates customer satisfaction is improving.

Some managers in our study saw conflicts between providing great customer satisfaction and achieving high productivity. For instance, incentive structures sometimes placed equal values on sales and on customer service. But as one manager noted: "If you want to achieve 100% [satisfaction], you don't have time for selling. It's questionable whether you can score 100% on service quality and 100% on [sales] objectives."

In any kind of business, there comes a point at which a service recovery can become excessive in the company's eyes, and be seen as giving away the store. However, many customers don't want a payoff. They simply want to have their problem fixed and to be reassured that it won't happen to other people in the future.

The Employee

Frontline service employees have the greatest job satisfaction when they believe they can give customers what they expect.

These workers have the difficult task of dealing with customers who hold them responsible even when the failures in question are completely out of their control. The attitudes of customer-service workers, positive and negative, spill over onto customers.

Yet companies do surprisingly little to support them.

To be successful, these workers need to feel that management is providing the means to deliver successful service recovery on a continuing basis. Alternatively, when employees believe management doesn't support them, they tend to feel they are being unfairly treated and so treat customers unfairly. They display passive, maladaptive behaviors and can even sabotage service.

This alienation is compounded when the workers believe that management is not improving the service-delivery process, which keeps employees in recurring failure situations. Even though complaining customers represent an opportunity to fix problems and improve satisfaction, alienated employees often see them as the enemy. In a study of a major European bank, employees in Switzerland consistently indicated that they did not consider reports of missing account statements to be complaints. As one said: "These things happen. There is nothing we can do about that."

At companies that reward low complaint rates, frontline employees become tempted to send dissatisfied customers away instead of admitting a failure has occurred.

Resolving the Tensions

Our experience with managers interested in improving service recovery indicates that most hope for a quick fix of some specific tensions. But quick fixes only treat the symptoms of underlying problems. Real resolutions should involve closer integration among the three stakeholders, such as gathering more information from customers and sharing it throughout the company, and adopting new structures and practices that make it easier to spot problems and fix them.

We suggest the following five strategies:

- **Create a "service logic" that explains how everything fits together.** This should be a kind of mission statement or summary of how and why the business provides its services. It should integrate the perspectives of all three groups:

  What is the customer trying to accomplish, and why?
  How is the service produced, and why?
  What are employees doing to provide the service, and why?

The results should serve as a guide both for delivering service and for help with service recovery. It should include a detailed study of internal operations; map out how the company responds to customer complaints; and describe how the company uses that information to improve service-recovery processes. Similar mapping should detail every step of customer experiences, including those of real customers with complaints, highlighting their thoughts, reactions and emotions along the way. Highly skilled managers and employees who can think outside the box are a must.

TNT NV, a Netherlands-based global delivery company, developed a service logic to help it grow in a mature market. Using a small, high-powered management team backed up by customer discussion forums, the company mapped its processes from a customer point of view, including a map of customer emotions during both regular processes and service recovery. The mapping exercise and the service logic that it produced led to a redesign of processes by managers and field staff that cut across traditional functional boundaries.

For example, previously a driver running late for a scheduled delivery had to call into the control center, which would then contact customer services, which would then contact the customer. Such calls often arrived after the delivery already had been made, thus further annoying the customer and embarrassing the driver. Since the process redesign, however, a driver running late is allowed to contact the customer directly. TNT drivers frequently visit the same customers almost every day, so their customers know them and appreciate the personal contact. The drivers also appreciate being able to make the calls directly.

- **Draw attention to the successes of customer-service groups.** Companies use in-house publications, intranets and training programs to share stories that emphasize their values and culture. Employees who come up with cost-saving ideas, for example, are often singled out for praise. But rewards and recognition also should flow to heroes in service-recovery stories. Such heroes can be on the operations side, helping to develop cost-efficient systems for handling complaints, and on the marketing side, giving a customer extraordinarily helpful treatment after a service failure.

Singapore Airlines Ltd., in its in-house magazines, frequently tells stories about employees who have provided not only outstanding service, but exceptional service recoveries. Senior managers, too, will not hesitate to swoop in anywhere there is an issue, creating more stories about internal vigilance.

Recovery Mode

The Issue: Every business can expect complaints from customers. It's how a business handles the complaints that matters most, and many do so poorly.

The Problem: When companies don't give upset customers a fair hearing or some assurance that the problem won't happen again, they are putting repeat business, profits and growth at risk.

The Solution: The key is to address tensions that arise among front-line employees who handle complaints, the managers of those employees, and the customers themselves. Steps include starting a complaints database that managers can analyze and use to improve service, and rewarding service employees not for reductions in complaints but for providing exceptional solutions to problems.

When customer-service employees believe that their goals are in line with the organization's values, they are more willing to exert the extra effort required in a failure-and-recovery situation.

- **Give customer-service staff as much freedom as your business strategy allows.** When a business has very few routines and its ties to customers are based on individual relations, service representatives should have more autonomy in resolving complaints. For such businesses, spending more time on service recovery—and retaining customers—has a clear effect on the bottom line. By contrast, in a highly standardized business with purely transactional customer relationships, such as a fast-food restaurant, employees should adhere to procedures in resolving complaints. Customer satisfaction in such businesses is closely aligned with high productivity, so there is less to be gained by customizing resolutions of complaints.

Ritz-Carlton, for example, the luxury brand of Marriott International Inc., authorizes personnel at the front desks of its hotels to credit unhappy customers up to $2,000 without asking a supervisor's approval. On the other hand, in one of our consulting projects, a client reacted very negatively to this approach, claiming that such a policy would be too expensive for his company. We replied that the high cost of poor service is exactly what makes this system work so well: It forces management to eliminate service failures in the first place.

- **Collect as much data as you can, and share it widely.** Companies must gather more feedback about poor service, record it and make it accessible. Managers and other employees have to be armed with strong information to be effective at resolving disputes.

It should be easy for customers to file complaints. One way to achieve this is by offering many communication channels. A regional airline in Asia, for example, uses annual passenger surveys, interviews with frequent fliers, focus-group discussions, customer hot lines, critical-incident surveys, onboard suggestion leaflets and even live call-in radio shows.

Software should be used that serves as a database for both positive and negative communications with customers. Employees and managers should be trained to mine the data and put it to use easily and quickly.

- **Use meaningful measures of employee performance—rewards and demerits.** Positive reinforcement and incentives should be offered for solving problems and pleasing customers. A system for measuring customer satisfaction should be devised to help rate employee performance. Salary increases and promotions then should be linked to an employee's achieving certain levels. There also should be disincentives or demerits for poor handling of customer complaints. Performance reviews thus may include a balanced scorecard—one that recognizes the need for both productivity and customer satisfaction.

Critical Thinking

1. Summarize the perspectives of the three stakeholders involved in service recovery.
2. In your opinion, why is it important to empower customer-service employees?

Dr. Michel is associate professor of marketing at Thunderbird School of Global Management, Glendale, Ariz. **Dr. Bowen** is the Robert and Katherine Herberger chair in global management and a professor at Thunderbird. **Dr. Johnston** is professor of operations management at Warwick Business School, University of Warwick, Coventry, England. They can be reached at reports@wsj.com.

When Service Means Survival

Keeping customers happy is more critical than ever. Service champs economize on everything but TLC.

JENA MCGREGOR

Hertz couldn't ask for a better customer than Richard M. Garber. The Cleveland-based business development manager typically rents cars from the chain 20 to 40 times a year when traveling on business for materials manufacturer FLEXcon. But now Garber is rethinking that loyalty. In the past month he has returned Hertz cars to the Boston and Minneapolis airports only to find nobody waiting with a handheld check-in device. In Minneapolis, Garber had to drag his bags to the counter to return his car; in Boston, he finally tracked down an employee who came out and explained that some colleagues had just been laid off. "When you're rushing for an airplane, every minute counts," says Garber. "The less convenient they are, the more likely I am to try someone else."

As the economy plunges deeper into recession, many companies are confronting the same brutal choices Hertz faced when it announced layoffs of some 4,000 people on Jan. 16. While businesses may feel forced to trim costs, cutting too deeply can drive away customers. Hertz spokesman Richard Broome says the company has reduced "instant return" hours at some smaller airports but is making adjustments to restore that service in locations where it "might have gone too far." Says Broome: "You try to create the right balance."

Across the business world, managers are trying to pull off the same perilous high-wire act. Just as companies are dealing with plummeting sales and sinking employee morale, skittish customers want more attention, better quality, and greater value for their money. Those same customers are also acutely aware that their patronage is of growing importance to companies as others decrease their spending. BMW Vice-President Alan Harris argues that in the current environment, consumers expect "that anyone who is in the market with money to spend is going to get treated like a king."

Keep the Front Lines Strong

The reality, of course, is that the opposite is often true. From retailers such as Talbots, which have stiffened their rules on returns, to airlines that now charge for checked bags, companies are stretching budgets in ways that can make things tougher for customers.

But the best performers are actually doing more to safeguard service in this recession. Bruce D. Temkin, principal analyst for customer experience at Forrester Research, says about half of the 90 large companies he recently surveyed are trying to avoid cuts to their customer service budgets. "There's some real resilience in spending," says Temkin.

That's especially true for many of the winners of our third annual ranking of Customer Service Champs. Top performers are treating their best customers better than ever, even if that means doing less to wow new ones. While cutting back-office expenses, they're trying to preserve front-line jobs and investing in cheap technology to improve service.

If anything, the tough economy has made starker the difference between companies that put customers first and those that sacrifice loyalty for short-term gain. In this year's ranking, based on data from J.D. Power & Associates, which, like *BusinessWeek,* is owned by The McGraw-Hill Companies, more than half of the top 25 brands showed improved customer service scores over last year. Among the bottom 25 of the more than 200 brands surveyed, scores mostly fell.

Cutting just four reps at a call center of three dozen can send the number of customers put on hold for four minutes from zero to 80.

Smart players have learned from previous downturns. Companies used to go after customer reps with the same blunt ax used elsewhere. Now managers are starting to understand the long-term damage created by such moves, from eroded market share to diminished brand value. The International Customer Management Institute, a call center consultant, has done studies that show eliminating just four reps in a call center of about three dozen agents can increase the number of customers put on hold for four minutes from zero to 80.

A better strategy is to get more out of the people you have. USAA, the insurance and financial services giant that caters to military families and ranks at No. 2 on our list, started cross-training its call center reps in 2007. Some 60% of the agents who answer investment queries can now respond to insurance-related calls. Not only did such training curb call transfers between agents, which drive up the cost of running a call center, but it also improved productivity. Even with Hurricane Ike and the stock market's financial crisis prompting a flood of calls to USAA's contact centers last year, the cross-training meant the company didn't have to expand its call center staff. Existing reps are more empowered to deal with customers, even if they may also have to do more work. No. 25 JW Marriott is training administrative assistants to step in as banquet servers when needed. And in November, brokerage Charles Schwab, No. 21 on our ranking, launched a "Flex Force" team of employees such as finance specialists and marketing managers at its San Francisco headquarters to handle calls on days of, say, rapid market fluctuations.

For those that slash costs, the challenge is keeping customers from noticing. Putting call center reps under one roof, for example, can eventually save as much as 35%, says Scott Casson, director of technology services at consultant Customer Operations Performance Center. On Feb. 12, USAA announced it will combine its six call centers into four; companies such as No. 11 KeyBank and Ace Hardware, No. 10, have also consolidated operations in the past year. Ace plowed the savings from that move into longer evening and weekend hours for customer calls. "During tough times there are plenty of other pressures customers face," says Ace Vice-President John Venhuizen. "We don't want a customer service issue to be what makes them blow their cork."

Safeguarding Service

Times are unquestionably tough. But cutting too deeply may only make things worse. Here are four ideas for keeping costs down and customer service solid:

Flex Your Workforce

Cutbacks in staffing levels may be necessary as sales slow. But to keep service quality high, make the most of the workers you have. Cross-train employees so they can step up to fill a variety of needs—and you can avoid making new hires.

Spoil Surviving Staff

Slashing jobs and benefits can wreak havoc on morale. If you must cut back, keep the front lines happy with flexibility and other rewards. American Express, for example, now lets call center reps choose their own hours and swap shifts without supervisors' approval.

Invest in Simple Technology

It may not be the best time to upgrade your call center with pricey software. But easy self-serve solutions such as in-store Web cams that link customers with remote tech experts can serve multiple locations at minimal cost.

Baby Your Best Customers

Now is not the time for equal treatment. Keep your most active buyers coming back with faster service, extra attention, and flexible rules. As business travel slows, Marriott, for instance, is extending elite status to its best guests even if they don't qualify under normal rules.

Pleasing Repeat Buyers

Hoteliers also are trying to trim in ways customers are unlikely to detect. They're increasingly combining purchasing power to get better deals across properties that are within the same chain but may have different owners. Some hotels in the Four Seasons chain, No. 12, are joining up to buy goods and services such as coffee, valet parking agreements, and overnight cleaning contracts that each hotel once bought on its own. JW Marriott hotels are teaming up to buy landscaping services that would be costlier if contracted for separately. The Ritz-Carlton, No. 5, is doing laundry at night to save electricity and replacing fresh flowers at posh properties with potted plants. With occupancy rates falling, notes Ritz COO Simon F. Cooper, "you have to get better because you're forced to."

As the game changes from acquiring new customers to keeping old ones, companies are shifting more resources to their steady patrons. They're the ones who pay the bills. And while first-time guests may not miss the absence of fresh flowers, repeat customers probably will. "It's the little things that often got you in the crook of those loyal customers' arms," says Jeanne Bliss, a former Lands' End service chief who now coaches customer service execs. That has led to a renewed emphasis on "tiering"–routing elite-level customers to better agents, nicer surroundings, or faster service.

A Road Warrior's Story: Four Stars for the Four Seasons

Last April, I was visiting top tech companies in Austin, Tex., while working for the World Economic Forum. On the flight in, after the attendant said: "Please put your laptop away. This is the fifth time I've told you," I closed my laptop and put it down beside me. I was jet-lagged and super tired.

The next thing I know, I'm in my room unzipping my bag, thinking "Where's my laptop?" I was at the Four Seasons, so I call the concierge, Steven Beasley, and tell him what happened. Two seconds later, he calls back and says he has American Airlines on the phone. I explain the problem, and they say nothing has come up on the system. About five minutes later, the concierge phones me back and says he's called the San Francisco airport to alert them to check the plane when it arrives there.

By that time I've given up. I go down to have dinner, and I'm having a predinner drink when the concierge turns up at my table and says: "Mr. Mulcahy? I've got your laptop," and hands it to me. "Would you like me to take it to your room?" I'm like "what the—what?" He'd taken it upon himself to keep badgering American. They did another check, and in fact they still had the laptop in Austin.

The concierge could have just left a message. I was so grateful to him for having gone this obscenely extra mile.

A Social Networker's Story: The Zappos Ceo and Ups Step in

I usually get packages sent to the office, but in December I ordered a big 110-pound storage unit from Target and needed it delivered to my house. I called UPS to check on it, and the rep said that sometimes during the Christmas season packages don't arrive until 9 P.M.

Getting agitated, I posted on Twitter about waiting for UPS and mentioned how I couldn't take my dog, Ridley, for a walk. After 9 P.M., I got a message from Tony Hsieh, CEO of Zappos, who started following my Tweets [comments on Twitter] after we met last year. He was having dinner with UPS's president for the Western region and sent a message saying the guy would call me. I got a call in the next five minutes. The UPS exec got me in touch with an operations manager to arrange for a delivery the next morning so I could make a scheduled client meeting.

At 9 A.M. on the dot, the doorbell rings. Not only do they have the package, but there's a UPS guy with flowers and chocolates and another with treats and toys for Ridley. They even offered to assemble the unit and listened to my suggestions for improving service. I now go out of my way to use UPS—and I bought shoes the next day at Zappos.

Consider No. 7, Zappos.com, the online shoe retailer whose devoted fans rave about its free shipping on both orders and returns. The retailer had typically upgraded both first-time and repeat customers to overnight shipping even though it wasn't advertising that perk. But starting in 2009, Zappos will no longer offer overnight upgrades to first-time visitors. Instead, CEO Tony Hsieh is moving those dollars into a new VIP service for Zappos' most loyal shoppers. Launched in December, the site, which for now can only be accessed by loyal customers who receive an invitation, promises overnight shipping and plans to offer earlier access to sales and new merchandise than the plain-vanilla site. (Repeat customers who aren't yet asked to join the VIP service will continue getting the overnight upgrade for now.) "We decided we wanted to invest more in repeat customers," says Hsieh. "We're shifting some of the costs that would have gone into new customers."

Some are also getting tougher on suppliers who serve their most frequent customers. No. 24 L.L. Bean dropped Bank of America as its vendor of store-branded credit cards in July 2008. The outdoor outfitter says the bank wasn't measuring up in terms of its vaunted customer support. Complaints about long hold times and call transfers between the bank's customer service agents were "endless," says Terry Sutton, L.L. Bean's vice-president for customer satisfaction. (Bank of America says it doesn't comment on specific relationships but is "focused on providing competitive products and exceptional customer service.") L.L. Bean switched to Barclays, which meant customers had to reapply. The risk that some might not take the time was high. "From a service standpoint, it was loaded with land mines," says Sutton. But she felt the move was worth it, especially since Barclays gave them a say on agents' scripts and set up its call center in the retailer's home state of Maine. Over 60% of cardholders have already switched.

Some companies are experimenting more with cheap technology, such as responding to customers via Twitter after they broadcast their complaints to the world. Other tech upgrades for customers can deliver unexpected cost savings. When No. 22 BMW rolled out Wi-Fi service at its dealerships last year, the move was intended to give customers a cheap way to pass the time while their cars were serviced. The cost was next to nothing since BMW just expanded the broadband dealers already used to run their businesses. But now that customers can use their waiting time productively, fewer are opting for free loaner cars, which are pricey for dealers to maintain. BMW's Alan

Harris says Wi-Fi, along with software that helps dealers better estimate loaner needs, has helped BMW cut its monthly loaner expenses by 10% to 15%.

When companies come up with simple, low-cost ways to trim costs while improving life for customers, they're likely to win in good times and bad. "I have a saying: 'Fix the customer before you fix the car,' " says Harris. "If you focus on fixing the customer's problem first, the rest is easy."

Critical Thinking

1. According to this article, why is it vital, in today's economy, for businesses to avoid cutting front-line service employees?
2. Describe some high and low satisfaction interactions you have personally had with service providers.

With Aili McConnon in New York and David Kiley in Detroit.

Become the Main Attraction

People go to summer events for music, food and fun—not for marketing materials.

Here's how you get them to pay attention to you.

PIET LEVY

There are hundreds, maybe thousands of people here. Many of them are just the types of customers you are looking for. But odds are that none of them are here to see you. Instead, the masses have gathered at this event to hear music, watch sports, eat food or, in the case of conferences, network and listen to keynote presentations.

The consumers are there for their reasons and you're there for yours: to market your brand and increase awareness and sales. In a sea of noise, surrounded by hordes of talking people, distracting attractions and numerous marketing booths and street teams competing for consumers' attention, you have to stand out. But in addition to turning heads, you have to open minds. Beyond handing out coupons or samples or tchotchkes, you must showcase the value of your product or service in an interactive and engaging way, which also means training the right people to serve as brand messengers. If you make sure you're memorable, when the event ends and the consumers go about their daily lives, they'll remember you, tell others about you and pay to experience your product or service.

Step Right Up

Event marketing is important because it "places your product or service face to face with your target audience," argues Brad Horowitz, vice president of marketing for Elite Marketing Group, an experiential agency with headquarters in New Hyde Park, N.Y. "Brands can have a conversation with consumers rather than delivering a monologue. Conversations allow for customized learning, which fosters purchasing behavior. Additionally, it allows for valuable feedback from consumers about the product or service and the perception out there in the real world."

To be the most effective event marketer, you have to go beyond just being at a popular event and set up shop in a premium position. "Juxtaposing your footprint to a high-traffic location at an event such as the entry or the food court will allow for the greatest reach and greatest amount of impressions," Horowitz says.

That's also where a lot of other marketing booths or street teams will be hanging out. But don't worry about them; worry about yourself, and calm those concerns by establishing a physical presence that pops.

Overland Pak, Kan.-based Sprint Nextel Corp., which sponsors the National Association for Stock Car Auto Racing's (NASCAR) Sprint Cup Series, incorporates a jumbotron, trophy replica and NASCAR driver appearances at its display at races, says Tim Considine, general manager of the sponsorship. To attract mechanics to its travelling display last year, the U.S. Air Force showcased customized vehicles that incorporated Air Force technology, says Kristin Krajecki, director of experiential marketing at the Air Force's experiential agency, GSD&M Idea City in Austin, Texas. For its presence at the National Religious Broadcasters Convention and Exposition earlier this year, TV Magic Inc., a San Diego-based broadcast solutions provider, presented a cross designed out of televisions at its booth, the sort of visual element that conference-attending pastors may want at their churches, says Stephen Rosen, president and CEO of the company. "You've got to make an impressive impression and let [consumers] feel that spending a few minutes with you of their very precious time is worth it," Sprint's Considine says.

You may not have the budget to bring your own jumbotron, super car, or elaborate TV display to an event, but you can find creative ways to cut costs. TV Magic actually reduced its trade show budget by 50% this year and was still able to replace its "worse than blah" booth from last year with one featuring the TV display, Rosen says. Savings came from two areas: TV Magic reduced the number of company representatives at the booth from seven to three, and the company partnered with electronic suppliers such as Sony and Panasonic to provide equipment at no cost, says Jeff Symon, President and CEO of San Diego-based Aim Agency, TV Magic's agency. In some cases, you may even be able to find a company partner to participate with you at the event and subsidize expenses, he also suggests.

Whatever you put together, make sure the element is relevant to the audience and reflective of your brand. The cars at the Air Force display appealed to gear heads, but given the Air Force-inspired modifications, including an ejection seat, vertical doors, and aircraft style controls, the brand was even more reinforced. In addition to the church-friendly TV display at its convention booth, TV Magic put together a system where pastors could be filmed and the video edited and broadcast to a TV, online, and mobile device on the spot as a way to demonstrate the type of service the company provides, Symon says.

It's also a good idea to make your display interactive to increase the odds and length of time that consumers will stick around. Incentives are another way to draw people in. Sprint stages racing video games on its jumbotron that people can participate in and offers free gifts to customers, Considine says.

You should also try to design the space to allow for easier traffic flow. Symon suggests removing any table separating consumers from brand messengers to allow greater interactivity and openness. Considine says the Sprint layout features no walls or interiors to better increase impressions and interaction, and the jumbotron is in place to increase the possibility of engaging people from the periphery.

Razzle-Dazzle Them

The wow factor and selling points are crucial event marketing criteria, but Considine argues that "the hand you shake, the kindness that you show to someone in an [event] marketing environment, may be more powerful than the information you present."

In addition to head-turning displays, you have to rely on your brand representatives to present the brand properly, yet oftentimes marketers may have to outsource for those services, as Sprint does for its NASCAR display.

To find the right people for the job, Aim Agency first profiles what the brand stands for and the type of people who would best represent it. Then comes an online evaluation process that serves as a screener to see if candidates match brand objectives, Symon says.

If you don't have the budget to recruit an agency to help you with staffing, use the interview process to determine which candidates are extroverted, upbeat, articulate, and professional, Considine and Symon say. Jessica Fisher, Senior Manager of events for athletic apparel company Reebok International Ltd. in Canton, Mass., says that before an interview begins it's important to have a casual conversation about the candidate's perspective of the brand to gauge his enthusiasm and understanding. It also helps to recruit people who can relate to the target audience. For its M&M's supporting street team at NASCAR races, Mars Chocolate North America utilizes two employees from the company's PR agency, Weber Shandwick, who are actual fans of NASCAR so their interaction with fans will be authentic, says Suzanne Beaudoin, Vice President of sponsorship and sports marketing for the Hackettstown, N.J.-based company.

Once your team is in place, make sure staff members dress the part to not only physically represent the brand but also attract consumers. The M&M's street team stands out with NASCAR-style jumpsuits, Beaudoin argues, to help communicate the brand's Most Colorful Fan website and Facebook page, which encourage NASCAR fans to submit photos displaying their love of the sport for a cash prize. Similarly, the Air Force tries to place its brand representatives in the most appropriate attire based on the event, says Captain Homero Martinez, the former chief of event marketing for the Air Force Recruiting Service. For a recent Memorial Day race, Martinez says, formal dress was appropriate given the holiday weekend's correlation with the Air Force. For more casual events like music festivals, staff wear more relaxed uniforms to reduce any consumer concern that they will be pressured to sign up.

By the Numbers

The Norwalk, Conn.-based Event Marketing Institute and Auburn Hills, Mich.-based experiential agency George P. Johnson Co. interviewed 108 sales and marketing management leaders for its EventView report, an annual study assessing the relevance of event marketing. Some key findings:

62% of respondents say their marketing budget for events has either remained constant or increased in 2010.

32% consider event marketing a "vital component" of their marketing plan.

64% cited event marketing as one of the top three elements for accelerating and deepening relationships, followed by social marketing (55%) and online marketing (54%).

Want a Ticket to Ride?

Follow These 10 Instructions For Successful Event Marketing:

1. Set up your booth or street team in highly trafficked areas.
2. Have a visual element that turns heads but connects back to your brand.
3. Find participating partners to subsidize costs.
4. Present an interactive element, like a game, so consumers stick around for a while.
5. Make your space as open as possible to maximize traffic and engagement.
6. Entice visitors with incentives like coupons or samples
7. Find upbeat, extroverted, professional, articulate people to act as brand representatives.
8. Cast people who can relate with the target demographic, like employing NASCAR fans for booths at NASCAR events.
10. Train representatives with quizzes and run-throughs, but don't overwhelm them with details.
11. Dress your staff so they stand out, but make sure they look approachable.

The U.S. Air Force paraded customized cars equipped with jet-inspired technology at events last year in an effort to attract mechanics for the Air Force on the spot, he says.

Beyond looking the part, training must be done so that brand representatives can act the part. Training should include quizzing participants about the brand and business objectives in addition to on-site run-throughs, Symon says, and participants should be encouraged to ask questions for clarification's sake. Fisher recommends giving representatives the product when applicable, so that when they are on site, "they are not just giving out words, but talking from their own experiences." It's ideal to have people who work for the company on hand to help address consumer questions, but for those assigned with attracting people with their presence and interaction, it's important not to overwhelm them with instructions during the training process. Considine says his advice boils down to one simple philosophy: Treat passing consumers like guests at your home. If they feel welcome, there's a greater chance they'll welcome your product or service into their lives.

Critical Thinking

1. What makes event marketing an attractive promotion option for businesses?
2. With a small group of peers from your class, design an event marketing plan for any business of your choice.

Beyond Products

More manufacturers are branching out into the service business. Here's how to make the move successfully.

STEPHEN W. BROWN, ANDERS GUSTAFSSON, AND LARS WITELL

For many manufacturers looking to boost their business, simply selling products doesn't cut it anymore.

Companies in a range of fields—from pulp and paper to telecommunications—have decided that they have to branch out into services to stay competitive. Some truck manufacturers, for instance, don't just offer vehicles; they also sell maintenance and service packages, as well as driver-training programs. In some cases, they even sell services that go well beyond caring for trucks, such as advising clients on ways to improve their logistics operation.

Why the push into services? In part, necessity. In the fiercely competitive global market, companies must do whatever they can to stand out. But companies that have successfully made the move say there are substantial benefits, too.

For one thing, unlike products, services often deliver a regular stream of income. They also require a lower fixed capital investment, and frequently bring higher margins, than products do. What's more, they can be tougher for rivals to copy—which can bring big competitive advantages.

Then there's marketing. Companies say they can build on their existing products, brand image and customer base when pitching a line of services. And when an existing customer buys services as well as products, it builds loyalty, since the two companies work together much more closely.

For all of that promise, though, making services work isn't easy, and success is far from assured. Many companies are unprepared when they make the move into new territory, and fall into a number of traps, such as introducing services the wrong way and focusing on the wrong points when pitching them to customers.

To learn the best way to do things, we surveyed hundreds of business-to-business manufacturers in a range of industries, interviewed many executives and developed several in-depth case studies. We looked at what made the unsuccessful firms stumble—and what helped the successful firms rise to the top.

Here's what we found, starting with what can go wrong.

Better Served

- **The Big Step:** Many manufacturers are starting to offer for-pay services in an effort to stand out in a competitive market and open up new streams of revenue.
- **The Pitfalls:** For all the promise that services hold, success is far from assured. Companies can fall into plenty of traps when entering this new territory—such as thinking the same strategies that worked for introducing new products will work for services.
- **The Road Map:** Successful companies use a number of common strategies, such as creating a separate division to handle services and devising generic service packages that customers can modify.

A Host of Hurdles

Many manufacturers in our research moved into the new territory without any clear strategy. For many years, they offered discounted or even free services to secure sales for their products, such as maintenance plans or training courses for the people who would be using the products. But later, when the companies tried to start charging for those services, they found that customers often weren't prepared to pay for something they used to get free.

Many companies also met internal resistance to their service plans. Sales forces were a particular challenge. For instance, sales teams often had incentive programs tied to meeting targets for product sales, and it was hard to incorporate services into that structure.

What's more, selling services is often more challenging than selling products. Aside from the fact that customers sometimes were used to getting the services free, it was much harder to show the value of an intangible offering and figure out how

Challenges and Payoffs

How surveyed manufacturing companies rated the severity of the hurdles to overcome in expanding their profitable service offerings (7 = most severe, 0 = not severe)

Organization not ready	**4.2**
Lack of experience	**4.1**
Pricing	**4.0**
Resistance from customers	**4.0**
Resistance from sales force	**3.8**
Lack of channels	**3.6**
Services are a cost driver	**3.6**
Economic potential	**3.5**

How the companies rated the benefits of making the transition to services (7 = high, 0 = low)

Improved customer relationships	**6.6**
Capturing a large share of the value life cycle	**5.8**
Meet the needs of customers to outsource	**5.6**
Response to changing customer needs	**5.4**
Achievement of competitive differentiation	**5.0**
Greater income stability	**5.0**
Profit margin for services	**4.7**
Response to decreased profit margin for hardware	**4.3**

Source: Stephen W. Brown, Anders Gustafsson, and Lars Witell.

to price it. And when the price finally got hammered out, it often led to disappointment. For people who are used to selling million-dollar equipment, it's tough to get excited about selling $50,000 maintenance contracts, even if they represent a recurring stream of income.

Meanwhile, moving into services often meant building up new sales connections within the customer's organization, often higher up the decision-making chain—and far removed from anyone who would actually be using the service.

The sales-force problem was just part of a larger issue: Many companies attempted to market new services the same way they sold new products—by giving employees new responsibilities while keeping the current structures, practices and incentives in place.

Different Knowledge Base

But people who have been focused on developing and selling products usually don't have the deep knowledge of a customer's operation they need to create and market services. To come up with an idea for a new product, for instance, you might only need to have a general knowledge of the industry and the problems that companies often face. But if you're trying to, say, take over a customer's maintenance operation or offer advice on improving logistics, you must know specifics about how companies do their job.

That wasn't the only big organizational mistake. Some manufacturers tried to get their whole operation behind the service effort, letting every department help in developing and delivering the new offerings. It seemed to be the best way to use the company's limited resources and ensure that products and services would work well together.

But this approach leads to lots of practical problems. When multiple departments are responsible for delivering services, it's tough to ensure a consistent level of quality—which could potentially lead to lots of grumbling from customers. It also can be tough to get managers from across the company to agree on standards for pricing and other factors.

The result of all this? Manufacturing employees often ended up focusing on developing new products—and then rushing out new services to complement them almost as an afterthought.

Keep Services Separate

Many of the successful companies in our study addressed these issues by taking one big step: They kept services separate from the rest of the operation, creating separate units to develop and deliver their new offerings.

Telecom giant Telefon AB L.M. Ericsson, for instance, gathered its various service businesses into a single unit, Global Services. The division, which now accounts for nearly a third of the total employees at Ericsson, offers services such as managing the networks that mobile-phone companies use.

Some companies took the idea of a separate services unit a step further, partnering with outside firms to help them develop and deliver services.

Why wall off services this way? Culture. As we've seen, in a manufacturing company, all of the processes and habits are geared toward making and selling physical goods. Changing the focus of an entire organization is extremely difficult—and usually only marginally successful.

As a senior executive at Ericsson observed: "Culture wins over strategy each time."

New Mindset

Consider how much has to change to make services work. One auto executive described how his company added services to the mix:

"If you go back to even a very short while ago, our whole idea of a customer was that we would wholesale a car to a dealer, the dealer would then sell the car to the customer, and we hoped we never heard from the customer—because if we did, it meant something was wrong. Today, we want to establish a dialogue with the customer throughout the entire ownership experience. We want to talk to and touch our customers at every step of the way. We want to be a consumer-products and services company that just happens to be in the automotive business."

Not many companies can pull off that kind of a makeover—retraining hosts of employees and getting them not only to learn new skills but also to change the way they approach their job. So, it's usually easier to build a service operation from the ground up, one that works far more closely with customers than the rest of the business does, and charge it with creating and executing the strategy.

Many successful companies kept services separate from the rest of the operation, forming separate units to develop and deliver their new offerings.

Beyond that, we found that successful companies tended to use similar strategies in developing and marketing their services.

Standardize—and Customize

Many companies often plunged into services by closely tailoring their offerings to each customer. Companies would come up with plans that fit the particulars of a customer's processes but couldn't be easily applied to another customer. And those kinds of services took a great deal of effort and significant costs to develop.

The more successful firms moved beyond this initial strategy and came up with generic service packages. These deals offer a standard set of services that clients can customize by adding or removing options. This lets the manufacturers balance customization and standardization—and keep costs down.

For instance, one truck maker offers a maintenance and repair package with standardized prices for spare parts and scheduling for service. But let's say a customer wants to use another company's replacement parts in the trucks. The service plan would let the client customize the plan by dropping the replacement-parts feature.

Look Beyond Costs

The successful firms in our research used another key strategy in crafting their services: They focused on more than helping customers cut costs.

Many companies in our work took a basic approach, pitching their services simply as a way for customers to save money. They might argue, for instance, that customers could lower overhead by outsourcing their maintenance operation.

The more successful companies found they did better by adding another dimension to their offerings. They looked for services that would help their customers provide benefits to their *own* customers—and thus boost business.

One truck company, for instance, sells its customers fleet-management services, such as monitoring fuel consumption and teaching drivers how to drive more fuel-efficiently. This, in turn, helps the company's customers sell themselves as environmentally friendly to potential clients. And that's often a crucial factor for many clients, such as government agencies.

Or consider Ericsson. When one of its phone-company clients wants to offer a new option to its subscribers—such as Internet connectivity over mobile phones—Ericsson can help develop the program and provide behind-the-scenes support.

Critical Thinking

1. In your perspective, how can services be used as a means for brand differentiation and competitive advantage?
2. Explain the phrase '*standardize and customize*'.

Dr. Brown is the Edward M. Carson chair in services marketing and executive director of the Center for Services Leadership at Arizona State University's W.P. Carey School of Business. **Dr. Gustafsson** is a professor of business administration at Karlstad University's Service Research Center in Karlstad, Sweden. **Dr. Witell** is an associate professor of marketing at the Karlstad Service Research Center. They can be reached at reports@wsj.com.

Imaginative Service

You need it more in tough times.

CHIP R. BELL AND JOHN R. PATTERSON

Take the hertz shuttle bus at the Atlanta Airport, and you might meet ***Archie Bostick.*** Archie greets you with a welcoming grin. Instead of a tip jar, Archie paper-clips dollar bills across the front of his shirt. Nothing subtle about that ploy—it's an attention-getter that announces *this is a unique experience.* Once on the bus, Archie delivers a comedy routine and uses any excuse to break into song. As Archie pulls up to the terminal, he announces, "Now, I may never see you again, so I want us all to say together, 'I love Hertz!' " And everyone hollers, "I love Hertz!" You witness a service innovator at work—he takes your breath away.

Value-added has been the service solution for many service exemplars—take what the customer expects and add a little more. Nordstrom sales clerk escorts you to another department. Southwest Airlines gives you free peanuts with slapstick humor. And Rosie's Diner refills your ice tea glass without you being charged.

But value-added extras have gotten more expensive. That free snack on a flight is now $8, and service charges are standard fare on most bills. Pursuing the extras can also send a mixed message. What do employees think when told to "wow" customers in the morning and are later informed of staff cutbacks and expense reductions? Challenging financial times call for a new approach: *value-unique service.*

Value-unique is different than value-added. For most customers, value-added means taking the expected to a higher-level: "They gave me *more* than I anticipated." But, value-unique is not about addition—it's about an imaginative creation.

When service people are asked to *give more,* they think, "I'm already doing the best I can." But, if asked to *pleasantly surprise* more customers, they feel less like worker bees and more like fireflies. If employees are asked to create a big customer smile instead of work harder, they feel a part of an adventure. And, when they get to create, not just perform, they feel prized. Just ask a Southwest, Disney, or Lexus dealership employee what they think of their job, and you will get a smiling "It's awesome," not a shrugging "It's all right."

Imaginative service is sourced in joy and fun. It comes from the same part of the soul that plans a prank, organizes a party, or helps a friend. When that part is used regularly, it raises self-esteem, increases resilience, and improves morale. Take a look at *Fortune Magazine's* annual *100 Best Companies in America to Work For*—Nordstrom, Container Store, Marriott, eBay, Zappos.com, and FedEx—and you see the great service-high morale link. They boast the lowest turnover (a cost saver), the best recruits (an investment), the highest productivity (another positive) and the greatest profits.

Five Ways to Deliver Unique Value

Here are five ways to foster service that takes your customers' breath away:

1. ***Project realness.*** Imaginative service is about *realness,* not *roleness.* The stereotypical leader gets caught up with looking, sounding, and "acting" executive, and employees get a message of "plastic power"—which may engender *compliance* but never *commitment.* Great leaders are unimpressed with the trappings of supremacy and more interested in communicating an authentic spirit and egalitarian style.

Imaginative service leaders know they get from employees the attitude they project. Employees do not watch the leader's mouth; they watch the leader's moves. As all leaders move in the floodlight of employee observation, their actions can telegraph either optimism or gloom; excitement or despair. An animated attitude is contagious. When we are around happy, upbeat people, we more easily join in the spirit—especially if the invitation comes from someone who prefers we enroll. An unbridled spirit has magnetic power on both customers and employees.

2. ***Protect customers.*** Tasks are important; rules are essential. But, revenue comes from customers. Imaginative service leaders encourage and empower employees to put customers (not procedures) first. This is not about deliberately violating rules or putting anybody at risk.

Zappos.com was founded in 1999 with goal of doing to on-line shoe apparel what Amazon.com did to online books. In 2000 they had $1.6 million in sales; in 2008 their sales exceeded $1 billion! CEO ***Tony Hsieh*** explains their growth this way: "We're aligned around one mission—to provide the best customer service possible. Rather than focus on maximizing short-term profits, we focus on how we can maximize the service to our customers. We are a service company that happens to sell shoes." They protect customers from being taken for granted or subjected to discomfort.

3. ***Proclaim joy.*** In times of frugality, staff reductions, cost controls, and cutbacks, employees tend to be somber. Optimism is replaced with anxiety; hope is overshadowed by fear. The receiving end of such dower dispositions are customers with money to spend. When customers most need a shot of enthusiasm, they are served by sleepwalking employees who seem indifferent and bored. The antidote to such melancholy is a leader with unmistakable passion and irresistible joy. "The ultimate measure of a man," said Martin Luther King, "is not where he stands in moments of comfort and convenience, but where he stands at times of challenge and controversy."

"To succeed," says ***Scott Cook,*** founder of Intuit, "you need people with passion. You can't just order someone to be passionate about a business direction." Passion comes from a deep sense of purpose—not the "ought to" sense of obligation that drives duty, but the "can't wait to" enthusiasm that sets an employee on fire. As Federal Signal President ***Alan Shaffer*** said: "Our goal is not merely to get buy-in. I want to put a lump in their throats and a tear in their eyes. I want to take their breath away."

The number one impact on customer relations is employee relations—happy employees create happy customers.

4. ***Provide trust.*** Imaginative service happens in a climate of trust—where people are considerate and supportive. If people are given license to criticize colleagues behind their back, the setting turns to suspicion. If manipulative or unfair behavior is tolerated, the climate turns to protection. It requires leaders disciplined to model thoughtfulness and hold others accountable.

Trustful cultures nurture appropriate risk-taking that leads to novel solutions and refreshing customer experiences. Trusting leaders view *error* as a chance to learn and *failure* as an invitation to try another approach. They treat employees as valued gifts, not indentured slaves. They empower and encourage. They are open about their own foibles and upfront when they make mistakes. The word embedded in *trust* is *us.* Trustful leaders care for their employees with the same humanity they give their family. *Family-like* doesn't mean entitlement, paternalism, or nepotism. It means attention to fairness, justice, and compassionate conduct.

5. ***Preserve integrity. S. Truett Cathy,*** founder of Chick-Fil-A, has elected to remain closed on Sunday and gained favor for courageously remaining true and faithful to his values.

"I like dealing with an organization whose leaders stand for something!" comment customers when asked what they like most. Chick-Fil-A, Southwest Airlines, USAA, and The Container Store receive high marks. Stand-for-something leaders aren't the loud, flamboyant, publicity-seeking types. Instead, they are clear, focused, courageous, and committed to stay their course and stand their ground.

Imaginative service leaders are grounded in complete, no-exceptions integrity. They reek of integrity. As ***Tom Peters*** says, "There is no such thing as a *minor lapse of integrity.*" They show their nobility when they courageously tell the truth, relentlessly do what they say they will do, and gallantly turn their backs on all shady actions. They send signals through their character.

Customers seek more value for their money. As you scramble to shore up value, the time is ripe for service with inventiveness—not just service with generosity. Leaders must ensure that the elements they add to their leadership advance service innovation.

Critical Thinking

1. What do the authors of the article mean by a *value-unique* service?
2. With a small group of peers from your class, come up with a list of other imaginative services based on your own experiences and observations.

Chip R. Bell and **John R. Patterson** are customer loyalty consultants and authors of *Take Their Breath Away: How Imaginative Service Creates Devoted Customers.* www.taketheirbreathaway.com.

Article 13

Service with a Style

The Ritz-Carlton Chicago puts guests in driver's seat.

KITTY BEAN YANCEY

The instant a cab pulls up to The Ritz-Carlton Chicago, Mark Farrell lunges to open the taxi door, takes charge of an overnight bag and welcomes this unannounced guest by name.

How did he know it?

"I peeked at your luggage tag," the doorman says with a grin.

Later, when a search for Marshall Field's department store to buy a quintessential Chicago souvenir—a box of Frango mints—proves futile, lobby attendant Rhonda Stacks comes to the rescue. Noticing this guest's confusion, she explains that the landmark is no more and insists on leading the way to the Macy's next door, where the minty chocolates now are sold.

Such non-random acts of hospitality occur daily at the Chicago Ritz, the only hotel in the USA to top *Condé Nast Traveler* magazine's Readers' Choice Awards seven times. The Ritz, actually run by the Four Seasons chain, doesn't have as high a profile as many other U.S. luxury hotels and often is confused with a Four Seasons a few blocks away.

"You might think (the readers' top hotel) would be in New York," says *Condé Nast Traveler* public relations manager Megan Montenaro. But, in fact, the No. 2 Readers' Choice hotel of 2007 (The Peninsula Chicago) also is here, underscoring what *Traveler* calls "a renaissance of sorts for the nation's second city."

Veteran Staff Excels at Personalized Service

In this convention and shopping mecca with no shortage of luxury hotels, why does the Ritz stand out?

The Ritz-Carlton Chicago (A Four Seasons Hotel) is not the city's most cutting-edge luxurious lodging. (The Peninsula, with impressive public spaces and spa/health club with glassed-in pool overlooking the city, might win that honor. A pricey Trump International Hotel & Tower is due to open next week.)

It's not the hippest (the Park Hyatt, Sofitel and Hotel Monaco emit a cooler vibe). Though it garnered five AAA diamonds and five Mobil stars for 2007, so did its sister Four Seasons Hotel Chicago and The Peninsula. It scored below The Peninsula and the other Four Seasons in *Travel + Leisure* magazine's 2007 "World's Best" readers' awards.

While the lobby does exude Old World elegance, boasting a large splashing fountain with a bronze sculpture of three wing-flapping herons, the 32-year-old hotel's décor and furnishings are dated. Even the elevators have marble floors and crystal chandeliers. The lobby's upholstered sofas would be more at home in granny's parlor.

Bathrooms in standard rooms ("deluxe" in Ritz parlance) were updated a few years ago with granite counters and sleeker fittings. But pending a renovation planned next year, room furnishings are downright dowdy—The Ritz's PR team prefers the word "traditional"—compared with many competitors.

Suite 3011, for instance, is a discordant symphony of colors and patterns: red-and-white-striped chair, yellow sofa, green rug, flower-patterned bedroom chair and curtains. The walk-in closet contains objects that are anachronisms on today's hotel scene—a tiny safe that opens with a key, an adhesive roller lint remover and spray starch.

TVs are the fat, old-fashioned sort that sit in bulky armoires. There's plug-in Internet access, but if you want Wi-Fi, you'll need to go to the lobby.

The hotel sits above the Water Tower Place shopping center, which is either convenient or slightly tacky, depending on your point of view. And the hotel's entrance (you take an elevator up to the 12th-floor lobby) isn't opulent.

But what sets the Ritz/Four Seasons apart, say Montenaro and loyal guests, is its service. Snippets from the

Four Seasons Score in 2007

The Ritz–Carlton Chicago (A Four Seasons Hotel) has been named the top U.S. hotel[1] seven times in the *Condé Nast Traveler* Readers' Choice Awards. Results of the 2007 survey of more than 28,000 readers:

Rank	Hotel	Score (out of 100)
1.	The Ritz–Carlton Chicago (A Four Seasons Hotel)	95.2
2.	The Peninsula Chicago	95.1
3.	The Stephanie Inn, Cannon Beach, Ore.	94.9
4. (tie)	Four Seasons Hotel New York Hotel Bel–Air, Los Angeles	94.3

1–The top U.S resort in the 2007 survey was the Four Seasons Maui at Wailea in Hawaii. with 96 points.

generally favorable reviews on TripAdvisor: "Their staff is absolutely top-notch." . . . "They actually care about customer service; it was a refreshing change to experience."

"My wife and I look at lists of best hotels, and this is it," Winthrop Carter, 61, a bespectacled periodontist from Portland, Ore., says while checking out on a recent Wednesday. "This is the fourth year I've stayed here, and the staff is great."

The 435-room hotel has 544 staffers. Spokeswoman Susan Maier says 40% have been here a decade or more; 20% have served 20 years or longer.

Low-key chief concierge Jon Winke, so effective that guests have asked him to make hard-to-get restaurant reservations in their home cities, has been here 32 years.

More than half the guests he deals with are repeaters, he says. First-timers often are confused by the hotel name, so he explains it.

Ritz-Carlton doesn't own the hotel or have anything to do with it. The owners leased the right to use the name and in 1977 hired the Four Seasons chain to manage it.

From a counter next to the reception desk, Winke does far more than answer queries. He has found a gospel group to sing at a guest's home and set up a practice session in the hotel ballroom for a visiting NBA team that wanted to keep plays secret. In recent days, he was busy helping doting parents of preteens track down $375 eighth-row seats for this week's Hannah Montana/Miley Cyrus concert.

Now 53, he was hired at 21 as a bellman. He had no hotel experience.

"Instead of doing a purely technical interview—like, can they do a certain job?—we do a behavioral interview to decide if a person is sincere about service . . . if they'll take care of the guest," says general manager Christian Clerc, contacted by phone after USA TODAY's stay. Employees are given guidelines but no scripts to use with guests, he says. They can make decisions on the spot to rectify a problem.

Plus, "people from the Midwest have a very warm, genuine approach," says Swiss hotel school-trained Clerc. "It is prevalent throughout the city and very helpful (for a hotel). What makes the difference in high-end hotels is service, the interaction with the staff."

Indeed, service differentiation is where the luxury hotel industry is headed, says *Hotels* magazine editor in chief Jeff Weinstein. Lodgings have "spent the last few years working on hard goods—the beds, bathrooms and TVs." Now they're focusing on personalized care, he says.

So does the Ritz/Four Seasons deliver?

Check-in on a recent Tuesday at 2 P.M. is swift. Front-desk receptionist Shannon Moore, an upbeat blonde, acting as if she has all the time in the world, steps from behind the counter to deliver the keycard and explain hotel layout when this guest declines a bellman's assistance.

Up on the 30th floor, a housekeeper in a crisp, gray-skirted uniform stops her chores to show the way to a hard-to-find room.

Here, an annoyance surfaces: the sound of hammering. "I'm so sorry, they're doing some work in the shopping mall," Moore says after investigating. "It should be over at 5. Would you like to change rooms?" No thanks—too much hassle.

Back in the serene lobby, the host of The Café offers a newspaper to read during a short wait for a $22 chicken Cobb salad. A server presents a black napkin to drape over a guest's dark pants (to avoid getting white napery lint on them).

A post-lunch trip to the spa/health club finds it unremarkable in size or décor. But a deep-tissue massage from Romanian-born, Europe-trained Livius Cazan is world-class. (When a massage costs $135 for 55 minutes, it should be.)

Next comes a walk around downtown to see how the Ritz measures up to the other Four Seasons and three competitors. Staffers are friendly when addressed at competing properties, but only the doormen at the Four Seasons Chicago and The Peninsula give unsolicited greetings. Public spaces at the newer Four Seasons Chicago, owned by the same realty company that owns the Ritz, are more intimate and less grand than the Ritz's, and its recently renovated rooms tend to be more expensive.

Back at the Ritz, a room-service dinner ordered at 8:34 P.M. arrives in 29 minutes—a minute earlier than promised—on a linen-draped table with heating compartment. The roasted organic chicken in red-wine sauce, served on Villeroy & Boch china, is fork-tender.

There's a message from a night-shift front-desk staffer checking that the construction noise has abated (it has) and apologizing again.

Then, personalized attention goes to the max. A man identifying himself as a hotel security staffer calls to say a server saw a guest believed to be from this room drop sheets of notebook paper in the lobby earlier. May he bring them up?

As this guest's stay nears an end, a contact lens pops out somewhere on the bathroom floor, counter or sink. It's hard to resist the urge to phone the front desk for help. Somebody would come up. And they'd probably find it.

Critical Thinking

1. With a small group of peers from your class, outline the service attributes that make The Ritz-Carlton Chicago superior.
2. Using the information presented in the article, come up with a slogan for The Ritz Carlton Chicago.

Marketers, Come on Down!

Let's play the grand-prize game.

Some people know how to play the marketing game like chess; they play so well that they can accurately predict—and prepare for—the marketplace's next move. Some people happen to come up with the right idea at the right time (we're looking at you, Mark Zuckerberg!), and some people are just plain lucky.

These six marketers and marketing researchers have won that trifecta—they're smart, timely *and* lucky. They've positioned their companies' services to respond to consumers' changing behaviors and marketers' needs (a real double-whammy!). They're the marketing minds behind the tools that other marketers want, and they deliver on what marketers and consumers need: value.

Read on to find out who's behind some of the most talked-about marketing and marketing research tools that are helping marketers and consumers win big.

Allison Enright and Elisabeth A. Sullivan

Vicki Lins

CMO of Canoe Ventures—SelecTV

If all goes as planned, 2011 will be a big year for SelecTV. Never heard of SelecTV? Don't worry, you will. Vicki Lins, CMO of New York-based Canoe Ventures and a veteran telecom marketer, is tackling the launch of the brand. Developed by Canoe Ventures with the support of a consortium of the nation's leading cable providers like Comcast and Cox Communications, the SelecTV brand is not a product but an industry-wide, consumer-facing brand that will appear on TV screens as an indication that the ad or program being viewed is interactive. It will be a "generic moniker for interactivity," Lins says.

The actual interactive elements will be managed by the viewer's respective cable provider or station programmer, but the education element for consumers needs to be equal among providers, Lins says. "We don't want to confuse the marketplace by sending mixed messages. If their interactive experience varies network by network and it is called something different, how confusing would that be? It benefits the industry, too, to align," Lins says.

"We are all moving forward in unison in 2011. It will be the year that interactivity hits scale and becomes significantly relevant in viewers' and advertisers' and marketers' lives," Lins says.

With the "brought to you by SelecTV" flag up and running, cable operators will be able to unify already-developed and to-be-developed interactive marketing platforms in a way that consumers will be able to recognize. For marketers, this means adding measurability and interaction to TV advertising and in-program product placements. Comcast Corp., for example, is already testing interactive TV advertisements in select markets whereby a viewer can click "OK" on his remote to request that information about the advertiser be mailed to him.

Lins is pretty familiar with Comcast. She worked there for seven years and led the rebranding of Comcast Spotlight, the company's ad sales division, as its senior vice president. During her last year there, she was tasked to work on "project Canoe," which then developed into Canoe Ventures. She ran between offices for that year as Canoe Ventures developed as an initiative that spans the entire cable community.

Despite the hard work it takes to get everyone moving in lockstep to develop the SelecTV standards and implement them, Lins is hopeful that the life of the SelecTV moniker is short-lived. She compares the purpose of its development to that of the HD label that was used to educate consumers about the difference between HD viewing and regular viewing. "If we do a good job and generate a lot of awareness and equity, it will go away very quickly," she says. Stay tuned.

Allison Enright

Alexander Muse

Co-founder of Big in Japan—Shopsavvy

Sometimes a marketing ploy can turn into big business. Just ask Alexander Muse, co-founder of Big in Japan, a Dallas-based mobile app developer.

When it launched in 2008, Big in Japan specialized in social Web development. But when mobile applications became all the

Survey Says

87% of U.S. Internet users subscribe to cable or satellite TV. Of those, 26% say they have seen an interactive TV advertisement, while one in four in this group has actually tried it.

Source: Marketing News' exclusive research conducted by research partner Lightspeed Research, Basking Ridge, N.J. The survey of 1,085 Internet users was completed using Lightspeed's U.S. omnibus panel in June 2010.

rage that year, Muse and his colleagues realized that they had to prove their worth as app developers. "We thought we better build something—a demo app—to show people that we have good skills and that they should hire us," Muse says. Nearly two years later, that demo app has become Big in Japan's "primary business," he says.

Big in Japan designed an app that would leverage all of the tools that mobile has to offer—a camera, access to the Internet and GPS capabilities. Called ShopSavvy, the app allows users to research products and compare retailers' prices while shopping in-store. "The idea is really simple: Point your phone's camera at a barcode and we'll tell you where you can buy it and for how much," Muse says. ShopSavvy also gives users access to consumer reviews and allows them to compile shopping wish lists.

What sets ShopSavvy apart from other price-comparison apps is that it gives users access to retailers' and manufacturers' own product and pricing data, rather than relying on third-party data aggregators, Muse says. ShopSavvy offers data from 20,000 retailers on 20 million products.

Marketers can use ShopSavvy to their advantage, Muse says. "We're strange bedfellows in many ways; we're creating price transparency," which could make marketers nervous. But "retailers want to manage how consumers see them," he says. Plus, ShopSavvy functions much like a loyalty card program in that consumers are willing to divulge data about themselves in exchange for value at the register, which means that marketers have access to real-time data on consumers' shopping behaviors.

ShopSavvy now offers marketers the chance to advertise through the app with "AdOns": ads that pop up on users' mobile phones when a product's barcode is scanned promoting relevant information, or a related product or service. For example, if a consumer scans a DVD's barcode, a Netflix ad might pop up offering him a chance to watch the movie's trailer, Muse says.

Big in Japan also recently signed a deal with Cellfire Inc., a San Jose, Calif.-based mobile coupon provider, to add grocery coupons to ShopSavvy.

ShopSavvy currently is used by about 5.5 million mobile phone users. Android is the most dominant platform for ShopSavvy, with 10,000 to 20,000 new Android users signing up each day, compared with 5,000 to 10,000 new iPhone users daily, Muse says.

ShopSavvy now is preloaded onto many LG and Samsung models, and featured in marketing messaging for carriers such as T-Mobile and Sprint. Primarily, though, Big in Japan has relied on word of mouth to generate awareness, Muse says. "We're free and we work pretty well. We're not perfect. We suck on groceries . . . but we rock on everything else."

Elisabeth A. Sullivan

Jamie Myers

Director of Marketing and Sales for Radius Global Market Research—Pricedeveloper

Setting the price point for your product or service is a marketing function, and it's not just a measure of cost plus a markup. Uncovering the optimal price point that reflects the value of the product or service matched with what consumers will pay for it is a way to maximize your investment and not leave any money on the table. Enter PriceDeveloper, a research service launched this April by New York-based Radius Global Market Research, which was ranked No. 31 in *Marketing News'* Honomichl Top 50 Report last month.

"Pricing is a strategic decision. A lot of marketers on the brand side of things see it as a separate issue and treat it tactically [to their detriment]," says Jamie Myers, director of marketing and sales at Radius. Myers has been with Radius (formerly Data Development Worldwide) for 11 years and developed his marketing know-how on the job. His background is in constructing and conducting research.

What's happening now in light of the recession is companies are taking second (and third and fourth) looks at their bottom lines and seeing where costs can be cut or reallocated for better use. It's also made PriceDeveloper one of Radius' top three most-requested services by clients. "It's a matter of the environment we are in. People are asking a lot more questions about this approach and how they can use it," Myers says. For example, a membership-based retailer used the PriceDeveloper service to research the value proposition of its annual membership fee relative to savings it provides to members among other member benefits. "Clients are wanting to position [their services] in a compelling way and justify the price that they are offering," Myers says.

While Radius has offered price research services to clients for several years, Myers has been learning a lot more about marketing because of the push behind the launch of PriceDeveloper and the general rebranding of Radius from DDW, which occurred in January but was in the making for about five years. Marketing doesn't always come easily to small market research forms, he says, but "today we are much more intelligent about having a marketing plan and adhering to touchpoints. We have

Survey Says!

More than one-third of U.S. Internet users say they use online/mobile price comparison tools to check prices elsewhere when shopping in a retail store—that percentage leaps to 49% among shoppers aged 18 to 34.

Source: *Marketing News*/Lightspeed Research survey, June 2010.

a strict calendar [we follow] to connect to customers and prospects in different ways." Presumably, all his marketing elements are priced accordingly.

A. E.

Bari Harlam

Senior Vice President of Member Engagement for CVS Caremark Corp.—CVS Coupon Centers

Familiarity doesn't breed contempt when it comes to taking care of your clients or customers; it's called good customer service. By listening and knowing its customer base as well as it can, CVS Caremark Corp., the Woonsocket, R.I.-based operator of more than 7,000 drug stores, is constantly launching new marketing initiatives to satisfy customers and keep them loyal. Well-known already is its CVS/pharmacy's ExtraCare loyalty program, which boasts more than 50 million members. An add-on service to the ExtraCare program launched nationally in April that encourages loyalty-card carriers to scan their cards before they shop at an in-store "coupon center" kiosk and print coupons that can be redeemed immediately. With consumers paying even more attention to value, the scan rate at the coupon centers was more than double CVS' goal by June, says Bari Harlam, senior vice president of member engagement for CVS Caremark.

Harlam has been integral in the research, development and launch of the initiatives since she came to CVS in 2000 from a career in academia that included faculty positions at Columbia University and the University of Rhode Island. In her academic career, her research interest areas centered on loyalty programs and methods by which research processes that were developed in the academic arena could be applied in corporate settings. Harlam discovered her "awesome match" with CVS during a sabbatical year and then went to work for them full time. "CVS is a very metric-driven, data-driven, get-to-the-facts kind of company where that is possible. I didn't come in needing to convince them that we should use this [loyalty and customer] data; there was already a hunger and thirst to do that better," she says.

The coupon center initiative was first tested in 2007, and the initiative was in direct response to what CVS' customer service and research staff was hearing from ExtraCare card holders. "The message was: 'How come I get these offers on the bottom of my receipt when I've already checked out? How about I get them before instead of after?' " Harlam says.

Survey Says!

73% of U.S. Internet users report using loyalty discount cards when shopping and the average consumer uses two to three different store cards regularly. 28% of respondents have encountered a coupon kiosk in the store. When a coupon kiosk is available, 32% always scan before they shop and 57% sometimes scan, while only 11% report never using it.

Source: *Marketing News*/Lightspeed Research survey, June 2010.

The customer intelligence area at CVS is prioritized in a way that research can lead or move in lockstep with what customers want, rather than be reactionary. "We very much think of it as an ongoing effort. We understand where [customers] are and where their heads are. We know their pulse all the time," Harlam says.

A. E.

Christina Norsig

Founder and CEO of Pop-Up Insider—Pop-Up Insider

You've seen the Halloween costume stores that suddenly appear in formerly vacant retail spaces in time for the holiday and then close just as quickly. Target, too, has given the temporary leasing tactic a try. This March the mega-retailer opened a temporary shop in New York's Times Square to preview new clothes and home goods from British brand Liberty of London. The shop reportedly sold out of inventory before its short-term lease expired.

In response to the evolving marketplace and recent economic pressures, many marketers are experimenting with pop-up shops: purposefully short-lived retail locations that are open for a matter of days, weeks or months. Pop-up shops can help marketers test out new business ideas or product lines, test new retail locations, promote vendors, liquidate overstock, learn more about target markets or connect with customers in person. They can help landlords, too, by generating buzz for a retail location, says Christina Norsig, founder and CEO of Pop-Up Insider, a temporary real estate resource and consultancy based in New York.

Norsig speaks from firsthand experience. A retail expert who has helped highend tabletop companies market their fine china, glass and silver, Norsig launched her own website, eTableTop.com, in 2003 to give retailers an online distribution platform. During her first year of operation, she decided to open a pop-up shop in New York to build awareness and loyalty for her online business. She leased a deli on Broadway in Manhattan, displayed fine china and crystal in the funky glass meat cases, and sent an e-mail to her customer base alerting them to the temporary discounts on offer. She liked the experience so much that she decided to incorporate pop-up shops into her ongoing marketing strategy.

In the midst of the recession in 2009, companies began calling Norsig and asking to be included in her next pop-up shop. Landlords contacted her, too, to offer vacant spaces. "That got me thinking," Norsig says. "What I really need to do is start putting these people together." Last year Norsig formed Pop-Up Insider. In February, she launched a website, PopUpInsider.com—a "portal for all things pop-up," she says—giving landlords with vacant retail space the opportunity to list it for $499 per insertion. Norsig helps connect those landlords with retailers interested in opening a pop-up shop. While she and her small team don't negotiate leases, they do offer consulting services on what kind of location would suit a specific business. Pop-Up Insider also offers a range of "concierge services" including marketing, staffing, legal, insurance and design resources. "Our role is to put the pieces together," Norsig says.

"This is the next evolution of retail," she says. "This is the new way to market products. . . . Bricks, clicks and 'quicks' make a lot of sense to me."

E. A.S.

Jean Davis

Co-Founder of Convesition Strategies—Evolisten

In many ways, consumers who use social media are a marketing researcher's dream: Not only do they talk openly and unprompted about products, stores and restaurants, but also they discuss their purchase behaviors and emotional responses. "These people are telling you what they're ordering, what they're drinking, where they're doing it and how they feel about it. . . . They just tell you. You don't have to go through 16 questions for that type of thing." Best of all? That data is ready and waiting for marketers to put to good use.

So says Jean Davis, co-founder of Conversition Strategies, a Toronto-based boutique social media marketing research firm. Together with her business partners, Tessie Ting and Annie Pettit, Davis founded Conversition in late 2009 to apply traditional research methodology to information compiled from social media. (The company is called Conversition rather than Conversation because "we put the 'i' where the 'a' was for intuition," Davis says.) She and her colleagues bring years of marketing research experience to their new venture; for example, most recently Davis served as president of Ipsos Online in North America. They wanted to get out in front of the trend toward deeper dives into social-media-mined data because they knew that 2010 would bring more interest in such online research.

Conversition's research offerings differ from other social media research services in that they go beyond tallying up brand mentions or counting keywords—which, for many companies, had been the norm until very recently, Davis says. "They were all about buzz counting," but such numbers "didn't mean anything" because they often don't account for meaningless brand mentions or irrelevant data.

The company now offers a social media research tool called Evolisten, which acts as a "refinery" to sort through data compiled by online data collection services. It incorporates sampling and weighting methodologies, traditional scoring methods, filters that help determine consumer sentiment, and a set of constructs that enable marketers to compare social-media-mined data across industry verticals.

Conversition also offers Tweetfeel, which allows marketers to get "quick and dirty feedback" on who's Tweeting about their brands and what the general consumer sentiment is; and Tweetfeel Biz, which is a subscription-based Twitter-reading research tool that allows users to chart the Twitter buzz over time and build their own constructs to categorize it. Recently, Conversition partnered with Peanut Labs Inc., a San Francisco-based social media sample provider, to offer Peanut Labs' clients the chance to pair their social media-based survey research with Evolisten's data refinement capabilities.

Applying traditional marketing research methods to consumer data culled from social media is an important step, but such online research will get better and better as marketers start to leverage the Internet's data power, Davis says. "I think we're just at the real tip of the iceberg as far as the type of information that this data holds."

A. E.S

Survey Says!

Two-thirds of social media users talk about their experiences with brands and products. 56% of them do so at least once a week.

Source: *Marketing News*/Lightspeed Research survey, June 2010.

Critical Thinking

1. In your opinion, what traits and qualifications make a successful entrepreneur or a visionary?
2. You have been assigned to interview a successful entrepreneur; list the questions you would ask during the interview.

Honest Innovation

Ethics issues in new product development could be stalling innovation growth.

CALVIN L. HODOCK

Product innovation is the fuel for America's growth. Two Harvard economists described its importance as follows: "Innovation is no mere vanity plate on the nation's economic engine. It trumps capital accumulation and allocation of resources as the most important contributor to growth."

Innovative initiatives are a high risk game; failures widely outnumber successes. While enthusiasm, conviction and creativity should flourish in the hearts and minds of the innovation team, judgments must remain totally, even brutally, objective. But unconscious and conscious marketing dishonesty may make this easier said than done.

Unconscious Marketing Dishonesty

People fall in love with what they create, including movies, television pilots, novels, art and new products. And all too often that love is blind: As objectivity eludes the creator, normally rational people become evangelical rather than practical, rational marketing executives.

The Coca-Cola executive suite was convinced that New Coke was the right thing to do. Procter & Gamble's research and development (R&D) believed that Citrus Hill was a better-tasting orange juice than Tropicana and Minute Maid. The spirited Pepsi Blue team overlooked the obvious knowledge that colas should be brown. Ford's MBA crowd believed in a "cheap Jag" strategy. And Motorola's engineers were misguided in their devotion to the Iridium satellite telephone system.

Crest Rejuvenating Effects was fake innovation: It basically was just regular Crest with a great cinnamon vanilla flavor and feminine packaging, positioned for the "nip and tuck" generation of women aged 30 to 45. Similar to Rice Krispies' famous "snap, crackle, and pop" campaign, it encountered a tepid reception, but the brand's custodians believed that America was ready for "his and hers" tubes of toothpaste in their medicine cabinets.

These were well-meaning people who wandered off course because they became enamored with what they created. But let's face it, optimism has limits. The marketplace disagreed, and that's the only vote that counts in any innovation effort.

Conscious Marketing Dishonesty

Conscious marketing dishonesty is more insidious. Blinded passion may still be part of the equation, but in this case the innovation team consciously pushes the envelope across the line of propriety. Before long, there are disquieting signs or signals that all is not well with the new product.

Unfavorable data or information might be ignored, perhaps even suppressed. There might be the blithe assumption that some miracle will surface, and make it all right. Successful innovation initiatives are not products of miracles, but simply take a good idea and execute all the basic steps that are part of the discovery process. The reward goes to those who excel in executing the thousands of details associated with the dirt of doing.

Either way, conscious or unconscious, marketing dishonesty means resources are wasted, valuable time and energy are lost forever and shareholder value may be diminished (depending on the magnitude of the mistake). Often, nobody takes the blame—and many get promoted, because activity gets rewarded over achievement.

There's often no accountability, even though the new product blueprint is peppered with the fingerprints of many. New product assignments are similar to a NASCAR pit stop. The players are constantly moved around the chess board. The brand manager working on a new product for six to nine months moves to mouthwash. The mouthwash brand manager moves to shampoos. And what we have is a game of musical chairs, with no accountability. It is understandable why innovation teams are willing to "run bad ideas up the flag pole" in lassiez-faire-type innovation environments.

While there are supposed to be security checkpoints in the development process, the marketing "id" finds ways to maneuver around them. When important marketing research findings are ignored or rationalized away, because the innovation team is racing toward a launch date promised to management, the spigot of objectivity is turned off because reality might get in the way. Innovation initiatives build momentum to the point where nothing will stop the new product from being launched—not even dire news.

Marketing Dishonesty

There are eight recurring errors associated with flawed innovation. The most disingenuous is marketing dishonesty, where the innovation team consciously engages in deception—even though there is a red flag flapping in the breeze, indicating that a new product is ill. Six marketing dishonesty scenarios are outlined here.

Campbell's Souper Combo

Souper Combo was a combination frozen soup and sandwich for microwave heating; it tested extremely well as a concept. The product was test marketed, and national introduction was recommended.

Two forecasts surfaced. The new product team estimated that Souper Combo would be a $68 million business. The marketing research department viewed it differently: It would be a $40 million to $45 million business, due to weak repeat purchase rates. Nobody challenged the optimistic forecast. Senior management trusted what they heard, while being fed a bouillabaisse of marketing dishonesty. The national introduction was a disaster, and Souper Combo died on the altar of blemished innovation in nine months.

Crystal Pepsi

Pepsi's innovation team ignored focus group participants who hated the taste of this clear cola. It was forced through the Pepsi distribution system on its journey to failure. When was the last time you saw Crystal Pepsi on the store shelves?

Apple Newton

The Newton was the first (but flawed) PDA rushed to market, because then-CEO John Scully viewed it as his signature product—knowing that Apple loyalists were dismayed that a "Pepsi guy" was running the company. Scully wanted to establish a technical legacy that endured long after he left the Apple campus.

The first Newtons were shipped to market with more than a thousand documented bugs. Nobody had the courage to tell Scully and the Apple board about this.

Arthritis Foundation Pain Relievers

This was a line of parity analgesics, involving a licensing agreement where the company paid the Atlanta-based Arthritis Foundation $1 million annually for trademark use. This analgesic line was a positioning gimmick destined for a law and order encounter, and that doesn't mean the NBC television program. Nineteen states attorney generals said the proposition was deceptive. The drugs contained analgesics common to other pain relievers, and were developed without assistance from the Arthritis Foundation. The Foundation was paid handsomely for the use of its name.

Although McNeil Consumer Healthcare admitted no wrong doing, the case was settled for close to $2 million.

Pontiac Aztek

This was considered the ugliest car ever, and the research verified this. While the research predicted that the Aztek was a hopeless cause, the project team sanitized the research sent to senior management to make the situation look better than it was. Decisions about the Aztek's fate were based on intelligence that was heavily modified and edited. Get it out became more important than "get it right."

Aztek-type decisions became regrettably common in the General Motors culture. John Scully never heard the bad news about the Newton, and the General Motors executive suite didn't want to hear any bad news about their cars. It is a heck of way to run one of America's largest corporations and a bad deal for General Motors shareholders, when a culture of intimidation fuels marketing dishonesty. No wonder things are grim at GM these days.

Polaroid Captiva

This camera was similar to Polaroid's original goldmine product the SX 70, but with a smaller film format. It was priced at $120, although marketing research indicated it would not sell if priced over $60. In this scenario, marketing sold a bad idea supported with a specious assumption; marketing research couldn't sell the truth.

Captiva's potential sales were inflated with an assumption about high levels of repeat purchases after introduction. Selling cameras is different than selling cookies or shampoo, products that need replacement. Captiva perished in the marketplace, as the company violated its cardinal principle: Make the cash register ring selling film, while offering the cameras at cost.

Ethics Issues

While these new products had varied product deficiencies, they all share a common denominator: an optimistic sales forecast. An innovation team can manipulate the numbers to get any sales level it wants. It's easy to do, use optimistic assumptions. New product teams can, and do, cook the books with creative number crunching.

Most new product failures are heavily researched. It is used to justify moving a bad new product forward. In a recent *Advertising Age* article, Bob Barocci, the CEO of the Advertising Research Foundation, remarked, "There is a general belief

Executive Briefing

Jeffery Garten, former dean of the Yale School of Management and *BusinessWeek* columnist, graded briefing business schools with a C + in teaching ethics. Sweeping bad news about new product initiatives under the rug can be more costly than embezzlement, and it is just as unethical. A *USA Today* survey says that 52% of students working on their master's of business administration degrees would buy stock illegally on inside information. Business schools need to emphasize ethics training far more than they do now, particularly since unethical behavior can be an underlying dynamic in new product failures.

that over 50% of the research done at companies is wasted." He attributed this to the desire to "support decisions already made." All too often, innovation teams push questionable new products through the pipeline with the support of "justification research."

Another ethical issue is targeting. It is difficult to imagine that ad agencies and their clients did not know Vioxx and Celebrex were overprescribed drugs, sold to consumers with minor aches and pains who could have used less expensive alternatives like Advil and Aleve. Both clients and agencies mutually formulated target strategies with Celebrex and Vioxx as examples. These drugs were developed for senior citizens with chronic pain. But the target segment was too small, so the focus shifted to aging baby boomers with clients and agencies in agreement on the reconfiguration.

Prescriptives

Here are seven recommendations:

1. **Innovation committee.** Boards have finance, audit, nominating and compensation committees. Why not an innovation committee composed of outsiders who are not board members? Their role is to assist the board in assessing innovation initiatives. The board can then decide what action should be taken, including pressing the "kill button."

   Companies sometimes do postmortems after failure. The innovation committee should perform pre-mortems early in the development process, before bad ideas soak up lots of money. There is a rich reservoir of people resources to serve on innovation committees (e.g., academics, retired senior executives, industrial designers, and product and industry specialists). But one thing that they should not be is cronies of professional management.

2. **Find a value-added marketing research department.** The prior case histories illustrate that bad research news often is ignored or rationalized away. Hire a research director who knows how to develop and steward a value-added research department, and that has senior management's respect. The respect factor will protect the function from retribution, should the news be bad. Such a person will not be easy to find. One company's solution was to hire a consultant from McKinsey & Company to steward their research department.

   In the early days, pioneer researchers such as Alfred Politz and Ernest Dichter presented their findings to boards of directors. Marketing research lost it status on its journey from infancy to maturity. Today's market research is frequently unseen by the board. The right person in the function—think one with management respect—gives marketing research an influential voice in the innovation process that it currently does not have.

3. **Reinforce the unvarnished truth.** Senior management needs to embrace skeptics, rather than surround themselves with "yes people." Before management reviews a new product plan, key players—manufacturing, finance, marketing, and marketing research—should sign off that the plan's assumptions, the underlying source for rosy sales forecasts, are truthful.

4. **Ethics boot camp.** Corporations spend millions on employee training, but how much is focused on ethics to help marketers navigate through gray areas? The innovation team should attend an ethics boot camp early in the development process. This should include everybody, including the ad agencies. Manipulating the forecast for a new product is unethical. It cheats the shareholders even more than it cheats the public.

5. **Teaching new product development.** In academia, new product courses are taught with a focus on best practices; a different perspective is required. The abysmal failure rate is due to worst practices. Classroom discussions of best practices aren't doing much to reduce failure. Class lectures should focus on ethics issues, like manipulating forecasts and justification research used to keep bad ideas afloat.

6. **Ethics test.** Business schools screen candidates based on their graduate management admission test (GMAT) scores. But there is another much-needed test that business schools should implement: an ethics test. Ethics scores should carry equal weight with GMATs. This demonstrates to candidates that ethics are important, and represent a significant prerequisite for admission. As evidenced in new product cases, ethics is more than simply the despicable acts of WorldCom's Bernie Ebbers and Enron Corporation's Andrew Fastow. And, most important, this should help business schools turn out students with a stronger moral compass—ones who don't feed management a duplicitous forecast for a flawed new product.

7. **Corporate endowments.** Corporations interact with business schools on many different levels. They make sizable donations, fund basic research and send their executives to workshops and seminars. They also need to endow ethics chairs with dedicated academics who are interested in ethics scholarship. Corporations should not hesitate to open up their vaults of information to these academics. What are the ethical patterns that underscore an endless stream of new product failures?

Final Thoughts

Failure is inevitable in product innovation. Perfect success is impossible, even undesirable, because it impedes reaching for the stars like Apple did with iPhone or Toyota with the Prius. Perfect success would be a dull agenda of safe bets like a new fragrance or a new flavor. This means the company has elected to play small ball.

This was the trap that Procter & Gamble fell into for close to three decades, despite having 1,250 PhD scientists churning out a treasure chest of patents—leading to 250 proprietary technologies. Despite all this patent activity, very few marketplace hits that made the company famous—think Tide or Pampers as examples—had surfaced from this scientific capability. The innovation focus had drifted to minor product improvements, until the newly anointed CEO A. G. Lafley came along to change all that.

Lafley mandated that P&G be more aggressive, expect failures, and shoot for an innovation success rate in the range of 50% to 60%. And that means having only 4 out of 10 new products fail at Procter & Gamble, well below the industry norm.

The statistic—nine out of 10 new products fail—has hovered over the marketing landscape for six decades. It is estimated that the food industry loses $20 billion to $30 billion annually on failed new products. Would it not be refreshing to attempt to scale this back with a healthy dose of marketing honesty?

Critical Thinking

1. Define *unconscious marketing dishonesty*. Do you agree with the author's distinction between unconscious and conscious marketing dishonesty?
2. List some additional examples, beyond what's in the articles, of conscious and unconscious marketing dishonesty.

Calvin L. Hodock is former chairperson of the American Marketing Association board, author of *Why Smart Companies Do Dumb Things* (Prometheus Books, 2007), and professor of marketing at Berkeley College, based in West Paterson, N.J. He may be reached at calhodock@hotmail.com.

Article 16

Trust in the Marketplace

JOHN E. RICHARDSON AND LINNEA BERNARD MCCORD

Traditionally, ethics is defined as a set of moral values or principles or a code of conduct.

> . . . Ethics, as an expression of reality, is predicated upon the assumption that there are right and wrong motives, attitudes, traits of character, and actions that are exhibited in interpersonal relationships. Respectful social interaction is considered a norm by almost everyone.
>
> . . . the overwhelming majority of people perceive others to be ethical when they observe what is considered to be their genuine kindness, consideration, politeness, empathy, and fairness in their interpersonal relationships. When these are absent, and unkindness, inconsideration, rudeness, hardness, and injustice are present, the people exhibiting such conduct are considered unethical. A genuine consideration of others is essential to an ethical life. (Chewning, pp. 175–176).

An essential concomitant of ethics is of trust. Webster's Dictionary defines trust as "assured reliance on the character, ability, strength or truth of someone or something." Businesses are built on a foundation of trust in our free-enterprise system. When there are violations of this trust between competitors, between employer and employees, or between businesses and consumers, our economic system ceases to run smoothly. From a moral viewpoint, ethical behavior should not exist because of economic pragmatism, governmental edict, or contemporary fashionability—it should exist because it is morally appropriate and right. From an economic point of view, ethical behavior should exist because it just makes good business sense to be ethical and operate in a manner that demonstrates trustworthiness.

Robert Bruce Shaw, in *Trust in the Balance,* makes some thoughtful observations about trust within an organization. Paraphrasing his observations and applying his ideas to the marketplace as a whole:

> 1. Trust requires consumers have confidence in organizational promises or claims made to them. This means that a consumer should be able to believe that a commitment made will be met.
> 2. Trust requires integrity and consistency in following a known set of values, beliefs, and practices.
> 3. Trust requires concern for the well-being of others. This does not mean that organizational needs are not given appropriate emphasis—but it suggests the importance of understanding the impact of decisions and actions on others—i.e. consumers. (Shaw, pp. 39–40)

Companies can lose the trust of their customers by portraying their products in a deceptive or inaccurate manner. In one recent example, a Nike advertisement exhorted golfers to buy the same golf balls used by Tiger Woods. However, since Tiger Woods was using custom-made Nike golf balls not yet available to the general golfing public, the ad was, in fact, deceptive. In one of its ads, Volvo represented that Volvo cars could withstand a physical impact that, in fact, was not possible. Once a company is "caught" giving inaccurate information, even if done innocently, trust in that company is eroded.

Companies can also lose the trust of their customers when they fail to act promptly and notify their customers of problems that the company has discovered, especially where deaths may be involved. This occurred when Chrysler dragged its feet in replacing a safety latch on its Minivan (Geyelin, pp. A1, A10). More recently, Firestone and Ford had been publicly brought to task for failing to expeditiously notify American consumers of tire defects in SUVs even though the problem had occurred years earlier in other countries. In cases like these, trust might not just be eroded, it might be destroyed. It could take years of painstaking effort to rebuild trust under these circumstances, and some companies might not have the economic ability to withstand such a rebuilding process with their consumers.

A *20/20* and *New York Times* investigation on a recent *ABC 20/20* program, entitled "The Car Dealer's Secret" revealed a sad example of the violation of trust in the marketplace. The investigation divulged that many unsuspecting consumers have had hidden charges tacked on by some car dealers when purchasing a new car. According to consumer attorney Gary Klein, "It's a dirty little secret that the auto lending industry has not owned up to." (*ABC News 20/20*)

The scheme worked in the following manner. Car dealers would send a prospective buyer's application to a number of lenders, who would report to the car dealer what interest rate the lender would give to the buyer for his or her car loan. This interest rate is referred to as the "buy rate." Legally a car dealer is not required to tell the buyer what the "buy rate" is or how much the dealer is marking up the loan. If dealers did most of the loans at the buy rate, they only get a small fee. However, if they were able to convince the buyer to pay a higher rate, they made considerably more money. Lenders encouraged car dealers to charge the buyer a higher rate than the "buy rate" by agreeing to split the extra income with the dealer.

David Robertson, head of the Association of Finance and Insurance Professionals—a trade group representing finance managers—defended the practice, reflecting that it was akin to a retail markup on loans. "The dealership provides a valuable service on behalf of the customer in negotiating these loans," he said. "Because of that, the dealership should be compensated for that work." (*ABC News 20/20*)

Careful examination of the entire report, however, makes one seriously question this apologetic. Even if this practice is deemed to be legal, the critical issue is what happens to trust when the buyers discover that they have been charged an additional 1–3% of the loan without their knowledge? In some cases, consumers were led to believe that they were getting the dealer's bank rate, and in other cases, they were told that the dealer had shopped around at several banks to secure the best loan rate they could get for the buyer. While this practice may be questionable from a legal standpoint, it is clearly in ethical breach of trust with the consumer. Once discovered, the companies doing this will have the same credibility and trustworthiness problems as the other examples mentioned above.

The untrustworthiness problems of the car companies was compounded by the fact that the investigation appeared to reveal statistics showing that black customers were twice as likely as whites to have their rate marked up—and at a higher level. That evidence—included in thousands of pages of confidential documents which *20/20* and *The New York Times* obtained from a Tennessee court—revealed that some Nissan and GM dealers in Tennessee routinely marked up rates for blacks, forcing them to pay between $300 and $400 more than whites. (*ABC News 20/20*)

This is a tragic example for everyone who was affected by this markup and was the victim of this secret policy. Not only is trust destroyed, there is a huge economic cost to the general public. It is estimated that in the last four years or so, Texas car dealers have received approximately $9 billion of kickbacks from lenders, affecting 5.2 million consumers. (*ABC News 20/20*)

Let's compare these unfortunate examples of untrustworthy corporate behavior with the landmark example of Johnson & Johnson which ultimately increased its trustworthiness with consumers by the way it handled the Tylenol incident. After seven individuals, who had consumed Tylenol capsules contaminated by a third party died, Johnson & Johnson instituted a total product recall within a week costing an estimated $50 million after taxes. The company did this, not because it was responsible for causing the problem, but because it was the right thing to do. In addition, Johnson & Johnson spearheaded the development of more effective tamper-proof containers for their industry. Because of the company's swift response, consumers once again were able to trust in the Johnson & Johnson name. Although Johnson & Johnson suffered a decrease in market share at the time because of the scare, over the long term it has maintained its profitability in a highly competitive market. Certainly part of this profit success is attributable to consumers believing that Johnson & Johnson is a trustworthy company. (Robin and Reidenbach)

The e-commerce arena presents another example of the importance of marketers building a mutually valuable relationship with customers through a trust-based collaboration process. Recent research with 50 e-businesses reflects that companies which create and nurture trust find customers return to their sites repeatedly. (Dayal. . . . p. 64)

In the e-commerce world, six components of trust were found to be critical in developing trusting, satisfied customers:

- State-of-art reliable security measures on one's site
- Merchant legitimacy (e.g., ally one's product or service with an established brand)
- Order fulfillment (i.e. placing orders and getting merchandise efficiently and with minimal hassles)
- Tone and ambiance—handling consumers' personal information with sensitivity and iron-clad confidentiality

- Customers feeling that they are in control of the buying process
- Consumer collaboration—e.g., having chat groups to let consumers query each other about their purchases and experiences (Dayal . . . , pp. 64–67)

Additionally, one author noted recently that in the e-commerce world we've moved beyond brands and trademarks to "trustmarks." This author defined a trustmark as a

> . . . (D)istinctive name or symbol that emotionally binds a company with the desires and aspirations of its customers. It's an emotional connection—and it's much bigger and more powerful than the uses that we traditionally associate with a trademark. . . . (Webber, p. 214)

Certainly if this is the case, trust—being an emotional link—is of supreme importance for a company that wants to succeed in doing business on the Internet.

It's unfortunate that while a plethora of examples of violation of trust easily come to mind, a paucity of examples "pop up" as noteworthy paradigms of organizational courage and trust in their relationship with consumers.

In conclusion, some key areas for companies to scrutinize and practice with regard to decisions that may affect trustworthiness in the marketplace might include:

- Does a company practice the Golden Rule with its customers? As a company insider, knowing what you know about the product, how willing would you be to purchase it for yourself or for a family member?
- How proud would you be if your marketing practices were made public. . . . shared with your friends. . . . or family? (Blanchard and Peale, p. 27)
- Are bottom-line concerns the sole component of your organizational decision-making process? What about human rights, the ecological/environmental impact, and other areas of social responsibility?
- Can a firm which engages in unethical business practices with customers be trusted to deal with its employees any differently? Unfortunately, frequently a willingness to violate standards of ethics is not an isolated phenomenon but permeates the culture. The result is erosion of integrity throughout a company. In such cases, trust is elusive at best. (Shaw, p. 75)
- Is your organization not only market driven, but also value-oriented? (Peters and Levering, Moskowitz, and Katz)
- Is there a strong commitment to a positive corporate culture and a clearly defined mission which is frequently and unambiguously voiced by upper-management?
- Does your organization exemplify trust by practicing a genuine relationship partnership with your customers—*before, during, and after* the initial purchase? (Strout, p. 69)

Companies which exemplify treating customers ethically are founded on a covenant of trust. There is a shared belief, confidence, and faith that the company and its people will be fair, reliable, and ethical in all its dealings. ***Total trust is the belief that a company and its people will never take opportunistic advantage of customer vulnerabilities.*** (Hart and Johnson,pp. 11–13)

References

ABC News 20/20, "The Car Dealer's Secret," October 27, 2000.

Blanchard, Kenneth, and Norman Vincent Peale, *The Power of Ethical Management,* New York: William Morrow and Company, Inc., 1988.

Chewning, Richard C., *Business Ethics in a Changing Culture* (Reston, Virginia: Reston Publishing, 1984).

Dayal, Sandeep, Landesberg, Helen, and Michael Zeissner, "How to Build Trust Online," *Marketing Management,* Fall 1999, pp. 64–69.

Geyelin, Milo, "Why One Jury Dealt a Big Blow to Chrysler in Minivan-Latch Case," *Wall Street Journal,* November 19, 1997, pp. A1, A10.

Hart, Christopher W. and Michael D. Johnson, "Growing the Trust Relationship," *Marketing Management,* Spring 1999, pp. 9–19.

Hosmer, La Rue Tone, *The Ethics of Management,* second edition (Homewood, Illinois: Irwin, 1991).

Kaydo, Chad, "A Position of Power," *Sales & Marketing Management,* June 2000, pp. 104–106, 108ff.

Levering, Robert; Moskowitz, Milton; and Michael Katz, *The 100 Best Companies to Work for in America* (Reading, Mass.: Addison-Wesley, 1984).

Magnet, Myron, "Meet the New Revolutionaries," *Fortune,* February 24, 1992, pp. 94–101.

Muoio, Anna, "The Experienced Customer," *Net Company,* Fall 1999, pp. 25–27.

Peters, Thomas J. and Robert H. Waterman Jr., *In Search of Excellence* (New York: Harper & Row, 1982).

Richardson, John (ed.), *Annual Editions: Business Ethics 00/01* (Guilford, CT: McGraw-Hill/Dushkin, 2000).

———, *Annual Editions: Marketing 00/01* (Guilford, CT: McGraw-Hill/Dushkin, 2000).

Robin, Donald P., and Erich Reidenbach, "Social Responsibility, Ethics, and Marketing Strategy: Closing the Gap Between Concept and Application," *Journal of Marketing,* Vol. 51 (January 1987), pp. 44–58.

Shaw, Robert Bruce, *Trust in the Balance,* (San Francisco: Jossey-Bass Publishers, 1997).

Strout, Erin, "Tough Customers," *Sales Marketing Management,* January 2000, pp. 63–69.

Webber, Alan M., "Trust in the Future," *Fast Company,* September 2000, pp. 209–212ff.

Critical Thinking

1. Formulate your own definition for ethics in business.
2. With the prevalence of e-commerce, do business ethics take on new meaning or dimensions?

Dr. John E. Richardson is Professor of Marketing in the Graziadio School of Business and Management at Pepperdine University, Malibu, California. **Dr. Linnea Bernard McCord** is Associate Professor of Business Law in the Graziadio School of Business and Management at Pepperdine University, Malibu, California.

Green Fallout

The era when green marketing meant sunny logos and big environmental claims is over.

JASON DALEY

When sweet, red crude began sticking to the marsh grass in coastal Louisiana in May, it was the end of an era for many people, including shrimpers, fishermen and a huge swath of the Gulf Coast tourism industry. But it was also, at least symbolically, the end of an era for the marketing world.

For more than a decade, BP had flooded the media with advertisements showing solar panels, windmills and waving fields of grass without a drop of oil in sight. It changed its name, KFC-style, from British Petroleum to BP to deemphasize its claim to fame: hydrocarbons. The company adopted a stylized green sun as its logo and rolled out the slogan "Beyond Petroleum."

But when the company's Deepwater Horizon offshore well began blowing tens of thousands of barrels of crude into the Gulf of Mexico each day, no outlay of advertising dollars could change the cold, hard facts: The company that had cultivated the greenest image in the oil industry still derived more than 99 percent of its revenues from gas and petroleum. For consumers who had been fed the image of the company out tending windmills, the revelation was almost as shocking as the images of oil-soaked pelicans.

The BP blowout was the swan song of an old style of green marketing, one in which companies could make green claims and hope that no one would look over their shoulders. In the last five years, a new type of green marketing has taken hold, and it has high standards.

It's no longer enough to say you're green in your advertising. It's not even enough to have one or two flagship green products in your line or to screw in a few compact fluorescents and send out a press release. In a time when consumers and watchdogs measure the environmental impact of raw materials and industrial processes, packaging and transportation, a company marketing itself as green needs to have sustainability built into its DNA, or at least painstakingly retrofitted into its culture. But even more important, green products have to be good products.

Research has shown that consumers don't respond simply because something is environmentally friendly. "Being green in and of itself isn't a differentiator except with a small group of consumers," says Joel Makower, executive editor of GreenBiz.com and author of *Strategies for the Green Economy*. "Green succeeds only to the extent that it means better—it's cheaper to buy, it operates better, it lasts longer, it's cooler for my image. People do want to do the right thing, but they don't want to go out of their way to do that. They love 'change' when it's a noun; they hate it when it's a verb."

Back in 2006, Matt Kolb, a real estate agent in Boulder, Colo., had his "change" moment when a client decided to ride around town on a rented bike to look at houses. Kolb lost the client when he went with a private seller he'd met on his bike ride, but the encounter led Kolb to form Pedal to Properties, a real estate firm that offers agent-led bike tours to houses for sale. Last year, after the company became a major player in the Boulder area, Australian entrepreneur Tim Majors approached Kolb and bought half of the company to help franchise the concept around the country. Their green twist of using bicycles is what helps Pedal to Properties stand out in the homogenous, blazer-clad real estate sector, but Majors says it's more the company's overall quality.

"When I bought into the company, I realized we had to be more mainstream to be successful," he says. Majors helped recruit some of the highest-earning agents in the Boulder area and persuaded Terabitz, a market leader in real estate software, to help Pedal to Properties develop a next-generation real estate platform that uses social media. That has helped Pedal to Properties become not only a greener alternative, but also a company with strong fundamentals. It has launched locations in Northampton, Mass., and Sonoma, Calif., with more on the way.

And the bike tours, which are optional, aren't just a green gimmick. Majors says they offer buyers a real advantage. "Biking slows down the buying process and gives clients a feeling for the community. They get to see what it's like to bike to local schools or churches. It's a great differentiation from other real estate firms."

But the company is cautious about calling itself "green," even though it's made strides in becoming paperless by handling massive real estate documents electronically and have pushed the idea to others in the industry.

"I would never say we're absolutely 100 percent green," Majors says. "But we understand the responsibility of a green company, and we're very environmentally conscious."

That's another distinction between old-school green marketing and today's generation of green salespeople—a willingness to reveal exactly what the practices are and a willingness to admit strengths and weaknesses to customers. That's the basis of "radical transparency," a practice in which a company allows consumers to examine its manufacturing processes, warts and all. The outdoor gear and clothing company Patagonia, for example, created a mini site called The Footprint Chronicles in which consumers can track individual products and their carbon footprints from their raw materials to their delivery to store shelves.

"Making a change like that is like turning a gigantic ship—it doesn't happen fast," Makower says. "No company is or likely will be perfect. There's no such thing as a sustainable company yet in the truest sense of the word. We have to accept our green status as imperfect or be paralyzed by imperfection."

In many respects, green transparency is being forced on the corporate world. Sustainability stats are likely to become as common as food nutrition labels when Wal-Mart implements its sustainability index during the next few years. The index will assess the environmental effect of all of the 100,000 products Wal-Mart sells, from Coca-Cola to Black & Decker. That's the type of large, mainstream change that can drive other companies to improve their green bona fides.

Government is getting involved, too. After almost 15 years without a revision, the Federal Trade Commission is updating its guidelines for green claims, creating verifiable definitions for buzzwords such as "sustainable" and "biodegradeable." It's begun calling out greenwashers, too. Last year, the FTC fined four companies for selling bamboo-derived rayon clothing as 100 percent pure bamboo and hit Kmart for improperly marketing paper plates as biodegradable. More states are implementing strict laws to cut down on greenwashing, meaning that green marketing needs to focus on honesty and transparency.

Easy access to information, understandable definitions and a crackdown on greenwashing are essential if green marketing is to overcome its weak link: consumers.

In an Eco Pulse survey conducted this spring by The Shelton Group, a Tennessee-based marketing firm that tries to mainstream green products, 64 percent of participants said they were interested in buying green, especially low-cost, low-risk items such as cleaning products and recycled paper products. But, in practice, green products haven't caught fire; according to the survey, only about 20 percent of respondents said they are "consistently green in their behaviors or purchases." Part of that is because consumers are confused about which companies are truly green. In a 2009 BBMG Conscious Consumer Report, survey participants rated Wal-Mart both the greenest and least green company. All of those green "seals of approval," green bottles and eco-sounding product names make it difficult for consumers to determine which products are the real deal. So, they often simply cut green out of their decision making.

"Twenty-five percent of our respondents said they had no idea how to decide if a product is green," says Lee Ann Head, Shelton's vice president of research. "The vast majority of people still make their decision based on reading labels—but at the same time they don't trust the labels. There's still a sense of buyer beware with green products."

And because consumers don't understand exactly what green means, they often conclude that the green product won't perform as well.

In the service industry, selling yourself as green can be an expensive endeavor, especially if there is no guaranteed payoff. That's why Joey Terrell went it alone when he decided to refresh his Joliet, Ill., Denny's by building a LEED-certified restaurant in 2009. (LEED stands for Leadership in Energy and Environmental Design, an independent certification program run by the U.S. Green Building Council.)

Denny's gave him permission to build the green restaurant as long as it cost about the same as a regular store, he says. The project turned into a marketing boon itself as Terrell's Denny's raced a nearby McDonald's to become the first green-certified restaurant in the country.

When it was all said and done, Terrell says, he came in $40,000 under budget and is saving about $20,000 a year in energy and water conservation. Plus, he's benefiting from a marketing boost. "We're seeing double-digit sales increases over last year. It's a surprise for us, we weren't anticipating that. People generally come into the restaurant and tell us it's because it's green," says Terrell, who is planning to turn his Mokena, Ill., Denny's green, too.

"People tell us they love eating in the restaurant but can't pinpoint why," he says. "Maybe it's because the air is fresh with reduced contaminants, and the skylights make it feel like you're eating in a meadow."

In many ways, green marketing has transcended marketing. To market itself as green, a company has to do the often difficult work of actually being green, not simply flashing pictures of windmills.

But unlike the first generation of green marketing, which imploded when the expensive products failed to live up to customer expectations, today the momentum is so strong, and the benefits often so compelling, that companies aren't likely to abandon their green efforts. In fact, much of the most successful environmental advances have happened under the radar as companies have squeezed waste and inefficiency from their manufacturing processes and reduced packaging. For instance, the aluminum can is a third lighter than it was 20 years ago, a remarkable green achievement that doesn't show up in Budweiser advertisements.

Green marketing eventually will fade away, and if innovation continues at the current pace, that will be sooner rather than later. Not because green marketing is ineffective but because green is becoming the status quo. When all cleaning products are nontoxic, when every appliance is an energy sipper, when all toaster ovens are 100 percent recyclable, green will cease to be a factor. Until then, marketers need to plug their green achievements without making that their only notable selling point.

"Green is no longer a trend, it's inextricably linked to how companies do business, design, use and dispose of products," Makower says. "In 10 years, you won't be able to sell a car without electric assist. Green will be part of the fabric. It's those other differentiators, like cost and performance, that will still be important."

Critical Thinking

1. In your perspective, as a consumer, what constitutes a "green" product?
2. Assess the Pedal to Properties and Patagonia websites for evidence of "green" culture.

Jason Daley is a freelance writer based in Madison, Wisc.

UNIT 2

Research, Markets, and Consumer Behavior

Unit Selections

Learning Outcomes

- As marketing research techniques become more and more advanced, and as psychographic analysis leads to more and more sophisticated models of consumer behavior, do you believe marketing will become more capable of predicting consumer behavior? Explain.
- Where the target population lives, its age, and its ethnicity are demographic factors of importance to marketers. What other demographic factors must be taken into account in long-range market planning?
- Psychographic segmentation is the process whereby consumers markets are divided up into segments based upon similarities in lifestyles, attitudes, personality type, social class, and buying behavior. In what specific ways do you envision psychographic research and findings helping marketing planning and strategy in the next decade?

Student Website

www.mhhe.com/cls

Internet References

Canadiabun Innovation Centre
www.innovationcentre.ca

BizMiner—Industry Analysis and Trends
www.bizminer.com/market_research.asp

Small Business Center—Articles & Insights
www.bcentral.com/articles/krotz/123.asp

Maritz Marketing Research
www.maritzresearch.com

USADATA
www.usadata.com

WWW Virtual Library: Demography & Population Studies
demography.anu.edu.au/VirtualLibrary

If marketing activities were all we knew about an individual, we would know a great deal. By tracing these daily activities over only a short period of time, we could probably guess rather accurately that person's tastes, understand much of his or her system of personal values, and learn quite a bit about how he or she deals with the world.

In a sense, this is a key to successful marketing management: tracing a market's activities and understanding its behavior. However, in spite of the increasing sophistication of market research techniques, this task is not easy. Today a new society is evolving out of the changing lifestyles of Americans, and these divergent lifestyles have put great pressure on the marketer who hopes to identify and profitably reach a target market. At the same time, however, each change in consumer behavior leads to new marketing opportunities.

The writings in this unit were selected to provide information and insight into the effect that lifestyle changes and demographic trends are having on American industry.

The first unit article in the *Marketing Research* subsection describes how as more companies are refocusing more squarely on the consumer, ethnography and its proponents have become star players. The second article, "Bertolli's Big Bite," presents a case where Unilever's brand underwent marketing research resulting in a significant increase in its market share.

The articles in the *Markets and Demographics* subsection examine the importance of demographic and psychographic data, economic forces, and age considerations in making marketing decisions.

The articles in the final subsection analyze how consumer behavior, social attitudes, cues, and quality considerations will have an impact on the evaluation and purchase of various products and services for different consumers.

© Blend Images/Getty Images

What Post-Recession Behavior Means for Marketers Today

New Research Predicts How We Will Spend

MICHAEL FRANCESCO ALIOTO, PHD

Given the magnitude of the current recession, there continues to be ongoing discussion about what the post-recession consumer will look like. Will consumers return to pre-recession spending and continue to stimulate new growth in the near-future economy? Or will they fundamentally change their habits, ultimately altering the next stage of national and global economic development?

A majority of economic analysts and futurists perceive that we are in the midst of a fundamental paradigm shift in our economic behavior. They suggest that similar to the Great Depression of the 1930s, the current mentality and habits of consumers will indeed change, resulting in long term attitude and behavior modifications that likely will give rise to an economy less dependent on consumer purchasing as a stimulus or economic growth.

The Consumer-Purchasing Model

It has long been thought that consumer spending, and the purchasing of both common disposable and durable goods, was a main driver of economic growth and business development. Many manufacturers and retail outlets have depended on robust consumer spending as a main impetus for economic growth.

The current recession, however, has placed us on a different path—one that is more global in nature. At the same time it also has exposed major weaknesses in the domestic economy as it relates to consumer purchasing habits and lifestyles. Massive governmental intervention has become a critical tool in the stimulation of future economic growth, both in the United States and global markets. However the real question is whether the global economy can depend on consumer spending to drive economic growth. This was a fundamental condition of the pre-recession economy, but will it return and to what extent?

The Grounding of Consumers

In conjunction with macro-level lifestyle changes (e.g., the severity of unemployment, particularly among Boomers and educated sectors, as well as in security about global economic performance), it is the "new" consumer that will challenge manufacturers and retail stores alike as we move into the post-recession period. This may be the difference between a more robust economic recovery and a prolonged economic down turn.

Several key shifts in the mindset of the consumer have already begun to take place:

- **Consumers are purchasing less in terms of goods and services:** The idea of "less is more" is now in vogue.
- **Brands will be required to offer "proof of value":** Brands must add value to the products and services they represent. Many consumers will not purchase products and services based solely on brand reputation.
- **Consumers are conducting their own research:** The Internet and other information sources enable pre-shopping research and decision-making. Often, the targeted product consideration set has been narrowed or even decided upon before the customer has physically entered the store or the purchase decision stage of the shopping cycle.
- **Consumers are consistently becoming "value-driven" buyers:** They are looking more critically at bundled products and services, as well as deep-discount pricing.
- **Values are shifting:** From the more egocentric "me," to group and family "we," or even to the community "us."
- **Many consumers are becoming procrastinators:** Consumers are delaying the purchase of durables, technology and other high-ticket items.
- **Concern about the U.S. middle class:** The current recession has threatened the very existence of the middle class. Will it survive or, more importantly, will it continue to be a major driver of the domestic and global economies?

While we cannot change consumer purchasing habits or predict the post-recession economy, a number of analysts—ourselves included—offer the following recommendations for marketers as we all move toward post-recession strategic planning:

- **Know your customer:** This is even more critical in a post-recession market. We need to get close to customers and be prepared for both micro and macro attitudes and behavioral changes. We need to continue to research customers and understand their lifestyles and values. Organizations that are flexible and nimble will be able to survive and prosper in the next-generation economy, and a realistic view of the customer will enable this.
- **Embrace innovation and ideation:** We will need to do more "co-creation" and develop other consumer-centric approaches for the development of new products and services. It will be critical to get it right the first time, as consumers will have less tolerance for missteps or missed opportunities.
- **Continue to build and reinforce your brands:** Leverage emotional connections to create psychological attachment, while enhancing your brand's promise. Iconic brands are "top of mind" with customers. One should always strive for iconic status.
- **Accelerate new projects to "now":** This is the time to come to market with innovative concepts—before somebody else does or the market passes you by.
- **Do not necessarily reduce prices:** Rather, add value.
- **Think globally:** Both European and North American markets have become saturated in terms of products and services. The next hot markets will most likely continue to rise from the developing, not the developed, world.

While the next wave of economic activity associated with the post-recession consumer may be fundamentally different from current realties, manufacturers and retailers should not just strive to stay alive, but with pioneering planning and thought, they can actually flourish.

While the next wave of economic activity associated with the post-recession consumer may be fundamentally different from current realties, manufacturers and retailers should not just strive to stay alive, but with pioneering planning and thought, they can actually flourish.

This will be both the challenge and opportunity in the way we conduct business in a post-recession environment. One day as we look back on this era, we may say that we didn't just survive the next great depression, but that we forged the next great opportunity.

Critical Thinking

1. Summarize the post-recession consumer attitudinal and behavioral shifts outlined in this article.
2. In your perspective as a consumer, are these shifts short-term or long-term ones? Justify your answer.

MICHAEL FRANCESCO ALIOTO is vice president of analytics at Gongos Research in Auburn Hills, Mich. He can be reached at malioto@gongos.com.

Bertolli's Big Bite

How a Good Meal Fed a Brand's Fortunes

High-quality ingredients make for a satisfying meal, and for more than 100 years the Bertolli brand delivered this through its lines of olive oils and sauces. But as time-pressed consumers shifted away from home cooking and toward convenience options, Bertoll's marketing team saw a gap in the frozen meal landscape it knew it could fill, now Bertolli commands 38.6% of the market.

JEFF BORDEN

Baby boomers and Gen X-ers have been cocooning and nesting since the '90s—fueling, among other trends, a voracious appetite for savory meals prepared at home that are as convenient as take-out.

Bertolli Brand North America has had a name in the U.S. market since the 1890s with its pasta sauces and olive oils. But scanning sales figures for prepared meals, Bertolli executives saw a fast-growing segment where the company had zero presence.

"It was very clear to us that we were not playing in an area that was really growing," says Lori Zoppel, brand development director of marketing for Bertolli Brand North America, based in Englewood Cliffs, N.J. "All the food trends were toward convenience and serving working-couple homes. Here was an area that fit consumer desires, but there was no brand with an upscale name."

As the average number of hours worked each year grows—by 26% to 2,300 hours in 2006, compared to the workload in 1992—the number of frozen meals that Americans eat has also risen, by more than 47% to 82 meals a year, according to Chicago-based market research company Mintel. The huge $5.7 billion market already was dominated by several brand heavyweights, including Nestlé's Stouffer's lines, ConAgra's Banquet brand and Birds Eye.

The largest segment of the overall frozen meal category is single-serve options, with about 75% of the category. Multi-serve frozen entrées and dinner—the market eyed by Bertolli—represents about 20% of the category, but is the fastest-growing segment, Mintel reports. Clocking 16% growth between 2003 and 2005, the lure for Bertolli was irresistible.

"Whenever we're looking at a new product, we always look for the category drivers," Zoppel explains. "Is it a big space or a growing space, or both? Do we have a brand that can play and compete in that space? And, if so, what difference can we make? We saw a chance to leverage our brands into a new area. We needed to compete in complete meal solutions."

Bertolli's new product, Dinner for Two, offers frozen dinners for home preparation with such tasty titles as Shrimp, Asparagus & Penne and Spicy Shrimp Fra Diavolo & Penne.

Once the decision to enter the frozen entrée fray was made, Bertolli turned to ethnographic research in 2000 to help design meals that would stand out from competitors—that would mark its products as an upscale, luxurious end to a busy day, not just a convenience.

Zoppel worked closely with Debbie Weiss Clark, a research manager at Unilever, Bertolli's parent company. Clark has since joined GfK Market Measures in East Hanover, N.H.

"There is no substitute, when you want to learn about how people eat and cook, than going and observing them and talking to them while they are eating and cooking and experiencing things," Clark says. "It's so much better than a laboratory setting, where it's all so artificial and you cannot capture what is turning them on and turning them off."

Teams of Bertolli researchers hired subcontractors to identify families willing to participate in the research; participants were paid about $150. Researchers accompanied them to grocery stores to observe their shopping habits, and watched them cook and eat traditional frozen meals to learn areas of complaint and dissatisfaction.

Anatomy of a Package

As it prepared to introduce products nationally, Bertolli researchers paid considerable attention to packaging as it sought to cast its products as fresher and upscale.

An appetizing photo of the product and a glass of wine is meant to convey that the product quality is on par with that of a restaurant. The on-pack "Ready in 10 Minutes" tag emphasizes convenience.

What Bertolli heard was that polybag meals already on the market had mushy pasta and didn't taste fresh. Participants also complained that the packaging was unappealing and seemed downscale.

While ethnographic marketing research was not the "make or break" factor in the success of the polybag meals, Zoppel doesn't discount its importance. "The ethnographic issue was critical to combine the product and the consumer," she explains. "It helped us gain some insights and sell it internally. Not starting out with words on paper and asking people, but actually giving people food in their mouths and having different members of the team there to observe . . . added a lot of power to our plan."

Meanwhile, other researchers visited traditional Italian restaurants in Manhattan's Little Italy and the Bronx's Arthur Avenue, to see what kinds of ingredients chefs used in their dishes. Researchers also visited popular Italian chain restaurants, including Romano's Macaroni Grill and Olive Garden.

"We were looking for trends and the little things, the key ingredients, that add something," Clark says. "For example, using portabello mushrooms instead of standard mushrooms, or pecorino Romano instead of Parmesan cheese."

Even without the results of the research, Bertolli enjoyed a significant advantage when entering the frozen food arena: A popular Unilever brand in Italy, Quattra Salti En Padella, already had proprietary technology that produced fresher-tasting entrees. Furthermore, the Italian firm had a way to freeze the pasta in a ball-shaped form, a detail that differentiates Bertolli from its competitors.

"There's nothing better than a proposition where you can come in and differentiate your brand as a higher-quality brand," Zoppel says.

With the market research complete, the Bertolli team decided to bring the Dinner for Two concept to market. The product's initial offerings—such as Chicken Parmigiana & Penne—were test-marketed in New England for two years, beginning in January 2003. While under development Bertolli's marketing team made sure it paid equal attention to the packaging of the meals as was paid to the recipes. Designers placed a photograph of the cooked entrée against a sepia-toned background of the hills of Tuscany. There's also a glass of wine on the package, meant to underscore the idea that the food inside is on par with a restaurant meal.

"The message is that this product is worth paying more for because there is better quality inside," Clark says.

What's for Dinner?

Despite the choices available to consumers to make the task of putting dinner on the table quick and easy, most continue to take the time to cook up meals from scratch. An online survey of 2,000 adults asked: "How often do you do the following for your evening meal in a typical week?"

	Mean number per week
Cook a meal from scratch	2.6
Bring home carry-out	0.8
Eat at a full-service restaurant	0.7
Leftovers	0.6
Make a frozen entrée	0.5
Make a salad	0.5
Make dinner using a meal kit	0.4
Call for delivery	0.4
Eat canned soup	0.2
Skip dinner	0.2
Other	0.1
Total	7.0

Source: Mintel International Evening Meals (July 2006) report.

The message is that this product is worth paying more for because there is better quality inside.

Consumers and food experts alike raved about the taste and the convenience, even as they cringed at the products' nutritional information in nearly the same breath. Since the Bertolli meals are made with richer ingredients—part of the effort to make them more indulgent and position them as an at-home version of a restaurant Italian meal—the original versions of Grilled Chicken Alfredo and other meals have more fat and sodium than some competitors in the category.

Bertolli recently launched a second-generation Mediterranean-style line featuring lighter sauces using more olive oil and wine. Among the four new offerings launched in 2007 are Shrimp &

Penne Primavera and Rosemary Chicken Linguine & Cherry Tomatoes.

"We took a look at how we could reduce fat from the Alfredo meals without sacrificing quality by adding a little less cream and a little less butter," Clark says.

All those efforts have produced a significant success story for Unilever.

Since launching nationwide in January 2005, Bertolli-brand frozen entrees have carved out a 38.6% share of the multi-serve polybag market, besting both Stouffer's and Birds Eye. In U.S. grocery stores, Bertolli accounts for eight of the top 11 best-selling polybag dinners, according to AC Nielsen.

Meanwhile, the line has become a new growth driver for Unilever with sales rising more than 185%, from $70 million in its first year to a projected $200 million plus in 2007.

There've been other benefits, too.

"This product has revolutionized our relationships with retailers," Zoppel says. "We were really able to come in and say we were participating in this segment, which was so important to consumers. We put together a marketing plan and delivered. We're leveraging our global footprint."

Critical Thinking

1. With a small group of peers from your class, outline the new product development process undertaken by Bertolli when it introduced *Dinner for Two.*
2. In your opinion, what demographic, psychographic, and lifestyle shifts in the United State attribute to Bertolli's *Dinner for Two success?*

Article 20

Youth Marketing, Galvanized

Media & Marketers Diversify to Reach A Mercurial Market

Daniel B. Honigman

Ten years ago, marketers looking to target the youth segment didn't need to look much further than one channel: MTV. But changing media consumption habits are splintering media buys, shards of which are being claimed by other networks, experiential promotions and social networks. The fight to claim the bleeding edge of youth marketing is fierce and is forcing marketers to innovate beyond the pale.

"People live and breathe advertising and marketing in a different way now; they relate to it individually," says John Koller, senior marketing manager in charge of Sony's PlayStation Portable (PSP) video game console.

In 1998, the multimillion-dollar PlayStation marketing budget allocation was 75% broadcast, 20% print, and 5% events and online. "It's splintered significantly since then," Koller says, reporting that the allocation is now closer to 55% broadcast and 20%–25% online. The last quarter is split across mobile, outdoor and retail channels.

"Broadcast is great for awareness, but it's not a 100% driver to the retail environment. Working with PR and great editorial or being able to have a PSP truck outside a Wal-Mart, those are some of our drivers [now]," Koller says.

This splintering of media budgets is common across all segments, but figuring out how to balance these spinning plates is essential to brand survival, says Andrew Frank, research vice president of New York-based Gartner Research. "Anyone who's trying to reach the youth market can't put their eggs in one basket," he says. "Fragmentation has led to a situation in which there's not one seller of ad services that can reach it all. The most successful brands are using a variety of techniques to reach young consumers, but the challenge is keeping them all integrated and complementary."

One such innovator is Cartoon Network, a cable network created in 1992 by Atlanta-based Turner Broadcasting System Inc. Its heavy-hitting, late-night Adult Swim block of programming is the largest draw for men aged 18–34, according to Nielsen Media Research. Despite being a single cable outlet, it offers a mixed bag of marketing touch points for media buyers to choose among.

John O'Hara, senior vice president and general sales manager for Cartoon Network, attributes Adult Swim's success to the network's overall wackiness quotient. But even more, he says, is its pickiness when selecting and integrating an advertiser—and its campaign—into its lineup. This, he says, helps Adult Swim maintain credibility in the youth segment. "You can become uncool with this segment quickly," he says. "We want to make sure we do things with a partner that makes sense and [with whom] we can work something . . . that maintains that 'cool' element."

To do this, Adult Swim takes alternative paths for its ads. For example, in December 2007 its program *Aqua Teen Hunger Force* featured an in-show ad for XM Satellite Radio. The show's plot featured the main characters hijacking the signal of a fictitious hard-rock satellite radio station. During the program, viewers could tune in to the XM channel for a "live" broadcast, and XM posted a fake complaint letter against the program's characters on its Web site.

For an experiential promotion, Adult Swim teamed up with Virgin Mobile and video game developer Activision Inc. to sponsor a 12-show college tour featuring faux-hard rock band Dethklok from the program *Metalocalpyse.* At the band's stage shows, students—who received free tickets—got a chance to play the video game *GuitarHero III: Legends of Rock* and use Virgin cell phones to text messages that were viewable on the stage's video screen.

When it comes to engaging the youth segment, Adult Swim usually incorporates humor and music, but creativity is what advertisers look for most. "Adult Swim [shows have] some off-the-wall characters, and the sky's the limit for us," O'Hara says. "So creativity, in terms of what we can do with an advertiser across our platforms, will lead to engagement. If you start out with an audience that's so engaged with the network, you'll find a way to engage them with your product."

Utilizing the Web is no different. Simply measuring eyeballs, MTV.com drew 7.5 million unique viewers in October 2007, which pales in comparison with social networks MySpace and Facebook, which drew 123.4 million and 40.1 million unique visitors, respectively, according to Nielsen

Online. MTV.com traffic also trails music giants like Yahoo! Music and Project Playlist. MTV declined to comment for this story.

"You can become uncool with this segment quickly," he says. "We want to make sure we do things with a partner that makes sense and [with whom] we can work something . . . that maintains that 'cool' element."

Anastasia Goodstein, founder and editor of Ypulse.com and author of *Totally Wired: What Teens And Tweens Are Really Doing Online,* says a big reason why MTV is trailing online is because it missed the boat with social networking. "You have the long-tail effect of people going to smaller sites or checking out their friends' blogs, all of which nibble away at MTV's Web properties," Goodstein says. "[And] MTV also [can't compete with] some of the authentic grassroots sites that are created by people within specific subcultures. [For marketers] trying to reach influencers in the snowboarding community, for example, they should find out what site or publication is embraced by the core group within that subculture."

This is not to say that MTV and its Web properties haven't responded to the more segmented markets. "From a youth marketing perspective, is MTV still the place to go? Of course it is," says Josh Weil, partner at Ramsey, N.J.-based youth marketing research firm Youth Trends. "They've made great inroads in the college market with mtvU, they're launching a ton of vertical Web sites against different music genres and, at some point, they're going to launch a social network. They consistently reach, through their TV channels, mobile and online, more people than any other platform." For MTV, it's just a matter of figuring out a combination that works for its audience and its advertisers. "On the digital end, like everyone else, MTV is trying to figure out how to best leverage its digital assets. Right now, its strategy is to throw a bunch of [stuff] up there and see what sticks," Weil says.

Peter Gardiner, partner and chief media officer with New York-based ad agency Deutsch, agrees. "It would be a bit over-blown to say MTV doesn't work anymore," he says. "Ten years ago, youth marketing started and ended with MTV, but while MTV isn't what it used to be in terms of its dominance over the youth market, it's still an incredibly powerful part of the mix."

In the end, however, whether marketers use MTV, Adult Swim, online or targeted verticals, media channels are only a part of what marketers need to do to effectively reach the youth market. "You hear a lot from marketing executives about the fracturing of media," says Sony's Koller. If you can parse the youth demographic into the smallest segment and can market to [each segment accordingly], you'll be ahead of the game."

Critical Thinking

1. How homogeneous is the youth (18–34) consumer segment?
2. In your opinion, what promotional appeals or themes appeal to today's youth segment?

It's Cooler than Ever to Be a Tween

They're a hot market, they're complicated, and there are two in the White House.

SHARON JAYSON

The prepubescent children of days gone by have given way to a cooler kid—the tween—who aspires to teenhood but is not quite there yet.

Tweens are in-between—generally the 8-to-12 set. The U.S. Census estimates that in 2009, tweens are about 20 million strong and projected to hit almost 23 million by 2020.

Among them now are Malia Obama, at 10 already a tween, and sister Sasha, who turns 8 this year. With the Obama daughters in the White House, the nation's attention will focus even more on this emerging group—and the new "first tweens" will likely be high-profile representatives of their generation.

"My daughter is really excited that there's a girl in the White House the same age she is," says Courtney Pineau, 31, of Bellingham, Wash., mother of fifth-grader Sophia, age 10.

Retailers know tweens are a hot market for clothes, music and entertainment. But now psychologists and behavioral researchers are beginning to study tweens, too. They say tweens are a complicated lot, still forming their personalities, and are torn between family and BFFs, between fitting in and learning how to be an individual.

Tweens have "their own sense of fashion in a way we didn't have before and their own parts of the popular culture targeted toward them," says child and adolescent psychologist Dave Verhaagen of Charlotte. How will this shape their personalities? "Time will tell. We don't know."

Research has shown that middle school is where some troubles, particularly academic, first appear. Also, a 2007 review of surveys in the journal *Prevention Science* found that the percentage of children who use alcohol doubles between grades four and six; the largest jump comes between fifth and sixth grades.

"They're kids for a shorter period of time," adds psychologist Frank Gaskill, who also works with tweens in Charlotte. "More is expected of them academically, responsibility-wise."

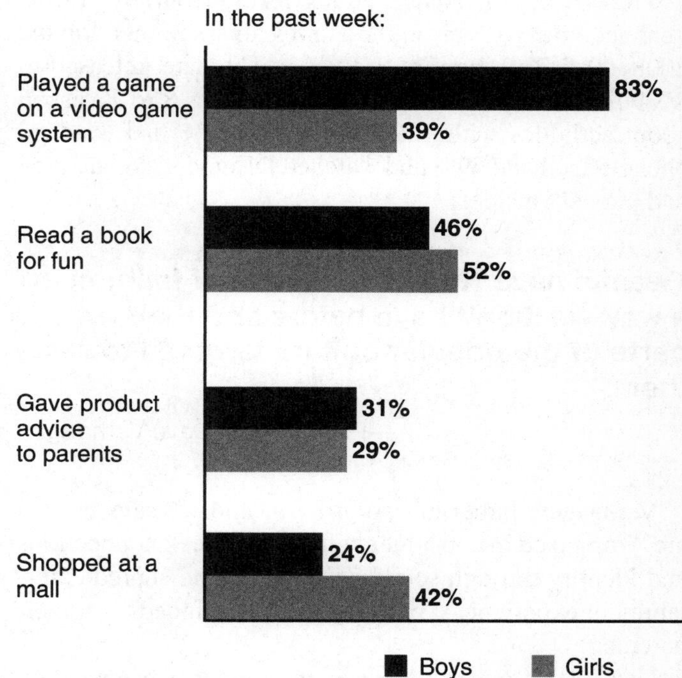

What tweens are doing.

Source: Youth Trends (based on in-person interviews with 1,223 8-12-year-olds in December. Margin of error ±2.8 percentage points).

Many parents, including Beth Harpaz, 48, of Brooklyn, are well aware of this short-lived time. Her older son is 16 and a high school junior; her younger son is 11 and in fifth grade.

"I'm trying really hard to save his childhood. I want him to enjoy little-boy things and don't want him to feel that he has to put on that big hoodie and wear the $100 sneakers and have that iPod in his ear listening to what somebody has told him is cool music," says Harpaz, author of *13 is the New 18*.

Gender Differences

Boys haven't been the main target of marketers hawking all things tween, from clothes and makeup to TV shows and music. But Disney wants to change that with its launch Feb. 13 of Disney XD, a "boy-focused" cable brand that includes TV and a website with themes of adventure, accomplishment, gaming, music and sports.

Until now, Disney has been "a tween-girl machine," Verhaagen says. "It may be that teen idols and celebrities are more inherently appealing to girls because it's all about personality and music and relational things that girls are more interested in. Boys at that age are more interested in sports and adventure and are not as easily marketed to by personalities and pop stars."

The Disney Channel and Nickelodeon are favorites, according to an online survey this summer for the 2008–09 GfK Roper Youth Report. The data, released to *USA Today,* found that of 500 tweens ages 8 to 12 asked about activities within the past week, 82% had watched Nickelodeon and 69% had watched Disney; 92% said they had played outside.

Tweens have "their own sense of fashion in a way we didn't have before and their own parts of the popular culture targeted toward them."

—Psychologist Dave Verhaagen

Verhaagen, father of two girls, 11 and 13, says tweens are "immersed in consumer culture" and seek connections and identity through social networking and shared entertainment experiences, but they're still "aligned with their parents."

New data from in-person interviews in December by Youth Trends, a marketing services company based in Ramsey, N.J., found 85% of the 1,223 respondents ages 8–12 agreed that "my family is the most important part of my life" and 70% said "I consider my Mom and/or Dad to be one of my best friends."

Elizabeth Hartley-Brewer, a parenting expert in London and author of *Talking to Tweens,* says the tween years are when young people begin to realize the wider world, and to see themselves as separate from their families. That's why the peer group is so crucial, she says.

Jade Jacobs, 12, of North Potomac, Md., is active in soccer, basketball, gymnastics and two cheerleading teams. "The main reason I do most of my sports is to hang out with my friends and to get exercise," she says.

She also loves to shop with friends. "It's not always about buy, buy, buy," she says. But, "if we have a little money, we'll find a cute accessory."

Her mother, Christina Jacobs, 43, says the idea of "mean girls" is part of the tween years, which is one reason girls worry about clothes. "Girls are looking at each other and seeing who is wearing what. They're harder on each other," she says. "Girls are looking at each other at 9 and 10, and boys are in la-la land."

Music Is Cool

Eleven-year-old Campbell Shelhoss, a fifth-grader in Towson, Md., says he's not in a hurry to be a teenager, even though he says he has outgrown some childhood pastimes.

"I feel like Pokémon is a little young," he says, and he puts cartoon toys and handheld video games in the same category.

He plays baseball and golf. He wanted a cellphone "for a few weeks" and then decided it wasn't that important to him.

Almost two-thirds (63%) of kids 8 to 12 do not have a cellphone, the Youth Trends study finds. It also finds that tweens spend 12.1 hours a week watching TV and 7.3 hours online.

The Roper report also asked tweens to rate 17 items as "cool or not cool." Music was at the top of the cool list, followed by going to the movies. "Being smart" ranked third—tied with video games—followed by electronics, sports, fashion and protecting the environment.

The "First Tweens"

"Right now, their friends and their status is everything to them," says Marissa Aranki, 41, of Fullerton, Calif. She is a fifth-grade teacher and has two daughters, 18 and 12.

"It's universal for the age, but they show it in different ways. For boys, the whole friendship thing is through technology and through sports," she says. "Girls like to talk, either about other girls or about boys. A lot of the girls are really boy-crazy. And some of the boys are not really girl-crazy yet. They're really out of the loop in that case. They've got their little guy friends and they're trying to be athletic, and that's what they care about."

Tweens are part of the larger generational group sometimes called Millennials or Generation Y. Those in their late teens through mid-20s are "first-wave" Millennials because they're the ones who set the trends that this later wave (born between the early 1990s and about 2003 or 2004) continues to follow, suggests historian and demographer Neil Howe, co-author of several books on the generations.

Verhaagen, author of *Parenting the Millennial Generation,* says older and younger Millennials share certain traits, such as comfort with technology and diversity, and being family-oriented.

He believes the struggling economy also will leave an imprint on both groups of Millennials; the younger ones could become less materialistic and consumer-driven.

Howe says tweens are even more interested in being protected and sheltered than their older Millennial siblings; he says this is because the parents of older Millennials tend to be Baby Boomers while parents of the younger group are often part of Generation X, in their 30s to mid-40s.

"These Xers are concerned about such things as safety and protection," he says. "They're not as worried as Boomers were about making their children paragons of perfection. Xers care less about that and try to do less. They're more pragmatic."

Howe counts Barack and Michelle Obama as Gen Xers, those born between 1961 and 1981. But many view the president and first lady as post-Boomers who are part of "Generation Jones," a term coined by cultural historian Jonathan Pontell for people born between 1954 and 1965.

Either way, it may be tough for the Obama girls to stay out of the spotlight, suggests Denise Restauri, founder of a research and consulting firm called AK Tweens and the tween social networking site AllyKatzz.com.

"They're in nirvana," she says. "Right now, (Malia and Sasha) are the most popular girls in school. It doesn't get much better than that when you're a tween."

Critical Thinking

1. Summarize the purchasing attitudes and habits of Tweens in the United State.
2. In your opinion, what current lifestyle shifts explain Tweens' purchasing patterns?

Sowing the Seeds

A deeper understanding of the customer buying process can drive organic growth.

MARK POCHARSKI AND SHERYL JACOBSON

Marketers love to talk about getting closer to customers. But the reality today for most companies is that they aren't very close at all to the people or companies that purchase their products or services. The problem: It's a complicated world out there. What was once a fairly straightforward buying process that consumers followed—comprising one or two channels and an orderly progression of steps from awareness to purchase—has now morphed into a complex and constantly changing ecosystem made up of multiple channels, more competition, and less-attentive and increasingly empowered customers.

As a result, traditional sales and marketing tools that have worked for decades are no longer adequate. Consider how the scope and complexity of the buying process has grown for a product as simple as a doorknob. Not so long ago, a homeowner would go to a local hardware store or a big-box retailer such as Sears, maybe speak with an associate and choose from perhaps a half-dozen different types of doorknobs.

Now the consumer might start with a Google search of "new doorknob," which would turn up literally thousands of information sources on buying and replacing doorknobs (home improvement sites such as HGTV or This Old House) along with myriad purchase options, ranging among the following:

- retail giants such as The Home Depot, Lowe's, Wal-Mart, and Target
- regional hardware stores such as Ace, Aubuchon, and True Value
- for-sale-by-owner sites such as eBay and Craigslist
- numerous e-retailers such as doorknobdiscountcenter .com and knobsandhardware.com

It's safe to say, however, that none of those retailers has deep insight about that potential consumer other than his perceived need for a new doorknob. Is he building a house or replacing a door? Does he want more security or is the new knob strictly for looks? How much of a factor is price? Did someone refer him to this brand? Beyond offering basic price information and product descriptions, most retailers are not likely to take any action to lead the consumer through a detailed buying process. And yet if companies don't invest in understanding where they can win or lose that customer in the buying process, then how can they invest in the marketing programs that matter most?

The irony is that marketers are being asked with increasing urgency to help drive organic business growth by acquiring and retaining customers—and by convincing them to buy more products or services. In many cases, however, their methods have yet to catch up with the madness of the current marketplace, in which consumers are less attentive to traditional messaging and just as likely to follow advice on a new product from a Web log (blog) or third-party Web site. Although most companies have a very good understanding of the transactions that a customer has historically engaged in, they have very little understanding of why an individual behaves in the way he does and what they could do to alter that behavior to their advantage.

Executive Briefing

With the increasing complexity of business today, many marketers have forgotten the fundamental principal that growth occurs only when you're able to change specific behaviors in customers during their buying process. That's harder today because the typical buying process is a complex ecosystem of channels, information sources, and marketing mix options—but it's absolutely essential. This article outlines specific ways companies can develop insights from the customer buying process and then focus their marketing efforts on the things that really matter.

Marketers need new tools that will help them develop deeper insights into customer behavior and identify key points in which they can influence purchase decisions. Conducting an in-depth analysis of the buying process to uncover these "leverage points" can help marketers define the best tactics to alter (or reinforce)—to increase sales and ultimately drive profitable growth.

New Buying Process

The proliferation of product choices, information sources, distribution channels, and marketing platforms has made the world a complex place for both buyers and sellers of goods and services. For marketers, it's the equivalent of moving from a simple game of checkers to trying to solve a Rubik's Cube and Sudoku puzzle simultaneously. Unfortunately, existing models for understanding the buying process—particularly the specificity of how a customer is motivated and influenced at each step along the way—are constrained by two significant flaws in conventional wisdom.

The buying process is nonlinear. The first flaw is viewing the buying process as a linear progression. Many marketing and sales teams still group the customer life cycle into orderly and discrete stages: awareness, trial, consideration, purchase, and repeat. They have systems in place to monitor what happens at each stage (e.g., customer relationship management, sales-force automation, loyalty analysis), but those systems don't show the numerous paths customers use to navigate throughout the process. That used to matter less when there were one or two ways of creating awareness or purchasing a product; the linkages then were fairly obvious. Now, however, the paths are so varied that companies cannot effectively track them. A customer might enter a store ready to buy a specific make and model of a computer after researching the product online, or he might be a novice looking for information and guidance. Those are two customers with very different purchase contexts that require two separate marketing approaches. Marketing tactics for the computer-savvy shopper might include word-of-mouth strategies, blogs, and third-party endorsements, whereas the computer-novice shopper might require aggressive sales promotions, in-store purchase displays, and endorsements from well-known media outlets such as *Consumer Reports.*

Compounding the problem: Marketing and sales personnel who treat the buying-process stages as a straight line (awareness leads to consideration, which leads to a purchase, which leads to repeat purchases) incorrectly assume that all buying processes begin with awareness and that success in one stage will naturally lead to success in the next. That attitude ignores other influences at various points in the buying process, which can lead a customer down an entirely different path.

Take, for example, a technology distributor that grew successfully over the years by following a simple marketing premise: that high-quality technical support was good for business, especially during the consideration phase. The company developed an unrivaled (online and offline) pre-sales technical support group to help customers configure complex technology solutions to meet their needs. Although this approach allowed the company to win customers and build share for a number of years, it also created a bloated cost structure that ate into margins. More alarmingly, the company was not aware of the increasing number of prospects—including some long-term customers—that were (1) using the distributor's best-in-class support to configure solutions but then (2) purchasing the solution from one of several new and lower-cost competitors that didn't offer technical support.

Acquisition and retention are interrelated. The second flaw involves treating customer acquisition and customer retention as independent processes. In too many companies, an artificial wall exists between the two. Sales and marketing will focus on the former (if sales are down) or the latter (if defection rates are high), but rarely does it examine the interdependencies between them. Viewing acquisition and retention separately ignores the fact that customers today may make frequent and often overlapping trips through the buying process and therefore cannot be categorized as either a prospect or an existing customer—they are often both.

How frequently do you see promotions from cell phone providers or credit card companies offering low rates or give-aways for new customers—deals for which long-term and loyal customers are not eligible? Companies spend billions on advertising and promotion to entice new customers while saddling existing customers with inferior prices, even when those current customers come with zero acquisition costs. Consumers are fighting back, either by canceling their subscriptions and re-engaging as new customers (to get the better prices) or by canceling their service altogether and purchasing a competitive offering.

A more subtle example comes from the pharmaceuticals industry. Many drug companies have developed a marketing approach of investing significant dollars into direct-to-consumer advertising—to convince patients to inquire about certain branded drugs with their physicians. In doing so, however, drug companies often overlook other, higher-potential growth opportunities. For example, recent research we conducted in the pharmaceutical industry showed that in some sectors, lack of patient compliance (e.g., taking less than the prescribed medication or stopping the medication early) was in fact the biggest barrier to long-term, profitable growth. By viewing acquisition and retention as interrelated processes we were able to demonstrate that focusing marketing and sales activities on compliance issues (targeted at doctors and patients to ensure patients took their full regimen of medication) rather than direct-to-consumer advertising would make certain drug classes grow faster and more profitably. The resulting marketing programs helped turn a negative-growth product into a 30% growth rate in just one year.

Understanding Buying Behaviors

As the examples here demonstrate, organic growth is driven by behavioral change in customers. A company can control and accelerate its growth rate only if it knows the specific customer behaviors it wants to change and focuses its marketing and sales teams on influencing the behaviors that have the highest potential for return.

How to begin the process of understanding customer behavior? The first step is developing a comprehensive understanding of where the leverage points exist in the buying process. Leverage points represent the place in the buying process where customers or prospects either enter or drop out of your process. By influencing prospects to move to the next stage instead of leaving, marketers can directly increase the purchase or usage of a product.

In many cases, leverage points are not obvious; they might even conflict with accepted beliefs about the business. Management teams often guess wrong about customer behavior because they neither see changes occurring in the marketplace quickly enough, nor have the data to challenge their operating assumptions. The following examples show how uncovering leverage points led to changes in marketing activities that provided a big payback.

The men's high-end fashion industry. For years, the prevailing wisdom was that men buy high-end clothing and accessories because they want to dress like Tiger Woods, George Clooney, or some other handsome and successful personality. One fashion retailer played this aspirational card to the hilt: investing heavily in celebrity-endorsed print ads in men's magazines and TV spots during sporting events, hoping to influence its target audience. However, after careful examination of the buying process, that retailer found that many of its targeted segments didn't buy fashion and accessories that way at all.

For many segments, purchase decisions were made in the racks of high-end specialty stores. The retailer's primary target group was gathering only 5% of its information from television and 7% from magazines. Its main influence was word of mouth; 68% of all information was gathered from the subject's wife, girlfriend, or mother. And at the point of sale, more than two-thirds based their purchase decision on the fit and feel of the product. If the consumer tried on the product, then he disproportionally bought it over competitors' brands. To address those behaviors, the company shifted a significant amount of its marketing spend from celebrity sponsorship to point-of-purchase promotion designed to experience the product. It has since tripled the annual growth rate of its core business.

A watch manufacturer. Not all companies should move their marketing dollars downstream to the point of sale; sometimes the best move is in the opposite direction. Another example is of a watch manufacturer that historically had invested heavily with retailers to create attractive in-store promotional displays and signage. The marketing team spent a robust 85% of its budget on point-of-sale tactics. However, as younger consumers (a critical segment for this company) started using cell phones instead of watches to tell time, the watchmaker was experiencing significantly lower growth rates. Yet a closer examination of customer behaviors revealed that (1) younger shoppers didn't see the value of using a watch to keep time and (2) the point-of-purchase displays were having little impact on them. After examining the data, the watchmaker realized that the key leverage point—the opportunity to influence the youth segment's buying decisions and change its behavior—came well before they entered the store. The company shifted more than 60% of its marketing resources toward a broad-based campaign to promote the benefits and style of wearing a watch. The shift of marketing tactics had a significant impact in turning the brand around and driving new growth.

As the clothing retailer and watchmaker both discovered, focusing on the leverage points in the buying process can help you understand where you are winning and losing your customers. An in-depth analysis of the buying process provides specificity around the behavior that a company seeks to change among its target audience. Those insights include how and why people make decisions leading to purchase—and ultimately usage—of the product or where and why people drop out of the process. They can illuminate (1) where competition is really happening and (2) its impact on winning or losing customers. Importantly, they identify the role of influencers—any word-of-mouth advocacy manifested in blogs, chat rooms, or other venues—on the customer's behavior.

Most companies are swimming in the wrong kind of data, or they're analyzing the right data the wrong way.

The spirits world. Such outputs convinced one spirits maker to change its in-store promotional tactics. The marketing team knew that most of the company's customers were men, and it knew that the segment bought spirits roughly once a month. It didn't know much more than that, so it performed a deeper analysis to uncover the motivations behind the monthly visits. It uncovered two main scenarios. The first was the "special-occasions run," made when friends were coming over at the last minute. The second was the "stock-up," done monthly to replenish the customer's inventory. The last-minute shoppers cared more about packaging: opting for specialized glass bottles, often in smaller quantities. And in that segment of customers, the spirits maker was losing ground to new competitors. With that insight in hand, the spirits maker changed its in-store packaging to reinforce special-occasions buying behaviors. The change resulted in close to doubling the growth and profit from its primary spirits brand.

Turning Insights into Action

A key point to remember is you need the data to act. It's incredibly tempting to think you already know how consumers behave and to simply assume that you can rely on your intuition, years of experience, and macro-trend analysis to come up with the best approach. That's a tempting and sometimes fatal mistake. Most companies are swimming in the wrong kind of data, or they're analyzing the right data the wrong way. As we've highlighted, typical models for understanding buying and usage behaviors are not rich enough; you must go deeper where it really matters. There are two points to bear in mind.

Be broader in scope when you start analyzing the situation. Look at multiple buying processes in all corners of the market. Think more broadly about competitors/substitutes, consumers, geographies, and occasions. Have an unconstrained view of the opportunity first; then use feasibility and economics to highlight the best leverage points.

Don't get lost in the woods. At the end of the day, data must be actionable to have value (e.g., there are too many customer segmentations out there in which sales can't find the target). It's important to use interactive, hypothesis-driven processes combined with managerial insight to cut through the data clutter. Translate those data into holistic, living and breathing representations of your customers. To find the best opportunities, it's important to keep three questions in mind:

- Would the desired behavioral change drive significant profitable growth for the company? Does it provide a large-enough opportunity? (Unless the desired behavioral change tilts customers to your brand and results in profitable growth, there is limited upside to focusing on it.)
- Are the required skills and capabilities resident in the organization to execute on this opportunity? (If you don't have the marketing capabilities to affect this behavior, then it is not feasible in the short term.)
- Will it be cost-prohibitive to obtain the expected gains? (If you cannot overcome barriers through appropriate and affordable marketing tactics, then you won't achieve the desired behavioral change.)

With the leverage points identified in the buying process, a marketing team can then define a few critical "behavioral objectives" that will form the foundation of a sustainable growth strategy. These behavioral objectives help reinforce or change a customer's behavior to increase purchase and usage of a product. It's what you want the customer to do differently or more frequently. A behavioral objective is more actionable than a traditional marketing campaign goal.

For a financial services company, "attract new customers to the category" is a broad objective that is difficult to build a campaign around. A more important and valuable behavioral objective, such as "convert automatic teller machine users to debit cards," will allow for greater precision in marketing programs. The same lesson applies for a telecommunications company: Refining the behavioral objective from "initiate new cell phone usage" to "make personal calls with cell phone instead of home phone" provides enough specificity for a more targeted—and ultimately more successful—campaign. The point is that you can't be specific enough in targeting what customer behavior to change or reinforce without knowing where the leverage point is in the first place.

Focusing on What Matters

Leverage points and behavioral objectives are important elements of a detailed buying-process analysis. Done right, that type of analysis will move marketing's collective mind-set away from assumptions, estimates, and "spread-your-bet" marketing plans—toward a focus on the customer behaviors it needs to change (and where). A buying-process analysis is particularly helpful in multichannel industries such as pharmaceuticals, technology, and financial services. In such industries, the multiple constituencies involved in decision making make it even more critical to understand the behaviors and opportunities at each stage.

Buying-process analysis can also help a management team pinpoint the greatest achievable economic opportunities instead of spending too much time on broad-based ideas such as customer loyalty, awareness, and satisfaction. It also enables a company to see the marketplace in a way that's different from competitors, which will open up new opportunities upstream or downstream—and away from a head-to-head battle over market share.

Think about the elements that drive top-line growth: getting customers to buy more frequently, buy more products, buy instead of browse, or purchase from you instead of your competitor. Changing or reinforcing behaviors that affect any of those drivers in a positive way will directly contribute to increased revenue. Although it's easy for a company to state that it is focused on understanding its customers better, executing on that mission is the true challenge. The most successful companies have made a real commitment to developing deep insights into customer behavior—and they are taking steps to influence that behavior. Only by understanding the different dimensions of the buying process can companies solve the puzzle of sustainable organic growth.

Critical Thinking

1. What developments account for the increasing complexity of business in today's "complicated world"?
2. In your perspective, what new sources of information do consumers turn to and rely on when making purchasing decisions?

Mark Pocharski is a partner of Monitor Group (which helps organizations grow by working with leading corporations, governments, and social sector organizations around the world on the growth issues that are most important to them) and leader of Monitor's marketing strategy unit, Market2Customer (M2C), in Cambridge, Mass. He may be reached at mark_pocharski@monitor.com. **Sheryl Jacobson** is a global account manager of M2C and may be reached at sheryl_jacobson@monitor.com. To join the discussion about this article, please visit www.marketingpower.com/marketingmanagementblog.

Article 23

A Shift in Meaning for 'Luxury'

More thought goes into purchases, markdowns sought—and tech reigns.

BRUCE HOROVITZ

Steve Hundley dumped his Jaguar convertible. He stopped taking Baltic cruises. And he stopped buying his wife pricey jewelry.

But last year, just as the recession raised its head, the San Diego resident paid $6,500 for an outdoor artisan pizza oven.

"We don't need the Jaguar or cruises to the Baltic," says Hundley, who at 56, is semiretired following a heart attack two years ago. "But cooking healthy food is a big priority."

"We don't need the Jaguar or cruises to the Baltic. But cooking healthy food is a big priority."

—Steve Hundley

Americans are dipping their toes back into the luxury pool—but with a mind-set smacked down and radically reshaped by the recession, the lure of new technologies and emerging lifestyle twists that are often as much personal as cultural.

"The luxury brands are all trying to reinvent themselves and deliver a better experience," says Milton Pedraza, CEO of the Luxury Institute, a research firm that consults for designer brands. "Apple is making all these companies rethink their business models."

It wasn't long ago that luxury primarily meant the accumulation of designer clothes, expensive jewelry and fancy cars. For some, it still does. But for many consumers, the new luxury is something seriously different.

For some, it's about owning top technology products. The four brands most admired by Americans with six-digit incomes in a recent survey by marketing specialist Affluence Collaborative were Apple, Microsoft, Best Buy and Sony.

For others, such as the Hundleys, the new luxury is about investing in a lifestyle experience that not only can help improve health but also escalate the experience of such mundane acts as baking a pizza at home.

Sales of outdoor artisan pizza ovens at Kalamazoo Outdoor Gourmet—similar to ovens used at pizza parlors—were up 48% last year and are up 74% this year.

"It creates an experience—and isn't consumable," says Pantelis "Pete" Georgiadis, president of Kalamazoo. "You can keep enjoying it for a long, long time."

For others, it's about buying luxury goods only when they're on sale—or at a steep discount.

Nearly three in four wealthy women say they'll only purchase luxuries if they can get a good deal, reports a recent survey by AgencySacks, a branding firm that consults for some of the nation's top luxury brands.

Slipping a Bit

Luxury spending slid 7.8% last year to $10.1 billion, says Spending Pulse, a consumer spending monitor from MasterCard. It's bounced back up for the first five months of 2010.

But even affluent customers continue to seek discounts, bargains and sales, says Tim Murphy, chief product officer at MasterCard. In a recent MasterCard poll, some 64% of all consumers said they were shopping sales.

"A few years ago, you'd just market access to the affluent. Now, you must market access with a discount," Murphy says.

All this was driven by the recession. "The recession made everyone stop and rethink luxury and value," Pedraza says. "Even though we're coming back, that realization has stuck."

The new world of luxury is less about designer labels and glitz and more about shopping savvy and an I-feel-good-owning-this mentality.

What luxury marketers want to know: Is this the "new normal"?

Pedraza certainly thinks so. He says that Apple and Sony are emerging as new luxury designer labels.

"With Apple, you get a better design, a better function and a better luxury experience than you do with most other luxury brands."

Pedraza recently asked the CEO of a European luxury apparel brand to name the company that the CEO sees as his toughest competitor. Without batting an eye, the CEO, (whose company Pedraza won't name due to client confidentiality) said it was Apple. Apple declined to comment.

Not a Need, but a Want

But Yolanda Cummings, who works as a finance professional in Columbus, Ohio, says that to her, there are few things closer to luxury than her new Apple iPad. "I don't need it. I just wanted it because it's new, different and intriguing," she says. She paid about $699 for it. She already has a $300 Apple iPod touch and $1,600 Apple MacBook.

"I used to go overboard buying clothes," she says. "Now, I'm more inclined to purchase new technologies."

Andrew Sacks, president of AgencySacks, says he bought an iPad the first week it was introduced.

"Part of it is escapist luxury," he says. "We're living in a world where it's difficult to control a lot of things, so there's a feeling that owning new technology allows me to be more organized, more efficient and have more time."

The recession, he says, has helped to reset his own definition of luxury.

Recently, Sacks says, he reached into his closet and discovered a black leather John Varvatos jacket that he'd casually purchased several years ago for $1,500 at a New York boutique. He put the jacket in his closet—and forgot about it.

But when he recently rediscovered it—post-recession—his view of the jacket had changed entirely. "I was a little embarrassed that I could take something so expensive and put it away and not even have it on my mind," he says. "Today, I'd do a lot more research before even considering such a purchase."

For Don Contreras, luxury is the flat-screen Sony TV that he plans to buy and install in the gazebo in his backyard.

On weekends, the federal government physician from Albuquerque likes to do yard work and prune the fruit trees in his backyard. But he also likes to watch sports on TV. By placing the TV in his gazebo, he says, he'll be able to do both.

He only wants a Sony, he says, because that's the only electronics brand that he trusts. But he's waiting to buy it until he finds a really good deal.

"I'm not an impulsive buyer," he says. "I can wait."

Executives at Sony have concocted a new term to describe what their brand offers: "functional" luxury.

In a tough economy, says Stuart Redsun, marketing chief at Sony Electronics, "You don't have to worry about your product breaking down quickly."

Beyond that, he says, the functional luxury is from the product providing a new experience—such as the new Sony Cyber-shot camera, which lets folks shoot panoramic photos or new 3D TV sets that let folks experience home viewing of movies in a new way.

Another example: Sony soon will be the first consumer electronics maker with a Google feature built into its TV sets. Folks watching any show will be able to use a special remote to do a Google search on the same screen.

Sony also has pushed the value message hard. Over the holidays, for example, it bundled a new Sony TV, PlayStation gaming system, game and Blu-ray movie for $900 less than it would cost to buy the items separately.

"We sold out of all the units in that promotion," Redsun says. Sony recently rolled out a similar bundled deal that ends July 17.

Value and luxury have become synonymous.

At Neiman Marcus, "our customer's way of shopping has changed," says Karen Katz, CEO of Neiman Marcus Stores. "She is responding well to the opening and middle price points."

For example, many Manolo Blahnik designer shoes at Neiman Marcus typically sell for at least $500—and some for upwards of $900. But in the spring, Neiman Marcus had great success selling a Manolo Blahnik ballet flat for $395. "Our customer was very happy to have a Blahnik shoe for under $500," Katz says.

Bargain in the Bag

It's no accident that Coach, whose handbags used to start at about $250—and whose average retail price for a handbag hit close to $350 before the recession—launched a new line last year, Poppy, which starts at $198.

Beyond that, Coach has added more bags at lower price points—and made them more functional for women carrying devices from iPhones to iPads, says Michael Tucci, president of Coach's North American retail division. "The last thing I want you to get from this is that Coach got cheaper. We got more compelling from a value standpoint."

Consumers have responded. Coach sales are up 8% for the first nine months of its fiscal 2010.

Value, of course, is in the eye of the purchaser.

To Lori Wachs, a hedge fund partner from Philadelphia, nothing says luxury value like getting top-notch designer clothing at 40% to 70% off—simply by visiting a website.

Several times a week, she visits the luxury discount site Gilt.com, where shoppers have 36 hours or less to order luxury goods before someone else beats them to the limited number of items.

While Wachs won't say exactly what she's spent in the past 18 months, she says she's spent "thousands" of dollars on the 100 or so items she's purchased. Among them, a Chloé handbag, originally priced at $1,500, that she snatched for about $600.

"There's an adrenaline rush when there is a certain brand that you love," she says, "and after you click on it, you wait to see if it's been added to your basket—or to someone else's cart."

In two years, Gilt Groupe has amassed more than 2 million members, CEO Susan Lyne says.

"A lot of people feel like chumps if they pay full price," Lyne says. "When you get a deal on a luxury item, it makes you feel smart."

Critical Thinking

1. Define customer value. How does value play a role in post-recession consumer decision making?
2. According to this article, how has the meaning of luxury changed after the recent recession?

UNIT 3

Developing and Implementing Marketing Strategies

Unit Selections

Learning Outcomes

- Most ethical questions seem to arise in regard to the promotional component of the marketing mix. How fair is the general public's criticism of some forms of personal selling and advertising? Give some examples.
- What role, if any, do you think the quality of a product plays in making a business competitive in consumer markets? What role does price play? Would you rather market a higher-priced, better-quality product or one that was the lowest priced? Why?
- What do you envision will be the major problems or challenges retailers will face in the next decade? Explain.
- Given the rapidly increasing costs of personal selling, what role do you think it will play as a strategy in the marketing mix in the future? What other promotion strategies will play increased or decreased roles in the next decade?

Student Website

www.mhhe.com/cls

Internet References

American Marketing Association Homepage

www.marketingpower.com

Consumer Buying Behavior

www.courses.psu.edu/mktg/mktg220_rso3/sls_cons.htm

"Marketing management objectives," the late Wroe Alderson once wrote, "are very simple in essence. The firm wants to expand its volume of sales, or it wants to handle the volume it has more efficiently." Although the essential objectives of marketing might be stated this simply, the development and implementation of strategies to accomplish them is considerably more complex. Many of these complexities are due to changes in the environment within which managers must operate. Strategies that fail to heed the social, political, and economic forces of society have little chance of success over the long run. The lead article in this section provides helpful insight suggesting a framework for developing a comprehensive marketing plan.

The selections in this unit provide a wide-ranging discussion of how marketing professionals and U.S. companies interpret and employ various marketing strategies today. The readings also include specific examples from industry to illustrate their points. The articles are grouped in four sections, each dealing with one of the main strategy areas: product, price, distribution (place), and promotion. Since each selection discusses more than one of these areas, it is important that you read them broadly. For example, many of the articles covered in the distribution section discuss important aspects of personal selling and advertising.

Product Strategy. The essence of the marketing concept is to begin with what consumers want and need. After determining a need, an enterprise must respond by providing the product or service demanded. Successful marketing managers recognize the need for continuous product improvement and/or new product introduction.

The articles in this subsection focus on various facets of product strategy. The first article describes a methodology pinpointing how to conduct the right product market investigations in the right way. "Brand Integrity" reflects that excellence is achieved when the brand, the talent, and the customer experience are all in alignment. The next article in this subsection delineates how obsession comes naturally to Mark Parker, CEO of Nike. "Everybody Loves Zappos" closes this subsection describing how Tony Hsieh uses relentless innovation, stellar service, and a staff of believers to make Zappos.com an e-commerce giant.

Pricing Strategy. Few elements of the total strategy of the "marketing mix" demand so much managerial and social attention as pricing. There is good deal of public misunderstanding about the ability of marketing managers to control prices and even greater misunderstanding about how pricing policies are determined. New products present especially difficult problems in terms of both costs and pricing. The costs for developing a new product are usually very high, and if a product is truly new, it cannot be priced competitively, for it has no competitors.

© Purestock/Getty Images

"Rocket Plan" relates how companies can fuel success with a rigorous pricing approach.

Distribution Strategy. For many enterprises, the largest marketing costs result from closing the gap in space and time between producer and consumer. In no other area of marketing is efficiency so eagerly sought after. Physical distribution seems to be the one area where significant cost savings can be achieved. The costs of physical distribution are tied closely with decisions made about the number, the size, and the diversity of marketing intermediaries between producer and consumer. The articles in this subsection scrutinize ways retailers can create value for their customers and be very competitive in the marketplace.

Promotion Strategy. The basic objectives of promotion are to inform, persuade, or remind the consumer to buy a firm's product or pay for the firm's service. Advertising is the most obvious promotional activity. However, in total dollars spent and in cost per person reached, advertising takes second place to personal selling. Sales promotion supports either personal selling and advertising, or both. Such media as point-of-purchase displays, catalogs, and direct mail place the sales promotion specialist closer to the advertising agency than to the salesperson.

The articles in this final unit subsection cover such topics as noteworthy advertising campaigns, the ubiquitous nature of infomercial products, 20 years of Super Bowl advertising highlights, and some of "Best and Worst Marketing Ideas . . . Ever."

The Very Model of a Modern Marketing Plan

Successful companies are rewriting their strategies to reflect customer input and internal coordination.

SHELLY REESE

It's 1996. Do you know where your marketing plan is? In a world where competitors can observe and rapidly imitate each other's advancements in product development, pricing, packaging, and distribution, communication is more important than ever as a way of differentiating your business from those of your competitors.

The most successful companies are the ones that understand that, and are revamping their marketing plans to emphasize two points:

1. Marketing is a dialog between customer and supplier.
2. Companies have to prove they're listening to their customers by acting on their input.

What Is a Marketing Plan?

At its most basic level, a marketing plan defines a business's niche, summarizes its objectives, and presents its strategies for attaining and monitoring those goals. It's a road map for getting from point A to point B.

But road maps need constant updating to reflect the addition of new routes. Likewise, in a decade in which technology, international relations, and the competitive landscape are constantly changing, the concept of a static marketing plan has to be reassessed.

Two of the hottest buzz words for the 1990s are "interactive" and "integrated." A successful marketing plan has to be both.

"Interactive" means your marketing plan should be a conversation between your business and your customers by acting on their input. It's your chance to tell customers about your business and to listen and act on their responses.

"Integrated" means the message in your marketing is consistently reinforced by every department within your company. Marketing is as much a function of the finance and manufacturing divisions as it is the advertising and public relations departments.

Integrated also means each time a company reaches out to its customers through an advertisement, direct mailing, or promotion, it is sending the same message and encouraging customers to learn more about the product.

Why Is It Important?

The interaction between a company and its customers is a relationship. Relationships can't be reproduced. They can, however, be replaced. That's where a good marketing plan comes into play.

Think of your business as a suitor, your customers as the object of your affection, and your competitors as rivals. A marketing plan is your strategy for wooing customers. It's based on listening and reacting to what they say.

Because customers' priorities are constantly changing, a marketing plan should change with them. For years, conventional wisdom was 'prepare a five year marketing plan and review it every year.' But change happens a lot faster than it did 20 or even 10 years ago.

For that reason, Bob Dawson of The Business Group, a consulting firm in Freemont, California, recommends that his clients prepare a three year plan and review it every quarter. Frequent reviews enable companies to identify potential problems and opportunities before their competition, he explains.

"Preventative maintenance for your company is as important as putting oil in your car," Dawson says. "You don't wait a whole year to do it. You can't change history but you can anticipate what's going to happen."

Essential Components

Most marketing plans consist of three sections. The first section should identify the organization's goals. The second section should establish a method for attaining them. The third section focuses on creating a system for implementing the strategy.

Although some plans identify as many as six or eight goals, many experts suggest a company whittle its list to one or two key objectives and focus on them.

"One of the toughest things is sticking to one message," observes Mark Bilfield, account director for integrated marketing of Nissan and Infiniti cars at TBWA Chiat/Day in Los Angeles, which handles national advertising, direct marketing, public relations, and promotions for the automaker. Bilfield argues that a

Illustration by Kelly Kennedy

focused, consistent message is easier to communicate to the market place and to different disciplines within the corporation than a broad, encompassing one. Therefore, he advises, "unless there is something drastically wrong with the idea, stick with it."

Section I: Goals

The goals component of your plan is the most fundamental. Consider it a kind of thinking out loud: Why are you writing this plan? What do you want to accomplish? What do you want to achieve in the next quarter? The next year? The next three years?

Like taping your New Year's resolution to the refrigerator, the goals section is a constant reminder of what you want to achieve. The key difference between a New Year's resolution and your marketing goals, however, is you can't achieve the latter alone.

To achieve your marketing goals you've got to convince your customers to behave in a certain way. If you're a soft drink manufacturer you may want them to try your company's latest wild berry flavor. If you're a new bank in town, you need to familiarize people with your name and convince them to give your institution a try. Or perhaps you're a family-owned retailer who needs to remind customers of the importance of reliability and a proven track record in the face of new competition.

The goals in each of these cases differ with the audiences. The soft drink manufacturer is asking an existing customer to try something new; the bank is trying to attract new customers; the retailer wants to retain existing customers.

Each company wants to influence its customers' behavior. The company that is most likely to succeed is the one that understands its customers the best.

There's no substitute for knowledge. You need to understand the demographic and psychographic makeup of the customers you are trying to reach, as well as the best methods for getting their attention.

Do your research. Learn as much as possible about your audience. Trade associations, trade journals and government statistics and surveys are excellent resources, but chances are you have a lot of data within your own business that you haven't tapped. Look at what you know about your customer already and find ways to bolster that information. Companies should constantly be asking clients what they want and how they would use a new product.

"If you're not asking people that use your end product, then everything you're doing is an assumption," argues Dawson.

In addition, firms should ask customers how they perceive the products and services they receive. Too often, companies have an image of themselves that they broadcast but fail to live up to. That frustrates consumers and makes them feel deceived.

Companies that claim to offer superior service often appear to renege on their promises because their definition of 'service' 'doesn't mesh with their customers', says Bilfield.

"Airlines and banks are prime offenders," says Bilfield. "They tout service, and when the customers go into the airport or the bank, they have to wait in long lines."

The problem often lies in the company's assumptions about what customers really want. While an airline may feel it is living up to its claim of superior service because it distributes warm towels and mints after a meal, a business traveler will probably place a higher value on its competitor's on-time record and policy for returning lost luggage.

Section II: The Strategy

Unfortunately, after taking the time and conducting the research to determine who their audience is and what their message should be, companies often fail by zooming ahead with a plan. An attitude of, "OK, we know who we're after and we know what we want to say, so let's go!" seems to take over.

More often than not, that gung-ho way of thinking leads to disaster because companies have skipped a critical step: they haven't established and communicated an internal strategy for attaining their goals. They want to take their message to the public without pausing to get feedback from inside the company.

For a marketing plan to work, everyone within the company must understand the company's message and work cooperatively to establish a method for taking that message to the public.

For example, if you decide the goal of your plan is to promote the superior service your company offers, you'd better make sure all aspects of your business are on board. Your manufacturing process should meet the highest standards. Your financial department should develop credit and leasing programs that make it easier for customers to use your product. Finally, your customer relations personnel should be trained to respond to problems quickly and efficiently, and to use the contact as an opportunity to find out more about what customers want.

"I'm always amazed when I go into the shipping department of some company and say, 'What is your mission? What's the message you want to give to your end user?' and they say, 'I don't know. I just know I've got to get these shipments out on time,'" says Dawson.

Because the success of integrated marketing depends on a consistent, cohesive message, employees throughout the company need to understand the firm's marketing goals and their role in helping to fulfill them.

"It's very important to bring employees in on the process," says James Lowry, chairman of the marketing department at Ball State University. "Employees today are better than any we've had before. They want to know what's going on in the organization. They don't want to be left out."

Employees are ambassadors for your company. Every time they interact with a customer or vendor, they're marketing your company. The more knowledgeable and helpful they are, the better they reflect on your firm.

At Nordstrom, a Seattle-based retailer, sales associates are empowered to use their best judgment in all situations to make a customer happy.

"We think our sales associates are the best marketing department," said spokeswoman Amy Jones. "We think word of mouth is the best advertising you can have." As a result, although Nordstrom has stores in only 15 states, it has forged a national reputation.

If companies regard marketing as the exclusive province of the marketing department, they're destined to fail.

"Accounting and sales and other departments have to work together hand in hand," says Dawson. "If they don't, you're going to have a problem in the end."

For example, in devising an integrated marketing campaign for the Nissan 200SX, Chiat/Day marketers worked in strategic business units that included a variety of disciplines such as engineers, representatives from the parts and service department, and creative people. By taking a broad view of the business and building inter-related activities to support its goals, Chiat/Day was able to

Getting Started

A Nine-step Plan That Will Make the Difference Between Writing a Useful Plan and a Document That Gathers Dust On a Shelf

by Carole R. Hedden and the *Marketing Tools* editorial staff

In his 1986 book, *The Goal,* Eliyahu M. Goldratt writes that most of us forget the one true goal of our business. It's not to deliver products on time. It isn't even to manufacture the best widget in the world. The goal is to make money.

In the past, making money depended on selling a product or service. Today, that's changed as customers are, at times, willing to pay for what we stand for: better service, better support, more innovation, more partnership in developing new products.

This section of this article assumes that you believe a plan is needed, and that this plan should weave together your desires with those of your customers. We've reviewed a number of marketing plans and come up with a nine-step model. It is perhaps more than what your organization needs today, but none of the steps are unimportant.

Our model combines some of the basics of a conventional plan with some new threads that we believe will push your plan over the edge, from being satisfactory to being necessary. These include:

- Using and improving the former domain of public relations, image, as a marketing tool.
- Integrating all the business functions that touch your customers into a single, customer-focused strategic marketing plan.
- Borrowing from Total Quality theories to establish performance measures beyond the financial report to help you note customer trends.
- Making sure that the people needed to deliver your marketing objectives are part of your plan.
- "Selling" your plan to the people whose support is essential to its success.

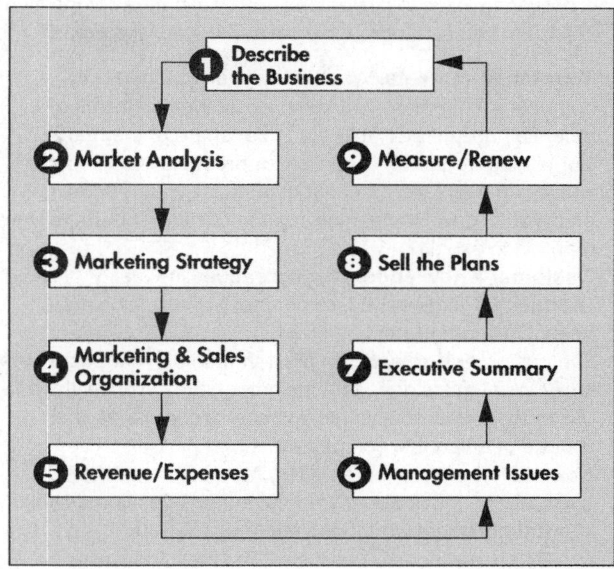

Taking the Plan Off the Shelf

First, let's look at the model itself. Remember that one of the primary criticisms of any plan is that it becomes a binder on a shelf, never to be seen again until budget time next year. Planning should be an iterative process, feeding off itself and used to guide and measure.

Whether you're asked to create a marketing plan or write the marketing section of the strategic plan for your business, your document is going to include what the business is trying to achieve, a careful analysis of your market, the products and services you offer to that market, and how you will market and sell products or services to your customer.

1. Describe the Business

You are probably in one of two situations: either you need to write a description of your business or you can rely on an existing document found in your annual report, the strategic plan, or a capabilities brochure. The description should include, at minimum:

- Your company's purpose;
- Who you deliver products or services to; and
- What you deliver to those customers.

Too often, such descriptions omit a discussion about what you want your business to stand for—your image.

This is increasingly important as customers report they are looking for more than the product or service; they're in search of a partner. The only way to address image is to know who you want to be, who your customers think you are, and how you can bridge the gap between the two.

Part of defining your image is knowing where you are strong and where you are weak. For instance, if your current yield rate is 99.997 percent and customers rate you as the preferred supplier, then you might identify operations as a key to your company's image. Most companies tend to be their own worst critic, so start by listing all your strengths. Then identify weaknesses or the threats you face, either due to your own limitations or from the increased competency of a competitor.

The description also includes what your business delivers to its owners, be they shareholders, private owners, or employees. Usually this is stated in financial terms: revenue, return on investment or equity, economic value added, cash generated, operating margin or earnings per share. The other measures your organization uses to monitor its performance may be of interest to outsiders, but save them for the measurement section of your plan.

The result of all this describing and listing is that you should have a fairly good idea of where you are and where you want to be, which naturally leads to objectives for the coming 6, 12, or 18 months, if not longer.

2. Analyze the Market

This is the section you probably believe you own. *Marketing Tools* challenges you to look at this as a section jointly owned by most everyone working with you. In a smaller company, the lead managers may own various pieces of this section. In a larger organization, you may need to pull in the ideas and data available from

(continued)

other departments, such as logistics, competitor intelligence, research and development, and the function responsible for quality control or quality assurance. All have two things in common: delivering value to customers, and beating the competition.

Together, you can thoroughly cover the following areas:

- **Your target markets.** What markets do you currently compete in? What do you know about them in terms of potential, dollars available, and your share of the market? Something frequently prepared for products is a life cycle chart; you might want to do the same for your market. Is it embryonic, developing, mature or in decline? Are there new markets to exploit?
- **Customer Knowledge.** Your colleagues in Quality, Distribution, Engineering, or other organizations can be helpful in finding what you need.
  The customer's objectives. What threats do your customers face? What goals does the customer have? Work with your customer to define these so you can become a partner instead of a variable component.
  How is the customer addressing her or his markets? Do you know as much about your customer's position as you know about your own? If not, find out.
  How big is each customer, really? You may find you're spending more time on a less important customer than on the customers who can break you. Is your customer growing or in decline? What plans does the customer have to expand or acquire growth? What innovations are in development?
  What does your customer value? Price, product quality, service, innovation, delivery? The better you know what's driving your customer's purchasing decision, the better you'll be able to respond.
- **Clearly identify the alternatives your customer** has. As one customer told employees at a major supplier, "While you've been figuring out how to get by, we've been figuring out how to get by without you." Is backward integration—a situation in which the customer develops the capability in-house—possible? Is there an abundance of other suppliers? What is your business doing to avoid having your customers looking for alternatives?
- **Know your competition.** Your competitors are the obvious alternative for your customer, and thus represent your biggest threat. You can find what you need to know about your competitors through newspaper reports, public records, at trade shows, and from your customers: the size of expansions, the strengths that competitor has, its latest innovations. Do you know how your competition approaches your customers?
- **Describe the Environment.** What changes have occurred in the last 18 months? In the past year? What could change in the near future and over a longer period of time? This should include any kinds of laws or regulations that might affect you, the entry or deletion of competitors, and shifts in technology. Also, keep in mind that internal change does affect your customers. For instance, is a key leader in your business planning to retire? If so, decision making, operations or management style may change—and your customer may have obvious concerns. You can add some depth to this section, too, by portraying several different scenarios:

- What happens if we do nothing beyond last year?
- What happens if we capitalize on our strengths?
- What might happen if our image slips?
- What happens if we do less this year than last?

3. The Marketing Strategy

The marketing strategy consists of what you offer customers and the price you charge. Start by providing a complete description of each product or service and what it provides to your customers. Life cycle, again, is an important part of this. Is your technology or product developing, mature or in decline? Depending on how your company is organized, a variety of people are responsible for this information, right down to whoever is figuring out how to package the product and how it will be delivered. Find out who needs to be included and make sure their knowledge is used.

The marketing strategy is driven by everything you've done up to this point. Strategies define the approaches you will use to market the company. For instance, if you are competing on the basis of service and support rather than price, your strategy may consist of emphasizing relationships. You will then develop tactics that support that strategy: market the company vs. the product; increase sales per client; assure customer responsiveness. Now, what action or programs will you use to make sure that happens?

Note: strategy leads. No program, regardless of how good it is, should make the cut if it doesn't link to your business strategies and your customer.

The messages you must craft to support the strategies often are overlooked. Messages are the consistent themes you want your customer to know, to remember, to feel when he or she hears, reads, or views anything about your company or products. The method by which you deliver your messages comes under the heading of actions or programs.

Finally, you need to determine how you'll measure your own success, beyond meeting the sales forecast. How will you know if your image takes a beating? How will you know whether the customer is satisfied, or has just given up complaining? If you don't know, you'll be caught reacting to events, instead of planning for them.

Remember, your customer's measure of your success may be quite different from what you may think. Your proposed measures must be defined by what your customer values, and they have to be quantifiable. You may be surprised at how willing the customer is to cooperate with you in completing surveys, participating in third-party interviews, or taking part in a full-scale analysis of your company as a supplier. Use caution in assuming that winning awards means you have a measurable indicator. Your measures should be stated in terms of strategies, not plaques or trophies.

(continued)

4. The Marketing and Sales Organization

The most frequently overlooked element in business is something we usually relegate to the Personnel or Human Resources Office—people. They're what makes everything possible. Include them. Begin with a chart that shows the organization for both Marketing and Sales. You may wish to indicate any interdependent relationships that exist (for instance, with Quality).

Note which of the roles are critical, particularly in terms of customer contact. Just as important, include positions, capabilities, and numbers of people needed in the future. How will you gain these skills without impacting your cost per sale? Again, it's time to be creative and provide options.

5. Revenue and Expense

In this section, you're going to project the revenue your plan will produce. This is usually calculated by evaluating the value of your market(s) and determining the dollar value of your share of that market. You need to factor in any changes you believe will occur, and you'll need to identify the sources of revenue, by product or service. Use text to tell the story; use graphs to show the story.

After you've noted where the money is coming from, explain what money you need to deliver the projected return. This will include staff wages and benefits for your organization, as well as the cost for specific programs you plan to implement.

During this era of budget cuts, do yourself a favor by prioritizing these programs. For instance, if one of your key strategies is to expand to a new market via new technologies, products, or services, you will need to allocate appropriate dollars. What is the payback on the investment in marketing, and when will revenues fully pay back the investment? Also, provide an explanation of programs that will be deleted should a cut in funding be required. Again, combine text and spreadsheets to tell and to show.

6. Management Issues

This section represents your chance to let management know what keeps you awake at night. What might or could go wrong? What are the problems your company faces in customer relations? Are there technology needs that are going unattended? Again, this can be a collaborative effort that identifies your concerns. In addition, you may want to identify long-term issues, as well as those that are of immediate significance.

To keep this section as objective as possible, list the concerns and the business strategy or strategies they affect. What are the short-term and long-term risks? For instance, it is here that you might want to go into further detail about a customer's actions that look like the beginnings of backward integration.

7. Executive Summary

Since most senior leaders want a quick-look reference, it's best to include a one-page Executive Summary that covers these points:

- Your organization's objectives
- Budget requirements
- Revenue projections
- Critical management issues

When you're publishing the final plan document, you'll want the executive summary to be Page One.

8. Sell the Plan

This is one of the steps that often is overlooked. Selling your plan is as important as writing it. Otherwise, no one owns it, except you. The idea is to turn it into a rallying point that helps your company move forward. And to do that, you need to turn as many people as possible into ambassadors for your marketing efforts.

First, set up a time to present the plan to everyone who helped you with information and data. Make sure that they feel some sense of ownership, but that they also see how their piece ties into the whole. This is one of those instances where you need to say your plan, show your plan, discuss your plan. Only after all three steps are completed will they *hear* the plan.

After you've shared the information across the organization, reserve some time on the executive calendar. Have a couple of leaders review the plan first, giving you feedback on the parts where they have particular expertise. Then, present the plan at a staff meeting.

Is It Working?

You may think your job is finished. It's not. You need to convey the key parts of this plan to coworkers throughout the business. They need to know what the business is trying to achieve. Their livelihood, not just that of the owners, is at stake. From their phone-answering technique to the way they process an order, every step has meaning to the customer.

9. Measure/Renew

Once you've presented your plan and people understand it, you have to continuously work the plan and share information about it. The best way to help people see trends and respond appropriately is to have meaningful measures. In the language of Total Quality, these are the Key Result Indicators—the things that have importance to your customers and that are signals to your performance.

For instance, measure your ability to deliver on a customer request; the amount of time it takes to respond to a customer inquiry; your productivity per employee; cash flow; cycle time; yield rates. The idea is to identify a way to measure those things that are critical to you and to your customer.

Review those measurements. Share the information with the entire business and begin the process all over again. Seek new ideas and input to improve your performance. Go after more data and facts. And then renew your plan and share it with everyone—all over again.

It's an extensive process, but it's one that spreads the word—and spreads the ownership. It's the step that ensures that your plan will be constantly in use, and constantly at work for your business.

Carole Hedden is a writer and communication/planning consultant living in Elmira, New York.

create a seamless campaign for the 200SX that weaves advertising, in-store displays, and direct marketing together seamlessly.

"When everybody understands what the mission is, it's easier," asserts Bilfield. "It's easier to go upstream in the same direction than to go in different directions."

After bringing the different disciplines within your company on board, you're ready to design the external marketing program needed to support your goals. Again, the principle of integrated marketing comes into play: The message should be focused and consistent, and each step of the process should bring the consumer one step closer to buying your product.

In the case of Chiat/Day's campaign for the Nissan 200SX, the company used the same theme, graphics, type faces, and message to broadcast a consistent statement.

Introduced about the same time as the latest Batman movie, the campaign incorporates music and graphics from the television series. Magazine ads include an 800 number potential customers can call if they want to receive an information kit. Kits are personalized and include the name of a local Nissan dealer, a certificate for a test drive, and a voucher entitling test drivers to a free gift.

By linking each step of the process, Chiat/Day can chart the number of calls, test drives, and sales a particular ad elicits. Like a good one-two punch, the direct marketing picks up where the national advertising leaves off, leveraging the broad exposure and targeting it at the most likely buyers.

While the elaborate 200SX campaign may seem foolproof, a failure to integrate the process at any step along the way could result in a lost sale.

For example, if a potential client were to test drive the car and encounter a dealer who knew nothing about the free gift accompanying the test drive, the customer would feel justifiably annoyed. Conversely, a well-informed sales associate who can explain the gift will be mailed to the test driver in a few weeks will engender a positive response.

Help Is on the Way

Three Software Packages That Will Help You Get Started

Writing a marketing plan may be daunting, but there is a variety of software tools out there to help you get started. Found in electronics and book stores, the tools are in many ways like a Marketing 101 textbook. The difference lies in how they help.

Software tools have a distinct advantage: They actually force you to write, and that's the toughest part of any marketing plan. Sometimes called "MBA In a Box," these systems guide you through a planning process. Some even provide wording that you can copy into your own document and edit to fit your own business. Presto! A boiler plate plan! Others provide a system of interviewing and questioning that creates a custom plan for your operation. The more complex tools demand an integrated approach to planning, one that brings together the full force of your organization, not just Sales or Advertising.

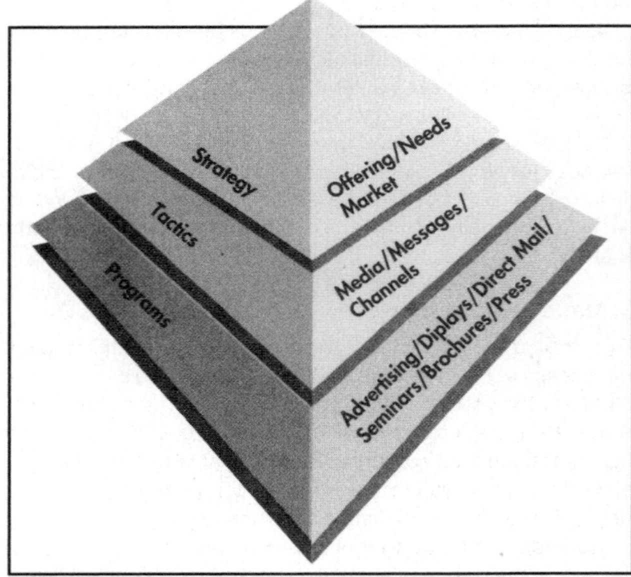

Pyramid Power: Plan Write's pyramid approach asks the user to define the messages for a business as part of the tactics.

1. Crush

Crush, a modestly named new product from a modestly named new company, HOT, takes a multimedia approach. (HOT stands for Hands-On Technology; *Crush* apparently stands for *Crushing the Competition*).

Just introduced a few months ago, *Crush* is a multimedia application for Macintosh or Windows PCs. It features the competitive analysis methods of Flegis McKenna, marketing guru to Apple, Intel and Genentech; and it features Mr. McKenna himself as your mentor, offering guidance via on-screen video. As you work through each section of a complete market analysis, McKenna provides germane comments; in addition, you can see video case studies of marketing success stories like Intuit software.

Crush provides worksheets and guidance for analyzing your products, customers, market trends and competitors, and helps you generate an action plan. The "mentor" approach makes it a useful tool for self-education; as you work through the examples and develop your company's marketing plan, you build your own expertise.

2. Marketing Plan Pro

Palo Alto's *Marketing Plan Pro* is a basic guide, useful for smaller businesses or ones in which the company leader wears

(continued)

a number of different hats, including marketing. It includes the standard spreadsheet capability, as well as the ability to chart numerical data. *Marketing Plan Pro* uses a pyramid process.

I liked the pyramid for a simple reason: It asks you to define messages for your business as part of your tactics. Without a message, it's easy to jump around, reacting to the marketplace instead of anticipating, leaving customers wondering what really is significant about your company or your product.

The step-by-step process is simple, and a sample plan shows how all the information works together. The customer-focus aspect of the plan seemed a little weak, demanding only sales potential and buying capacity of the customers. Targeted marketing is increasingly important, and the user may want to really expand how this section is used beyond what the software requires.

The package displays, at a glance, your strategy, the tactics you develop for each strategy, and the action plan or programs you choose to support the strategy. That could help when you're trying to prioritize creative ideas, eliminating those that really don't deliver what the strategy demands. Within each of three columns, you can click on a word and get help. Click on the heading program: a list of sample actions is displayed. They may not be what you're looking for, but if this is your first plan, they're lifesavers.

I also really liked *Marketing Plan Pro's* user's manual. It not only explains how the software works with your computer, it helps with business terms and provides a guide to planning, walking you through step-by-step.

3. Plan Write

Plan Write, created by Business Resource Software, Inc., is exponentially more powerful than *Marketing Plan Pro. Plan Write* brings together the breadth of the business, integrating information as far flung as distribution systems and image. And this software places your marketing strategy within the broader context of a business plan, the approach that tends to prove most effective.

As with *Marketing Plan Pro, Plan Write* provides a sample plan. The approach is traditional, incorporating a look at the business environment, the competition, the product or service mix you are offering, the way you will tell customers about that mix, pricing, delivery, and support.

Among the sections that were particularly strong was one on customer alternatives and people planning. Under the heading of customer alternatives, you're required to incorporate competitive information with customer information. If you don't meet the customer's needs, where could he or she go? Most often we look only at the competition, without trying to imagine how the customer is thinking. This exercise is particularly valuable to the company who leads the market.

The people part of planning too often is dumped on the personnel guy instead of being seen as a critical component of your organization's capabilities. *Plan Write* requires that you include how marketing is being handled, and how sales will be accomplished. In addition, it pushes you to define what skills will be needed in the future and where the gaps are between today and the future. People, in this plan, are viewed as a strategic component.

Plan Write offers a fully integrated spreadsheet that can import from or export to most of the popular spreadsheet programs you may already be using. Another neat feature allows you to enter numerical data and select from among 14 different graphing styles to display your information. You just click on the style you want to view, and the data is reconfigured.

Probably the biggest danger in dealing with software packages such as *Marketing Plan Pro* and *Plan Write* is to think the software is the answer. It's merely a guide.

—Carole Hedden

Section III: Execution

The final component of an integrated marketing plan is the implementation phase. This is where the budget comes in.

How much you'll need to spend depends on your goals. If a company wants to expand its market share or promote its products in a new region, it will probably have to spend more than it would to maintain its position in an existing market.

Again, you'll need to create a system for keeping your employees informed. You might consider adding an element to your company newsletter that features people from different departments talking about the marketing problems they encounter and how they overcome them. Or you might schedule a regular meeting for department heads to discuss marketing ideas so they can report back to their employees with news from around the company.

Finally, you'll need to devise a system for monitoring your marketing program. A database, similar to the one created from calls to the 200SX's 800 number, can be an invaluable tool for determining if your message is being well received.

It's important to establish time frames for achieving your goals early in the process. If you want to increase your market share, for instance, you should determine the rate at which you intend to add new customers. Failing to achieve that rate could signal a flaw in your plan or its execution, or an unrealistic goal.

"Remember, integrated marketing is a long-range way of thinking," warns Dawson. "Results are not going to be immediate."

Like any investment, marketing requires patience, perseverance, and commitment if it is to bear fruit. While not all companies are forward thinking enough to understand the manifold gains of integrated marketing, the ones that don't embrace it will ultimately pay a tremendous price.

Critical Thinking

1. What is the purpose of a marketing plan for a company?
2. Outline and briefly summarize the elements of the marketing plan.

Shelly Reese is a freelance writer based in Cincinnati.

Article 25

Surveyor of the Fittest

With the correct methodology, companies can effectively assess what market is viable and what market is not.

HONGJUN (HJ) LI

Industry research shows that 75% of new-product launches fail in the marketplace (visit www.microsoft.com to read its section about new-product development performance). That number does not even include product concepts that never successfully enter the market. There are many reasons for such failures, but lack of market demand for new products introduced is definitely the most important one.

According to an AMR Research Inc. report released in June 2005: Out of 20 large manufacturers polled about poor performance of product launches, 47% cited failing to understand and meet customer needs exactly—compared with 33% citing being late to market and 23% citing poor pricing.

No company will develop and introduce a new product if it knows beforehand that there will be no market demand. Unfortunately, most companies try to justify new-product development (NPD) expenditures by doing some market analysis—only to find out later that projected market demand has failed to materialize. Thus, a critical question to industry players is how they can become more effective in their market assessment efforts. This article offers a practical methodology that answers the question.

Executive Briefing

You might be surprised at how many new-product introductions fail every year. Unfortunately, such failure is not necessarily due to lack of market investigation. That is not to state, however, that market investigation is not relevant anymore. On the contrary: The industry's poor performance with new-product introductions pinpoints the importance of doing the right market investigation the right way. Here is a systematic, effective, and easy-to-follow methodology that illustrates exactly how to accomplish that.

Defining "New Product"

For the purpose of this article, "new product" refers to one of the following:

- a product that creates or implements a new technology
- a product that implements an existing technology on a new platform
- a product that integrates multiple technologies or functions into a single product for the first time
- a product that provides significant enhancements to an existing product category

The focus of our discussion is the overall market, not company-specific issues that can also lead to new-product introduction failures. There are many cases in which market demand for a new-product category exists but a particular company's product—falling into that category—fails in the market because of poor internal execution. Although internal execution is certainly critical, companies must first and foremost understand whether there will be a market for their new products being conceived or developed. Market investigation, in other words, remains highly relevant.

We will also assume that when a new product is introduced, it works—and its functionality conforms to original design requirements or intentions. Product failures attributed to unintended design flaws or quality problems are excluded from the scope of discussion. Again, such issues are internal and not market-related.

Common Pitfalls

Because so many new-product introduction failures can be attributed to lack of market demand, it is necessary to understand why companies fail to foresee them in the first place. Granted that market forecasting is sometimes a very difficult thing to do, companies can significantly reduce risks of new-product introduction failures if they do some basic market assessment homework the right way.

In general, the following are the common market assessment pitfalls into which companies fall:

- blind faith in one's capability to drive or create market demand
- looking at technological merits only
- selective use of incomplete, biased, or deceiving market data and feedback in line with product concepts or initial decisions
- taking input from direct customers only, without looking at demand from customers' customers (when applicable)
- relying on feedback or data of customer/consumer interest only, without looking at many other market factors that drive actual purchase decisions
- depending on third-party market forecasts only, without looking at or fully understanding the methodology used and assumptions made

Some companies might achieve market success even if they fall into one of these pitfalls, but such success requires really good luck and can hardly be duplicated in different settings.

Assessing the Market

Market assessment can be viewed as a science or an art. The challenge to market research professionals: Although some commonly used research techniques and tools exist, they might not be adequate to address the complete scope of market assessment required for sound business decision making. The challenge to senior executives is that they don't have the time to do detailed market investigations themselves. In addition, they might not have an effective framework for judging the quality and reliability of their subordinates' market assessments.

Both dedicated market research professionals and senior executives can use the methodology suggested here. The former can use it to investigate all the key aspects of a new product's market potential; the latter can use it to evaluate their subordinates' work. The methodology, if used the right way, can help companies avoid the aforementioned pitfalls.

The individual elements in the suggested market assessment framework are nothing new (see Figure 1). What might be new, however, are identification of all major market-related factors that affect demand for a new product, categorization of these factors within a systematic framework, and a step-by-step process that is easy to follow: (1) define target segment and needs, (2) analyze relative value, and (3) evaluate food-chain and ecosystem risks.

Figure 1 Framework for market assessment.

Note: Customers are those that make purchase decisions (in the case of business-to-business and business-to-consumer). Customers might be different from end users in the case of business-to-business-to-consumer.

Defining Target and Needs

With rare exceptions, a particular new product serves only a particular market segment or niche. This is especially true in the consumer-technology market. If a new product to be introduced simply targets "everybody," then it will most likely have a tough road ahead—because different segments and niches have different needs. There is a direct correlation between clarity of market-segment definition and ability to meet target customers' specific needs. Not surprisingly, the phenomenon of "shoot and aim" can explain why so many new products fail.

Defining the target market segment entails a detailed analysis of key segment characteristics such as size, demographics, and purchasing behavior. Without a clear understanding of the target segment, it will be difficult to identify the needs that a new product can meet.

Associating a generic need with a product is easy, and it can mislead companies into believing that their new product meets target customers' needs. To avoid that pitfall, companies can ask a simple question: What, exactly, is the problem that the new product solves?

Take the failed WebTV (a set-top box that consumers connect to their television sets, which allows dial-up Internet connection), for example. Consumers with a personal computer (PC) at home do not need it for Internet access. WebTV does allow non-PC households to access the Internet; unfortunately, the amount of non-PC households with such a need is very small. Moreover, WebTV cannot address that need well because of poor display of Web content on a standard-definition TV.

Even if the specific need for a new product is identified or defined, companies must assess the strength of that need, as different strength levels mean different market sizes. In general, two variables influence the relative strength of the need for a product: cognizance and perceived importance.

Cognizance. This determines to what extent target customers are aware of a particular need. There are two levels: explicit needs and implicit needs. Explicit needs are well-recognized and can be clearly articulated. They normally indicate a high level of need strength. Only new products with meaningful differentiation (to be discussed next) can turn these needs into corresponding market demand. Implicit needs, on the other hand, are not well-recognized or clearly articulated. They typically represent a new market that takes time, resources, and market education to develop.

Perceived importance. Depending on how strong the perceived importance of a particular need is, products meeting a particular need can fit into three categories: must-have, nice-to-have, and can-live-without. Must-have products meet the needs with the highest level of perceived importance and have the broadest market reach. Nice-to-have products address less-important needs and therefore have lower market demand. Can-live-without products generally have the lowest market-penetration rate.

Although measuring need strength can be difficult and subjective, it is a critical element of market analysis. A common method of need-strength assessment is conducting a quantitative survey to ask consumers their interest level in a particular new product or service. The challenge, however, is that different survey designs can yield significantly different results even if the same topic is addressed. Thus, as mentioned, understanding methodologies used and assumptions made is vital to appropriate interpretation of survey results.

One example of different survey results on the same topic is a study on consumers' interest in watching video on mobile devices. A survey by RBC Capital Markets shows that only 24% are interested, whereas a study by The Diffusion Group shows that 32% are interested. The delta can be attributed to differences in measurement scales (true/false versus a 7-point scale) and age groups of survey respondents (ages 21–65 versus ages 15–50). (Read "The Appeal of Mobile Video: Reading Between the Lines" under the TDG Opinions section at www.tdgresearch.com.)

Regardless of which is right (or closer to being correct), consumer interest is only one variable; other factors also drive market demand for a new product. This is why completing the following second step is essential, too.

Analyzing Relative Value

In today's environment, in which new technologies are rapidly emerging, consumers are having more and more choices that meet the same needs. For a new product to succeed in the marketplace, it will need to deliver a more compelling value proposition than alternative solutions by accomplishing at least one of the following: being a better product for a similar price and/or having a better price for a similar product. It is noteworthy that the higher market penetration alternatives have already achieved, the more important it is for new products to have strong differentiation in features/performance or cost.

The main reason voice over Internet protocol (VoIP) has been able to gain traction in both business and consumer markets is that it can deliver the same service as traditional wireline voice but at a lower cost. VoIP also enables certain features not available from "plain old telephone service" (POTS), but lower cost is the main driver of market adoption.

On the other hand, independent VoIP-over-broadband operators (at least those in the United States) have had difficulties quickly penetrating the consumer market without spending tons of marketing dollars. That is because of the availability of four primary alternatives: existing POTS, mobile phone service, Skype-type (a peer-to-peer Internet telephony network) services, and inexpensive VoIP phone cards. Those services either make voice communications an already fulfilled need or deliver cost savings similar to VoIP-over-broadband.

The same thing can be said of telcos' Internet protocol television (IPTV) service. In many markets, especially the United States, cable and satellite television have already made home-video entertainment a fulfilled need. If telcos' IPTV offers only me-too video services, then the most effective way for it to gain market share from cable and satellite television companies is to offer a lower price—as part of a discounted service bundle or a lower cost, stand-alone service. Alternatively, telcos can develop new applications: true video on demand and other innovative, compelling services that leverage the Internet protocol network.

Alternative solutions are not limited to similar products from direct competitors. They also include various other substitutes that address the same need. For example, the use of hands to turn lights on or off is an alternative to a lighting-control home-automation solution that requires a purchase—even though the former is less convenient. As taught in any Economics 101 course, substitutes create a negative impact on demand for a particular product.

Even if a cool new product has no or few existing alternatives and addresses a specific need, affordability or customers' price elasticity will determine its market penetration. A good example is high-end home-control (also called home-automation) systems. Of course they are not truly new products today, as a category, but they were when introduced about three decades ago. Those systems address consumers' need for comfort, convenience, safety, and prestige. However, because of high price tags (typically tens of thousands of dollars), high-end home-control systems have found success only in the custom-installed electronics market. And today's household penetration rate in the United States is still less than 2%, according to Parks Associates (an industry analyst firm).

Evaluating Risks

Suppose a new-product concept passes the test of the previous two steps; there is still no guarantee of market success. This third step prompts companies to identify market risks from a new product's food chain and its ecosystem. In this article, "ecosystem" refers to the interdependency of a certain set of infrastructure elements, platforms, devices, and other components that function as a whole to meet a particular need of customers.

From a market perspective, food-chain risks arise from direct customers' business model issues or uncertainty of demand from customers' customers. Although food-chain risks do not apply to everybody, they can be significant in certain sectors. For example, food-chain issues can explain the failure of some telecommunications equipment companies—and their products—that specifically targeted competitive local exchange carriers (CLECs) in the 1990s in the United States. Various newly developed products for CLECs, at that time, could certainly pass the test of the previous two steps. But they failed eventually because their CLEC customers did not have a sustainable business model after capital market bubbles burst.

Food-chain risks can also apply to a company in the business-to-business-to-consumer market. Assume that a service provider has just approached a vendor of videophones for the deployment of a new service. To assess how many units the vendor can actually sell, it will need to carefully assess consumers' potential take rate, partially based on the service provider's marketing and pricing plans. If the service provider cannot sign up many subscribers to the service that involves the use of a videophone, then the vendor will not be able to sell many units either—no matter how rosy the service provider's deployment plan appears to be.

A new product might also face significant market risks if it has too much dependency on certain ecosystem elements beyond the product developer's control. Products that enable delivery of online video to the television represent a good example. The main device that has such capability is the digital media adapter (DMA), a special set-top box that connects to both the television and a home network. For DMA to succeed as a product category, it will need support from at least the following ecosystem elements:

- wide availability of high-quality online video content, which is subject to Hollywood's receptivity to digital-content distribution and compatible digital-rights management solutions
- attractive pricing from content owners
- high penetration of robust, no-new-wire home networking solutions for multimedia distribution (beyond Ethernet and 802.11b/g, a wireless LAN standard)
- wide deployment of higher-bandwidth broadband access networks beyond ADSL1 or DOCSIS1.0 (Asymmetric Digital Subscriber Line, Data Over Cable Service Interface Specification)

DMA devices first appeared on the consumer market around 2003. Over the past few years, however, very few units have been sold (according to research from Parks Associates and NPD). The poor showing of DMA as a product category can be attributed to not only factors illustrated in the previous two steps but also poor ecosystem support (e.g., very limited availability of quality online video content, various home networking issues). Going forward, though, the DMA market is expected to gain stronger momentum—this time driven by positive developments of the ecosystem.

Implementing the Process

The person or team responsible for market intelligence should (1) develop detailed output based on the key questions in the three aforementioned steps and then (2) provide an overall assessment (see Figure 2). The market intelligence function should present to executives

Steps	Detailed output
Step No. 1: Needs of target market segment	• definition of the target market segment and estimate of the total size of the target segment • definition of the specific needs that the new product can address • categorization of the strength of the identified needs: level of cognizance and importance
Step No. 2: Relative value for the money	• list of alternatives to the new product and their market penetration rate • feature and price comparison between alternatives and the new product • target customers' price elasticity and estimated market adoption rate at specific price points
Step No. 3: Food-chain and ecosystem factors	• analysis of viability of target customers' business model specific to the new product • list of ecosystem elements that the new product depends on • the current status and projected future developments of the identified ecosystem elements
Overall assessment	• qualitative assessment of the viability of the new product's market • quantitative projections of the total available market in terms of units and revenues (if feasible and needed)

Figure 2 The market intelligence function's implementation.

Note: Certain items of the output list can be omitted only if relevant facts (1) are already common knowledge to everybody or (2) do not apply to a particular new product.

not only the overall assessment but also a summary of the detailed output—so they can see how conclusions are reached.

To judge the quality and reliability of the market intelligence function's work, executives can ask themselves three simple questions:

- Is there clear definition of the target market segment, the specific needs of target customers, and the strength of their needs?
- Is there adequate assessment of the impact from alternatives and customers' price elasticity?
- Are food-chain and ecosystem risks clearly identified and evaluated?

A tool for executive decision making. How should the three-step market assessment process be used for NPD decision-making purposes? As different companies have different business models, financial objectives, market power, and so forth, perhaps there is no clear-cut answer that applies to everybody. However, executives might find Figure 3's risk-assessment framework (based on the three-step process) a useful tool for distilling output from the market intelligence function and making decisions on NPD projects.

Market assessment results		Yellow light	Red light
Needs of target market segment	Difficult-to-define target market segment		X
	Difficult-to-define specific needs of target customers		X
	Implicit needs	X	
	Nice-to-have product	X	
	Can-live-without product		X
Relative value for the money	Presence of alternatives with a high market penetration rate	X	
	High price elasticity of target customers	X	
Food-chain and ecosystem factors	Questionable business model of target customers		X
	Too much ecosystem dependency	X	
	Lack of ecosystem support		X

Figure 3 New-product development risk assessment.

Yellow light: Market demand is limited or has substantial uncertainties.
Red light: Market demand is very limited or has very high uncertainties.

If yellow lights are associated with a new-product concept, then executives will need careful assessment of the new product's value proposition and market positioning before making a "go" decision on product development. If a new-product concept faces one or more red lights, then there will be high risks of market failure—and executives might be better off allocating development resources to an alternative new product that addresses a more viable market.

How often should the process be used? In fast-changing industries or markets, it is probably necessary for that market assessment framework to be used more than once for the entire NPD process. That will allow companies to not only reduce new-product introduction failure risks but also identify new market opportunities in a timely fashion.

Other participants in the market assessment process. Although the market intelligence function and executives are the most direct users of the recommended market assessment framework, a few other functions should be included: product management, sales, marketing, strategic planning, and engineering managers. Their inclusion can take the form of providing input, reviewing output, and communicating relevant findings to individual team members.

The more synchronized the internal communication, the more capabilities companies will have for developing and selling new products that meet market needs.

Avoiding the Trap

There have been too many cases in which companies developed new technologies or products looking for problems to solve. To avoid falling into such a trap, companies can complete the aforementioned three simple steps. Afterward, they will be in a much better position to assess the market viability of a new-product concept and whether product development resources should be committed to it.

Critical Thinking

1. In your opinion, what are some possible reasons for the failure of new-product introductions?
2. You have been assigned as a consultant for a business that is looking to develop a new product. Prepare a list of DOs and DON'Ts to help it design a new product development process and a successful market introduction.

Hongjun (HJ) Li is director of product marketing at the Plano, Texas, office of Kodiak Networks, a startup specializing in advanced mobile-communication applications headquartered in San Ramon, Calif. He may be reached at hli@kodiaknetworks.com or hongjunli888@yahoo.com. To join the discussion about this article, please visit www.marketingpower.com/marketingmanagementblog.

Brand Integrity

It starts with internal focus.

TOM PETERS AND VALARIE WILLIS

After the layoffs and budget cuts, now what do you do? Are you living up to your brand promises, or are you falling short on customer experiences? How can you sustain your brand and the power of your values? When you focus only on the bottom line and ignore people, your brand suffers—as your customers lose sight of what you stand for, and they no longer trust what you can deliver.

What About Your Brand?

The news is full of stories about downsizing, job evaporations, and budgets being slashed to shreds. So, what happens to your brand? Does it survive? Or is it bruised and battered? As a leader, you are responsible for the integrity of your brand. You need to pull your head out of the financial data long enough to assess the current state of your brand and of your talent.

When you experience a strong economic shift, your brand can easily become diluted, especially if no one is asking, "What about the brand?"

I*n the hub of your organization is your talent, and your talent is your brand.* It is the talent that brings your brand to life. If your people (talent) are no longer happy, if they are concerned about their own welfare, or they are hunkered down to stay out of sight, your brand may be on its last breath as well. And when the brand is struggling, the customer experience is compromised. Talent can become non-caring and cynical, and these attitudes permeate into how customers experience the brand.

Whenever you experience a strong shift, you must recalibrate and set the organization back on course. As a leader, you can best do this by taking these five steps: 1) revisit the ambition or goal of the organization and connect people to it; 2) spend time on the front lines talking to people and getting a handle on the issues; 3) re-state the brand promise and ensure that everyone knows how his or her job affects the promise; 4) look at the changes and assess the impact on the brand and the impact on the customer experience; and 5) design a course of action to put the brand back on track.

If your brand is bruised and battered, your customers may be headed to the competition—the exact opposite of your aims. In tough economic times, focus on keeping your current loyal customers and clients. Now is the time to re-think how to make the brand truly distinctive in the marketplace.

Excellence is achieved when the brand, the talent, and the customer experience are all in alignment.

Excellence Audit

To learn how your organization is doing, and if it needs recalibration, take our *Excellence Audit.* The 50 characteristics in the *Excellence Audit* describe the seven elements that interact in the *Future Shape of the Winner* model. As a mini-audit, answer these five questions:

- How can you keep focused on excellence in these tough economic times?
- Have you modified your ambitions in light of today's operating context?
- Are your team members fully committed to pursuing the agreed direction?
- Are your people totally focused on creating value for their customers?
- Is everyone on the payroll making their optimum contribution?

The *Excellence Audit* demystifies *excellence* for you by generating quantitative data on excellence. It identifies the most promising places to target improvement; reveals whether people agree about the priorities for improvement; exposes barriers to progress; helps you compile optimum improvement agendas that fit your context; generates joint agendas for management and professional teams determined to pursue excellence locally; helps you get your area focused and moving forward; and provides clarity and focus amid baffling complexity and conflicting demands.

Brand Inside's Effect on Brand

A cornerstone of our message about brand is that *your employees are also your customers.* We call this *Brand Inside.* We stirred up controversy over this notion by posting a PPT entitled *The Customer Comes Second.* The message is this: Since the customers in the firm serve the customers in the marketplace, put your employees first.

Matthew Kelly states: "Your employees are your first customers, and your most important customers."

Let me, Tom, get personal about all this. I *love* great customer or "end user" feedback! I am competitive to a fault in that regard and a slave to the market— after all these years.

At a higher level of marketplace engagement, I *love* a hearty business backlog, especially if it's based on repeat business—and I carefully measure it against the year-to-date of previous years. And I *love* a fee-per-event yield that exceeds last year, the year before, and so on. And yet, in an important way, I put the customer or end user second or third to employees.

It's simple and crystal clear to me: To give a high-impact, well-regarded, occasionally life-changing speech "to customers," I first, second, and third have to focus all my restless energy on "satisfying" *myself.* I must be physically, emotionally, and intellectually agitated and excited and desperate beyond measure to communicate, connect, compel, and grab people by the collar and say my piece about a few things, often contentious and not "crowd-pleasers," that, at the moment, are literally a matter of personal *life and death.*

I crave great customer feedback—but in no way, shape, or form am I trying to "satisfy my customer." I am, instead, trying to satisfy *me*—my own deep need to reach out and grab my customer and connect with my customer over ideas that consume me.

Hence, my "Job One" is purely *selfish and internally focused*—to be completely captivated by the subject matter at hand. That is Job One: *self-motivation.*

Warren Bennis, my primo mentor, said, "No leader sets out to be a leader *per se,* but rather to express him- or herself freely and fully. That is, leaders have no interest in proving themselves, but an abiding interest in expressing themselves."

So I'm back to my somewhat disingenuous message: To put the marketplace customer first, I must put the person serving the customer "more first." Excitement and self-stimulation first. Customer service second. That's my cause-and-effect scheme.

My message is that in order to *put the marketplace customer first, I must put the person serving the customer "more first."*

There is no great external focus unless a great internal focus is in place. I contend that finding and keeping and co-creating with great folks is not about clever tools to induce prospective "thems" to "shop with us," but a 99 percent internal effort to create such an exciting, spirited, entrepreneurial, diverse, humane "professional home" that people will line up by the gazillions (physically or electronically) to try and get a chance to come and live in our house and become what they'd never imagined they could become!

If you are serious about developing leaders, I suggest that you construct small leadership opportunities for people within days of their start on the job. *Everybody a leader* is entirely possible. So give you folks leadership responsibility from the outset, if not day #1 then within the first month. Hence, leadership development becomes a theme activity from stem to stern.

Boost Your Brand

Take this quick quiz (only 10 questions) for assessing your organization. Ask team members to rate themselves and the team against each question.

1. I know what my organization does to provide value to our customers.
2. I understand our products and services well enough to explain them.
3. I see how my job contributes to the value our organization creates.
4. I understand what a brand is.
5. I can tell the story of our brand.
6. I believe our brand is valuable.
7. We continually improve how we deliver products/services to customers.
8. I understand how my job brings our brand promise to life.
9. I can develop my talent while contributing to this organization's success.
10. I'm passionate about my work.

These questions investigate how connected you and your team feel to your *Purpose* and *Brand Promise.* The consolidated results can be used in a team discussion to identify the most promising targets for development.

Critical Thinking

1. In your perspective, what do the authors mean by "excellence is achieved when the brand, the talent and the customer experience are all in alignment"?
2. Do you agree with the following statement: "Your employees are your first customers, and your most important customers"? Justify your answer.

Tom Peters is CEO of The Tom Peters Company, and **Valarie Willis** is a Keynote Speaker, Facilitator, and Consultant. Visit www.tompeters.com.

Everybody Loves Zappos

Get Happy: How Tony Hsieh uses relentless innovation, stellar customer service, and a staff of believers to make Zappos.com an e-commerce juggernaut—and one of the most blissed-out businesses in America.

MAX CHAFKIN

"What would make you happier in your life?"

Tony Hsieh asks me this question as we sit at a booth with half a dozen young people in one of those absurdly lavish lounges that can be found only in Las Vegas. It's called Lavo, setting of recent Paris Hilton and Nelly sightings and the city's newest hot spot. The theme is an ancient Roman bathhouse, and so, in addition to the normal nightclub features—thumping bass, low tables, dim lighting—there's the distracting aspect of two scantily clad women performing a risqué bathing routine, complete with damp sponges and music.

It's a strange setting for an interview—especially for an interview with Hsieh (pronounced *Shay*). He's a thoughtful, low-key fellow who seems out of place in such a louche setting. Indeed, he seems oddly oblivious to his surroundings, which makes sense, given that he runs what is arguably the decade's most innovative start-up, Zappos.com. Hsieh helped start Zappos in 1999 as an online shoe store, and the company has since expanded to all manner of goods. Zappos booked $1 billion in gross sales in 2008, 20 percent better than the year before. It has been profitable since 2006.

At a time when most business leaders are retrenching, Hsieh is thinking big. In late 2006, he launched an outsourcing program to handle selling, customer service, and shipping for other companies, and last December, he started an educational website for small businesses that charges them $39.95 a month to tap Zappos executives for advice. Hsieh has said Zappos will eventually move beyond retail to businesses such as hotels and banking—anything where customer service is paramount. "I wouldn't rule out a Zappos airline that's just about the best customer service," he announced at the Web 2.0 conference last fall.

But Hsieh, 35, isn't interested in talking about any of this right now. He's still on the happiness thing. "On a scale of 1 to 10, how happy are you right now?" he asks, informing me that, right now, he's at about an 8.

I think for a second and then respond, "Maybe a 7?"

This isn't polite conversation for Hsieh. "I've been doing a lot of research into the science of happiness," he says. In addition to asking everyone he meets what makes him or her happy, he has also been studying books on the subject, especially Jonathan Haidt's *The Happiness Hypothesis,* which uses social psychology experiments to evaluate the world's great religions and philosophies and concludes that ancient wisdom and science are both useful tools in the quest for contentment. Hsieh is working on a system to supersede both. "I've been trying to come up with a unified theory for happiness," he says.

Unlike the world's great religions, the Tony Hsieh Unified Happiness Theory is not entirely settled. It involves establishing balance among four basic human needs: perceived progress, perceived control, relatedness, and a connection to a larger vision. And because Hsieh's life is his company, the test subjects are Zappos employees. "I've got a few different frameworks, and I'm just figuring out how to combine them," he says without irony or even a smile. "I think I'm pretty close."

Hsieh is widely regarded as one of the most innovative Internet marketers of all time. The Web entrepreneur and marketing guru Seth Godin has likened Hsieh's ability to use technology to connect with his customers to the Beatles' ability to animate their teenage fans. The blog Search Engine Land calls Zappos "the poster child for how to connect with customers online." And Hsieh's mastery isn't limited to marketing. Zappos's warehouse boasts a fleet of 70 brand-new robots that allows it to ship a pair of shoes in as little as eight minutes, earning reams of praise from logistics-industry trade publications.

But Hsieh has a hard time getting excited about any of this. What he really cares about is making Zappos's employees and customers feel really, really good. This is not because Hsieh is a nice guy (though he is a very nice guy), but because he has decided that his entire business revolves around one thing: happiness. Everything at Zappos serves that single end. Other business innovators work with software code or circuit boards or molecular formulas. Hsieh prefers to work with something altogether more complex and volatile: human beings themselves.

That single-minded focus on happiness has led to plenty of accolades for the company, which routinely scores high on lists of the best places to work. But Zappos's approach to workplace bliss differs significantly from that of other employee-friendly businesses. For one thing, Zappos pays salaries that are often below market rates—the average hourly worker makes just over $23,000 a year. Though the company covers 100 percent of health care costs, employees are not offered perks found at many companies, such as on-site child care, tuition reimbursement, and a 401(k) match. Zappos does offer free food to its employees, but the pile of cold cuts in the small cafeteria loses its allure faster than you can say *Googleplex.* Instead of buying his employees' loyalty, Hsieh has managed to design a corporate culture that challenges our conception of that tired phrase.

Hsieh's accomplishments are all the more impressive when you consider Zappos's origins. The idea of selling shoes on the Web may seem merely unoriginal today, but it seemed truly wrong-headed in 1999. "There wasn't an ounce of evidence to suggest it would work," says Michael Moritz, a partner with Sequoia Capital and the guy who backed Yahoo, Google—and, after initially passing on the company in 2001, Zappos. And yet, as Hsieh turned that daft idea into a business, his company transformed. Zappos now boasts systems that are breathlessly praised by academics, entrepreneurs, and, of course, the customers who seem eternally tickled by the company's free shipping and unbelievably responsive service. At many companies, talk of corporate culture dulls the luster, inducing cynicism among employees and creating hours of busywork for managers. At Zappos, the culture is the luster. And Hsieh—soft-spoken, deliberate, awkward—has emerged as a most unlikely business guru.

I first met Hsieh three years ago at a cocktail hour at the Inc. 500 conference. (Zappos had landed at No. 23, with revenue of $135 million.) We spoke for 10 minutes or so, and I remember being struck by the scope of his achievement. But I was even more impressed by the oddness of Hsieh's mannerisms.

Hsieh is hard to know and even harder to read. He's generous and smart, but so subdued in one-on-one conversation that it's easy to mistake his reticence for rudeness. When he does speak, it's in full paragraphs that sound as if they have been formulated in advance. He sometimes smiles—as he does when he's explaining the clever way Zappos manages its call center—but he doesn't laugh at other people's jokes and seldom tells his own.

And yet, this mild-mannered fellow leads a company that is entirely uninhibited. Interviews are held over vodka shots, bathrooms are plastered with "urine color" charts (ostensibly to ensure that employees are hydrated but also just to be weird and funny), and managers are encouraged to goof off with the people they manage. Zappos's 1,300 employees talk about the place with a religious fervor. The phrase *core values* can prompt emotional soliloquies, and the CEO is held with a regard typically afforded rock stars and cult leaders.

Hsieh tries his best to keep up with the goofy, libertine culture. Every day, he blasts a steady stream of playful messages to 350,000 people on Twitter. (Before taking the stage at a conference earlier this year, he posted this missive: "Spilled Coke on left leg of jeans, so poured some water on right leg so looks like the denim fade.") He has also become an accomplished public speaker who spends a good chunk of his time on the road giving talks, which are delivered without notes.

What most of Hsieh's admirers—and even some Zappos employees—don't know is that this openness doesn't come naturally. Hsieh has been exceptionally shy all his life and finds meeting strangers exhausting. (His trick to get over his shyness is to pretend he's interviewing you for a job.) Those seemingly off-the-cuff Twitter missives? He spends 10 minutes or so carefully composing each one. He takes his employees out to restaurants and bars not because he loves nightlife but because he thinks it sets a good example. "I just want to have a company where people can hang out together," he says, "and then come in to work the next day and not worry about whether they've done something stupid." Most CEOs make their companies in their own image; Hsieh seems to have designed his company to behave the way he wishes he could.

Hsieh has always been a little different. He grew up in San Rafael, California, and excelled from an almost creepily young age. In first grade, he taught himself to program, playing with a Radio Shack microcomputer that his father, Richard—a Chinese-born chemical engineer with a Ph.D., an M.B.A., and 29 patents to his name—brought home. The next year, Richard blew a month's salary and bought his son an IBM XT personal computer. By third grade, Hsieh's bedroom was littered with pages of software code for a bulletin board system—a precursor to today's Internet message boards, accessed by dial-up modem—that he ran for several years, tying up the household phone line and mystifying his parents. "He stayed in his room for hours at a time," says Richard Hsieh.

Hsieh started his first company, LinkExchange, shortly after graduating from Harvard with a degree in computer science. The company allowed amateur Web publishers to barter for advertising by agreeing to publish one another's ads. "It was just something to keep busy," he says. "But within a week, we knew we were onto something." In three months, Hsieh signed up 20,000 websites; he decided that the site could make money by selling ads as well as trading them. Though Link-Exchange was unprofitable, the idea had enough steam to pick up a $3 million investment from Sequoia Capital—Moritz led the investment. By 1998, the company, which had revenue of about $10 million, would be sold to Microsoft for a staggering $265 million. Hsieh was just 24 years old.

And yet, despite this success, Hsieh found himself depressed. "The easiest way to explain it was that going into the office started to feel like work," he says. He felt increasingly that the people he had hired were not committed to the venture's long-term growth. "The Silicon Valley culture is, 'I'm going to work hard for four years and make millions of dollars and then retire,'" he says. Work, which once had felt liberating, had become a chore. He resolved that his next company would not be about a short-term payday. It would be about long-term growth, about creating a place to which he and his employees would want to come every day.

When you visit Zappos's headquarters in Henderson, Nevada, it's easy to miss Hsieh's desk. Not only is it tucked into a row of cubicles in the middle of the floor, but it's also smaller and more cluttered than any CEO's desk I have ever seen. There are stacks of unopened mail, empty Styrofoam cups, several unopened liquor bottles, and a sizable collection of self-help books—titles include *Mastering the Rockefeller Habits, The Time Paradox: The New Psychology of Time That Will Change Your Life,* and *14,000 Things to Be Happy About.* There are a few science titles—part of Hsieh's quest for a happiness framework—a few on food and wine, and one on marathon running, which he recently took up.

Hsieh is a relentless self-improver, which may help explain why, after selling LinkExchange, he didn't start a new company. Instead, he started 27. In 1999, he and Alfred Lin, a Harvard classmate, launched something called Venture Frogs. Though structured as a venture capital fund, it was more ambitious. Hsieh and Lin leased 15,000 square feet of office space in the same San Francisco building in which they both owned lofts, and they gave the space to the start-ups in which they invested.

Hsieh's involvement in Zappos started with a voice mail from a young man named Nick Swinmurn, who said he wanted to start an online shoe company. Hsieh had never been particularly taken with the idea of online retail, but when Swinmurn mentioned that catalog companies sold $2 billion a year worth of shoes, Hsieh got interested. In 1999, Venture Frogs agreed to invest $500,000, if Zappos—the name is a play on *zapatos,* the Spanish word for *shoes*—could recruit someone with shoe experience. Swinmurn found Fred Mossler, then a Nordstrom buyer.

Six months later, Swinmurn was out of money, and the site offered only three shoe brands. (Most orders were initially filled by a few local retailers.) "We were down to the last day, essentially," says Mossler. "And Tony called." Hsieh said he would keep the company afloat and offered to help. By the summer of 2000, Hsieh and Swinmurn were co-CEOs, and Zappos was operating out of Hsieh's living room. Says Hsieh: "It was the most interesting opportunity, and the people were the most fun."

This is also a delicate way of saying that Hsieh was not especially happy as an investor. A few of Venture Frogs' investments succeeded—notably the search engine Ask .com and the restaurant reservation system OpenTable—but as the dot-com bubble burst, most struggled to survive, and some were shuttered. Hsieh had been attracted to investing because it seemed to bring all the fun of start-ups on a larger scale; instead, it became a treadmill of meetings full of bad news. "I think it was much harder than he first imagined," says Moritz. What Hsieh wanted, he realized, was the unstructured fun of a new company. As he puts it, "I wanted to be involved in building something."

Zappos's early years were a scramble. Footwear brands, which associated the Web with heavy discounting, resisted putting their merchandise on Zappos. Still, Mossler succeeded in signing up about 50 companies in the first year and a half. Hsieh wrote software code and focused on financing—he bankrolled the company until he secured a line of credit with Wells Fargo in 2003. Nobody had set jobs, nobody cared about titles, and everybody hung out with everybody else after work. The economy was falling apart around them, but somehow, even the struggle was fun.

The defining aspect of the Zappos customer experience—free shipping and free returns—was concocted out of necessity. Hsieh figured that there was no other way to get people to try the site. He also added a prominently displayed toll-free customer support number, a personal buying service, free socks—anything to help put skeptical customers at ease. Because the company could not afford to spend money on marketing, the sales strategy involved making customers so happy that they bought again or told their friends or both.

Though shoemakers were initially reluctant to sell to Zappos—Nike held out for more than seven years—by 2002, Mossler had lined up more than 100 brands, including Steve Madden and Converse, and the company was beginning to do a brisk business. Sales hit $32 million in 2002, up from $8.6 million the previous year. At the time, 25 percent of orders were shipped from manufacturers' warehouses; these orders were often delayed for days. Hsieh decided to stop listing these items on Zappos and opened a warehouse outside of Louisville.

A few months later, Hsieh moved the company from San Francisco to Las Vegas—70 of the company's 100 employees made the trip. The move made sense for lots of reasons, chief among them lower taxes and a lower cost of living. Hsieh also wanted to be in a city where restaurants and stores are open 24 hours a day, to accommodate call center reps who work the graveyard shift. The move corresponded with yet another jump in sales and helped put an end to any financial worries. In late 2004, the company, which sold $184 million worth of goods that year, landed $20 million from Sequoia Capital.

Such rapid growth was exciting. But it also led Hsieh to wonder how he could preserve Zappos's radical dedication to customer service and its fun, loose work environment. "We always hired for culture fit," he says. "But we were growing so quickly that managers who hadn't been around for very long might not know what our culture was." He wrote an e-mail to the entire company asking for help, and he distilled the responses into a list of 10 core values, including "Be humble," "Create fun and a little weirdness," and "Deliver WOW through service." Then he assigned and collected short essays from every employee on the subject of the company's culture and published them, unedited, in a book that he distributed to the staff.

Every year, all employees, both new and old, contribute a fresh essay to the book, which has grown to 480 pages. Hsieh uses it as a way not only to get employees thinking about the meaning of their work but also to show the outside world what he has built. Talk to Hsieh for five minutes, and he will inevitably try to get your address so he can mail you a copy. The book is painfully earnest and yet affecting nonetheless. There are all the clichés one might expect—acronyms, ridiculous overstatement (one call center rep compared Zappos to China's Ming Dynasty), and a fondness for the word *Zapponians.* It often goes way over the top. "Could you imagine if Zappos was more than an online retailer, or the job that pays the bills, but actually became a way of life?" wrote Donavon Roberson, a pastor who left the ministry before joining Zappos.

Most Zappos employees are familiar with all this history. In fact, despite all the research I did before heading to Las Vegas, I didn't know that Nike had spurned Zappos until I sat in on a two-hour Zappos history class—part of a four-week course on the subject—and watched as employees called out various milestones: 2002, $32 million in gross sales! 2006, the year the company recorded its first $3 million day! 2007, the year Nike joined Zappos!

This mastery isn't accidental. It's required. All new Zappos employees receive two weeks of classroom training. Then they spend two weeks learning how to answer customer calls. At the conclusion of the program, trainees are famously offered $2,000, plus time worked, to quit. The practice, Hsieh's idea, began in 2005, with a $100 offer. "Our training team had gotten good at figuring out who wasn't going to make it, and we were thinking, How do you get rid of those people?" says Hsieh. Paying them to quit saves the company money by weeding out people who would jump ship anyway and allows those who remain to make a public statement of commitment to their new employer.

All employees receive four weeks of training. Then they are offered $2,000 to quit.

More recently, Hsieh has overseen the development of an even more comprehensive curriculum. The first course, intended for employees who have worked at Zappos for two years or less, involves more than 200 hours of class time (during work hours) and mandates that students read nine business books. Topics include Sarbanes-Oxley compliance and Twitter use. Advanced students can take classes in public speaking and financial planning. "The vision is that three years from now, almost all our hires will be entry-level people," Hsieh says. "We'll provide them with training and mentorship, so that within five to seven years, they can become senior leaders within the company."

The Zappos headquarters takes up three modest buildings in a nondescript office park about a 20-minute drive from the Las Vegas Strip. Walk in, and it becomes immediately clear why for some entrepreneurs, visiting Zappos is of a piece with the buffet at the Bellagio or a trip to the top of the (replica) Eiffel Tower. In fact, Zappos hosts a tour of its headquarters every couple of hours, an operation that is staffed by 12 people and includes two SUVs and a bus with custom Zappos paint jobs. Call the company from your hotel, and someone will pick you up and ferry you to Henderson.

Zappos hosts a tour of its headquarters every couple of hours. Call the company from your hotel, and someone will pick you up.

My tour is led by Roberson, the former pastor, who wears jeans and a maroon polo shirt and carries a giant Zappos flag. We are joined by four consultants from Deloitte. In the lobby, Roberson points out the Reply to All Hat—a sort of dunce cap for employees who commit that venial office sin of the inadvertent mass e-mail—and takes us past the nap room, where three employees are stretched out on couches. At the office of the company's staff life coach, who also happens to be Hsieh's former chiropractor, we are each photographed while sitting on a throne.

But the most striking thing about the tour is the extent to which the company's long-term plan is on display. A sales chart in the lobby informs everyone in the building that the day before—March 4, 2009—Zappos sold $2.5 million worth of merchandise. A computer printout in the hallway notes that there are currently 4.1 million items, mostly shoes, in stock in the warehouse in Kentucky. At the conclusion of the tour, we are invited to peruse the company library, which is filled with multiple copies of two dozen business and self-help books. We are urged to take whatever grabs our fancy, a policy that applies to employees as well. Roberson explains that one of Zappos's core values is personal growth and that books are given out to help employees grow with the company.

When I tell Hsieh that Zappos strikes me as not unlike a religious cult, he doesn't disagree. "I think there's a lot you can learn from religion," he says. "This is not just a company. It's like a way of life."

Of course, nobody except Hsieh works at Zappos to save his or her soul. It's a job—and not a particularly glamorous one. Customer service reps start at $11 an hour, warehouse workers at $8.25. But even in its hiring process, Zappos creates wildly different expectations than do most companies. Prospective hires must pass an hour-long "culture interview" before being handed off to whatever department they are applying to. Questions include, "On a scale of 1–10, how weird are you?" and "What was your last position called? Was that an appropriate title?" (The first question makes sure that employees are sufficiently weird; the second, in which the interviewer is trying to goad the applicant into grumbling about his or her title, tests for humility.)

If there is a disagreement between HR and the manager doing the hiring, Hsieh personally interviews the candidate and makes the final call. His strategy is to get the applicant into a social situation to see if they can connect emotionally. Alcohol often figures in the hiring process. "I had three vodka shots with Tony during my interview," says Rebecca Ratner, Zappos's head of human resources. "And I'm not atypical." I asked Hsieh if this wasn't exposing the company to unnecessary risks. "It's a risk," he says. "But if we're building a culture where everyone is friends with everyone else, it's worth the risk."

After my tour, I spend a few minutes sitting in the Zappos call center with Grace Hale, a bubbly young woman with dyed black hair and a lip piercing. Unlike most call center operators, Zappos does not keep track of call times or require operators to read from scripts. Hale has a penchant for offering unsolicited commentary on customers' shoe selections—"They *are* beautiful," she coos during one call, as she pulls up a picture of a pair of Dr. Scholl's Asana heels that a customer found

10 Questions for Tony Hsieh

What's your favorite part of a typical day?
Anytime I'm building something new.

What's the least glamorous thing you do in the line of duty?
Going through airport security.

What skill would you most like to improve?
Humor. I've been researching the science of humor, and I think it can be learned like any skill.

What's the simplest thing you never learned to do?
To whistle.

What accomplishment are you most proud of?
Being involved in building the Zappos culture.

What keeps you up at night?
Trying to figure out how to make the company culture stronger as we get bigger.

Who is the smartest person you know?
I believe that people are smart in different ways. With everyone I meet, I try to figure out what they're smart about and learn from them.

If you could go back and do one thing differently, what would it be?
I would try to do everything faster.

What was the happiest day of your career?
Our company milestones—like when we signed Nike after trying to get them for eight years.

On a scale from 1 to 10, how happy are you right now?
8.5.

uncomfortable. Not only are reps encouraged to make decisions on their own—for instance, offering a refund on a defective item—they are supposed to send a dozen or so personal notes to customers every day. "It's all about P-E-C," Hale explains to me. "Personal Emotional Connection with the customer." (After a few hours at Zappos, you actually stop noticing this argot.)

Zappos does not track call times or require operators to read from scripts. "It's all about P-E-C: Personal Emotional Connection with the customer," says one rep.

All of this is designed to impress customers—or as Hale would have it, "wow them." Last year, Zappos stopped promising free overnight shipping on its website, but not because of the cost. In fact, the company *still* ships almost every order overnight, but Hsieh wanted customers to be surprised when they got the item the next day. According to Patti Freeman Evans, an analyst with Forrester Research, this has helped Zappos fend off challenges from copycat sites such as Amazon's Endless.com and IAC's Shoebuy.com, which offer similar perks and even lower prices. "A lot of companies talk about service. Zappos really does it," Evans says.

During Zappos's early days, long workdays would often spill into late-night socializing. Hsieh enjoyed this so much that he formalized it at Zappos: Managers are now required to spend 10 percent to 20 percent of their time goofing off with the people they manage. "It's just kind of a random number we made up," Hsieh concedes. "But part of the way you build company culture is hanging out outside of the office."

On my last night in Las Vegas, Hsieh offers to take me out and show me what he is talking about. We are joined by a couple of his friends and six Zappos employees and bounce from a bar to a lounge to a nightclub. By the time I beg out, at 2 a.m., Hsieh and a few others are heading to a dive bar to grab a late-night bite to eat. Though Hsieh seems to enjoy himself—and though he does indulge in a few shots of Grey Goose—he never really lets loose. For the first half of the evening, we chat seriously about happiness. Then he withdraws, eventually sitting down, playing with his BlackBerry, and watching the party with what looks like a smile.

In his speeches, Hsieh likes to point out that Zappos does not have specific policies for dealing with each customer service situation. He claims that the company's culture allows it to do extraordinary things. I saw him make this point earlier this year in New York City, when he told a story about a woman whose husband died in a car accident after she had ordered boots for him from Zappos. The day after she called to ask for help with the return, she received a flower delivery. The call center rep had ordered the flowers without checking with a supervisor and billed them to the company. "At the funeral, the widow told her friends and family about the experience," Hsieh said, his voice cracking and his eyes tearing up ever so slightly. "Not only was she a customer for life, but so were those 30 or 40 people at the funeral."

Hsieh paused to compose himself. "Stories like these are being created every single day, thousands and thousands of times," he said. "It's just an example that if you get the culture right, then most of the other stuff follows."

Critical Thinking

1. Visit Zappos website and discuss why it has been called "the poster child for how to connect with customers online."
2. Define corporate culture. According to the article, what makes Zappos corporate culture distinct?

Max Chafkin is *Inc.'s* senior writer.

Rocket Plan

Companies can fuel success with a rigorous pricing approach—one that measures customer value, the innovation's nature, and the product category life cycle stage.

MARK BURTON AND STEVE HAGGETT

Innovation is the fuel that drives growth. Any good sales executive can tell you that the quickest path to revenue growth is through new product innovation rather than fighting for share in existing markets. Innovation offers immediate differentiation and the chance to command a premium price. Yet the risks of failure are high. Consider this statement from Eric von Hippel, a professor of the Massachusetts Institute of Technology (*Harvard Business Review,* January 2007): "Recent research shows that the 70% to 80% of new product development that fails does so not for lack of advanced technology but because of a failure to understand users' needs."

A new-product launch enjoys many proud parents: the development team that followed a rigorous staged development process, the manufacturing organization that trained Six Sigma black belts, the marketing team that developed creative promotions and toured with industry trade shows, the public relations team that built a compelling publicity campaign, and the sales team that enthusiastically extolled the product's virtues to customers. So why are there high failure rates?

Many companies' innovation efforts are inwardly focused. The results are billions of dollars wasted developing offerings that have little to no appeal to customers. In business-to-business markets there are three principal reasons for that:

Failure to connect customer needs to value: financial, competitive, and strategic benefits to the customer. PictureTel was an early innovator in the videoconferencing industry 20 years ago, developing a breakthrough technology enabling live videoconferences. Its product launch focused on its leading performance and truly impressive technical capabilities. Yet after PictureTel's great investment and product differentiation, the market did not beat a path to its door. The early value propositions failed to translate the cost of the system into clear value for customers: revenue benefits of reaching more customers or cost savings from travel. In 2000, PictureTel lost $100 million; in 2001, a smaller and more profitable rival purchased it.

Executive Briefing

The majority of new-product launches fail. However, it is seldom the technology itself that's to blame. A rigorous pricing approach can improve customer adoption rates, grow profitability, and increase return on investment. A strategy that quantitatively measures customer value, evaluates the nature of the innovation (whether minor, major, or disruptive), and assesses the stage of the product life cycle can be the difference between success and failure. The authors describe an effective approach.

Use of product-based value propositions centering on technical ability over market needs. Iridium was a triumph of rocket science. In 1987, the wife of a senior Motorola technology leader fumed because she couldn't call home from a boat in the Bahamas. Eleven years and more than $2 billion later, Motorola had successfully launched a necklace of 66 satellites linking $3,000 phone sets for $7-a-minute calls. However, cell phone customers wanted increasingly small units, not 1-pound "shoe phones," and the market for people who needed a dedicated satellite system for $7 a minute was tiny. In 2000, the network was sold for around $25 million—about a penny on the dollar for Motorola's investment.

Overemphasis on the role of pricing in driving customer adoption. Petrocosm launched as an oil industry transaction platform with a $100 million investment from Chevron and top leadership from the oil equipment industry. It offered a cheap source of high-technology drilling equipment. But in an industry requiring billion-dollar offshore platforms poised over explosive hydrocarbon reservoirs, replacing the trust and experience that trained sales and service representatives offer with a low-cost transaction failed to gain a customer base. The customer base didn't want cheap; it wanted cost-effective. Petrocosm faded away.

The good news is that the pricing process is straightforward and will improve the returns on investment in innovations. Most successful innovators follow a few simple rules:

- Define the financial benefits that customers receive from adopting the new solution.
- Align price levels with financial and psychological drivers of customer value.
- Align pricing strategy with the specific nature of the innovation and the product category life cycle status.
- Create outstanding launch programs—taking the emphasis off price by mitigating perceived risks for customers.

Companies that adhere to those principles enjoy significant benefits over their competitors, including (1) a more effective screening process that enables them to focus resources only on those innovations that provide significant value to the customer, (2) compelling launch programs that communicate the business value of innovations, and (3) a coherent pricing strategy that prevents panic discounting to drive sales. Taken together, those benefits translate to greater success rates for new offerings and better pricing for those that make it to market.

The Value-on-Innovation Paradox

In B-to-B markets, technological possibility often drives innovation, not defined customer needs. Living on the uncertain edge of technology, it should be less risky to focus on what's possible rather than invest money in less-certain research based on customer wish lists—trusting in Moore's Law rather than Murphy's Law. (Moore's Law is the observation that the number of transistors on an integrated circuit for minimum component cost doubles every 24 months, described by Intel cofounder Gordon Moore. Murphy's Law states that anything that can go wrong, will.) But the results show the drawbacks of a technology-driven approach.

Often, market research is focused on projections of market size and growth based on customer intent-to-purchase studies. Although this information can be important, it overlooks the most fundamental issue of whether an innovation will be successful: Is there a compelling business reason for customers to go through the upheaval of changing how they do things—to get the potential benefits of adopting your innovation? In short, what value does the customer expect to get, and how does value compare with the costs of switching? That question sets a much higher standard for research. To address it, companies need to focus on the six areas in Figure 1.

Great innovators use the answers to those questions to draw a map of where innovation will have the greatest impact—at both the market and individual customer level. Not until they understand (1) the customer value their innovations create, (2) the barriers, and (3) enablers of adoption do they finalize specifications. These same insights are used to define high-impact value propositions and to establish pricing models and price levels.

Define customer objectives	• How do customers make money? • How do they plan to grow? • How do they differentiate their offerings? • What are their greatest challenges?
Define current solution	• Which business processes support critical customer objectives? • What is the current work flow? • Who are the process owners and what are their priorities?
Define problem solved	• How does our innovation improve performance against key customer objectives and performance of critical business processes? • What is the impact of solving the problem defined? Is it significant enough to go forward?
Define financial impact	• How does our innovation affect revenues and costs relative to current solutions?
Define barriers to adoption	• What and whom in the customer buying group would our innovation affect? • What are the switching costs? • Is our innovation compatible with customer processes and supporting technology? • What is the organizational or political impact of our innovation?
Define likely adopters	• Who will benefit most from a change to our solution? • Who has the power to push for the change?

Figure 1 Customer value.

Defining barriers to adoption and identifying likely adopters are critical. Companies commonly misread how their innovations change the buying center dynamics. Existing customer contacts might not be the right targets for an innovation when relationships with new decision makers and influencers need to be cultivated. Companies often call on the same old contacts and fail to anticipate that those contacts will not have the power to drive change and/or are very much invested in the status quo. When that happens, they find that those relationships actually impede their ability to sell innovations to their current customers.

The smartest road to profitable returns on innovations starts with an understanding of the customer; technology comes second.

Using Value Insights

Translating the results of customer value research into effective pricing for innovations requires answering some challenging questions about value to the customer. Importantly, it is not

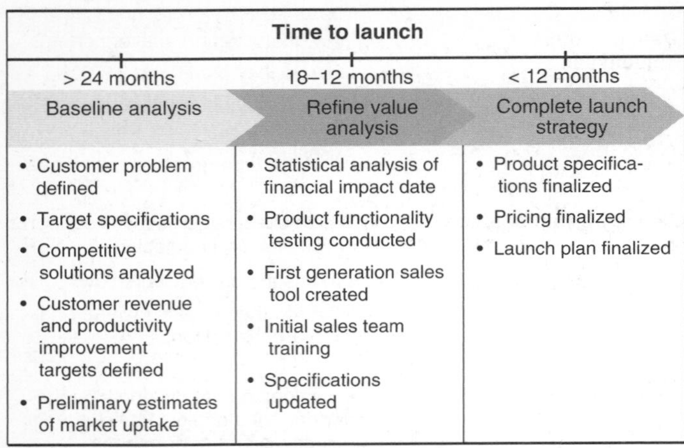

Figure 2 Preparing for effective launch pricing.

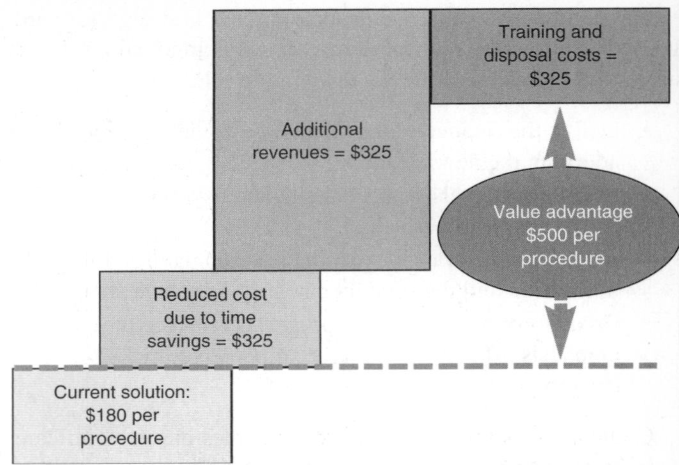

Figure 3 Use customer value data to determine your price.

necessary to exhaustively answer these questions at the start of your customer research and innovation development processes. In fact, one defining characteristic of many leading innovators is that they are comfortable with a certain amount of ambiguity to start. The key is that they continue to (1) ask hard questions about customers and value and (2) refine their views on offering specifications, value positioning, and pricing. They do it early and they do it often.

A leading manufacturer of dental equipment (disguised), which has built its business by entering new markets with innovative offerings, does exactly this. Figure 2 shows a summary of its process.

It is tempting to look at the timeline and say "Our product life cycles are too short for this to be practical." But the fact is that all windows of innovative advantage are shortening. For all companies, it is critical to do value homework and get launch pricing right. Although your business might require far more compressed timelines, the process of establishing and refining your view of value to the customer is the foundational element for successful introduction, pricing, and positioning of innovations.

When the manufacturer was able to employ new technologies, to replace reusable dental instruments with disposable ones, it knew it had a potentially valuable innovation to bring to market. Through direct customer interviews and operational studies, it determined that such a device would improve procedure-room utilization by reducing cleanup time. The device also provided a market opportunity for oral surgeons seeking to differentiate themselves by advertising that they use the safest and most advanced equipment.

Using this information to establish a range for pricing is a three-step process: Determine the total costs to the customer of his current solution options, define the financial benefits that your innovation delivers over and above current alternatives, and identify the switching costs for customers who want to move to your solution.

In the case of our dental equipment manufacturer, that meant determining the following:

- the cost per procedure of current solutions—by amortizing the total lifetime costs of current and reusable equipment over the number of procedures performed
- the cost savings due to greater procedure-room utilization
- the increases in revenues from patients brought in through oral surgeons advertising use of the new equipment
- switching costs (in this instance, disposal and training costs)

Its findings are summarized in Figure 3.

The results of customer value research yield a band of customer value and establish upper and lower boundaries for price range. Using that information about financial value, the manufacturer was then able to set an initial price that captured a fair share of the value created for customers. To do that, it first defined its value advantage over existing solutions: in this case, $500 per procedure. Next, it added the cost of the current solution to define the maximum range of price options available: $180–$680 (the $180 cost of the current solution plus the $500 value advantage).

To narrow down the range, the manufacturer analyzed the psychological elements of value from the customer's perspective. That included negative perceptions (e.g., risk from adopting the new technology, concerns about moving from the comfortable old solution to something new) and psychological benefits (e.g., pride in being on the cutting edge). Finally, the manufacturer needed to set a price that offered some incentive to purchase. At the end of the process, it decided on $400 per instrument. Although that was at the lower end of the possible range, it ensured a significant profit and gave customers a reasonable incentive to switch.

How do companies best select the right price within the range of customer value? Let's turn to that by looking more closely at pricing strategy.

Pricing Strategy Selection

To really refine the pricing decision, evaluate price ranges against a defined pricing strategy for your innovation. This is an iterative process of checking (1) pricing strategy against market research data and (2) possible price points against your pricing strategy. The best way to get your arms around the pricing strategy element is to think about the following two variables.

What is the nature of the innovation? Is it a minor improvement, such as an interim software update? Is it a major one, such as the introduction of flat-panel TV sets? Or is it disruptive, such as the current move to solid-state flash memory for applications previously covered by high-speed disk drives?

Understanding the nature of the innovation defines the degrees of freedom that the innovator has in selecting a pricing strategy. Minor innovations (e.g., line extensions) are often necessary, but they do little to create advantage over the competition. As such, they provide little to increase pricing power. Innovations that are recognized as major breakthroughs present much greater flexibility in choosing a pricing strategy. This is because companies can keep prices high to skim value until the market develops—and then bring prices down to drive growth.

With disruptive innovations, the decision is a bit trickier. In the groundbreaking article "Disruptive Technologies: Catching the Wave" (*Harvard Business Review,* January 2005), Clayton M. Christensen points out that such innovations fall into one of two categories.

Some, such as flash memory, offer significant performance advantages for niche markets (e.g., aerospace applications) but are too expensive for mainstream applications (e.g., laptop computers). The best approach for these products is to go upmarket and use a skim pricing strategy—until costs and complementary technologies make it possible to enter main-stream markets.

Alternately, some offer inferior performance on many key attributes but offer clear benefits in one or two areas for some customers. That was the case with 3.5-inch disk drives when they were introduced. In that instance, the best approach is to go down-market and use a penetration pricing strategy with prices set below established alternatives.

In what stage of the life cycle is the product category? This element is critical but often overlooked. Failure to consider the life cycle dimension can result in disastrous financial consequences. That happened with flat-panel TVs. Early entrants initially played the game well. Prices for the early sets were high, reflecting both costs and the value that enthusiasts placed on them. As process technologies improved, prices dropped precipitously and customer adoption took off. Unfortunately, as the market started to show signs of maturity, most manufacturers were slow to take their feet off the pricing gas. The result has been terrible margin pressures due to low prices and overcapacity—at exactly the time that consumers are becoming sophisticated enough to value and actively seek out differentiation.

Taken together, those two variables point to default pricing strategies for each combination type and stage of the product category life cycle.

Driving Customer Adoption

In addition to doing their homework on value to frame initial prices as fair and reasonable, great marketers take the focus off price by targeting the right customers, working to mitigate the risks of adopting a new technology, and making it easy for customers to see the value for themselves (as Figure 4 shows).

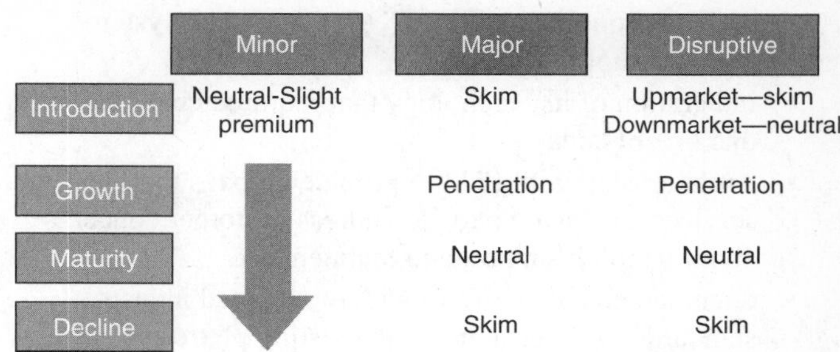

Figure 4 Pricing strategies change with market conditions.

When rolling out a true innovation, marketers are often focused on identifying and converting early adopters. Those customers are desirable because they become references for later adopters. The motivations for early adopters run the gamut from (1) exploiting the latest technologies to get ahead of the competition to (2) desiring to satisfy the emotional need to be on the cutting edge. Regardless of the specific motivation, early adopters are traditionally less price-sensitive. However, they are still concerned about the potential challenges in adopting an innovation; even the most motivated aren't completely careless about how much risk they will take on. And if the price is too high for an unknown product and its unproven benefits, then the product might never get off the ground.

To address those concerns, marketers should build their launches on what does drive adoption of new technologies. And they should use that knowledge to support sales. Key drivers of customer adoption include the following:

- compelling advantages over existing technology
- the ability to observe and measure the impact of those advantages
- the complexity of the new solution
- compatibility with existing processes and technologies
- the ability to try out an innovation before making a full commitment

Note that price is not on the list. What the list represents is customer desire to mitigate the risks inherent in adopting an innovative new technology. Too often, companies fail to take into account these drivers of adoption when launching an innovative new offering. Instead, the approach is: "Our specifications are set. Our product is so innovative that it's hard to prove value or understand risk until we get it into customers' hands. Once they have it, they'll see the genius of what we have created."

Consider how Azul Systems addressed adoption drivers in the launch of an entirely new server for handling Java applications. In addition to being a new player in the business, Azul's product did not replace any existing customer equipment—further squeezing already tight information technology budgets. Yet it enjoyed a successful launch. Here's how:

- an economic advantage program: "A free, private consulting engagement helps customers quantify the financial gains their organization will realize through a computer pool deployment." (See www.azulsystems .com for more information.)

- integration of its technology that required changing only one line of code
- a relationship with IBM to provide global support, services, and spare parts to address customer concerns about ongoing support and maintenance
- documented adherence to widely accepted industry standards for interfacing with existing platforms
- a no-cost 45-day evaluation program for qualified accounts

Successful introduction of new products is challenging, but some simple things can be done to greatly improve your chances. More than anything, companies need to understand what ease of adoption will mean to their customers.

An alternative method of enlightening customers is often absurdly low introductory price deals. That compounds the perception of risk by leading customers to think: "If this technology is so good, then why do they seem so desperate for customers?" Price dealing to get those early "reference accounts" can also dramatically affect future revenues. Once low prices are out on the street, it is very difficult to raise them.

Pricing for Success

Price strategy can be the lever that maximizes return on the risky investment or the velvet rope that bars customers from your service. Get it right and your company enjoys a commanding market position, increased profits, and well-earned confidence across the team. Get it wrong and your company limits both sales and profitability and suffers from a weakened market position, financial performance, and team capabilities.

Lessons from successful new-product launches demonstrate an effective process for innovation price strategy.

First, implement a customer-value measurement process as rigorous as the technology development process. Answers to the questions posed in Figure 1's six customer value areas will enable the company to (1) offer a quantified value message as compelling as the technology and (2) estimate a price range corresponding to customer value. Without a solid understanding of quantified customer value, the launch process is unnecessarily risky.

Second, within that range of customer value, set prices based on the interaction of the innovation's nature (minor, major, or disruptive) and the stage of product life cycle (introduction, maturity, growth, or decline). This simple matrix allows companies to plot a price point that maximizes both adoption and profitability.

The rules laid out here offer a guideline of where to set a price for a product or service innovation. That process can help companies overcome the long odds of new-product success—and fuel growth in both revenues and profitability.

Critical Thinking

1. How is price related to customer value?
2. How should pricing strategies vary as a product moves through the stages of the product life cycle?

Mark Burton is vice president of Holden Advisors in Concord, Mass., and may be reached at mburton@holdenadvisors.com. **Steve Haggett** is a client manager for Holden Advisors and may be reached at shaggett@holdenadvisors.com. To join the discussion about this article, please visit www.marketingpower.com/marketingmanagementblog.

Authors' note—*Pricing with Confidence: Ten Ways to Stop Leaving Money on the Table* (John Wiley & Sons), Mark Burton's book with co-author Reed Holden, will be published in February 2008.

Big Retailers Seek Teens (and Parents)

Hip fashions seen as key to fighting off specialty stores.

JAYNE O'DONNELL AND ERIN KUTZ

Having lost shoppers to hip specialty shops, department stores are reinventing themselves to attract both adults and their style-minded children.

J.C. Penney, Macy's, Bloomingdale's, Saks Fifth Avenue and Kohl's are all adopting approaches—from celebrity-designed fashions to mobile marketing to better fitting rooms—to try to lure young shoppers without turning off their parents.

With consumers cutting back on spending, many retailers have decided the best way to recapture them is to deliver a more cutting-edge experience and trendier clothing to attract their kids. The reasoning: Even as parents tighten their belts, they still spend freely on their children. If kids can get their parents to drive them to stores, the parents will end up shopping for themselves, too.

Middle-class teens, it turns out, represent a fairly recession-proof demographic, with outsize influence on household purchases.

That thinking has led J.C. Penney, long known as "my mom's store," to overhaul its teen merchandising, introduce new brands and redesign its teen departments. The retailer, which slashed its first-quarter earnings forecast by a third late last month and last week posted a larger-than-expected 12.3% March sales drop, will announce the changes today. Many of its rivals are taking similar steps, though the 106-year-old Penney chain, with its core clientele of middle-age and older shoppers, faces an especially stiff challenge and is making the biggest push.

While Penney says it commands the biggest share of the market for 13- to 20-year-old girls and women, CEO Mike Ullmann acknowledges his stores are most popular with teens until they get their own driver's license and credit card. At that point, Penney tends to lose them—until they grow up and return with kids of their own.

"With the teens, we have to capture them with a brand and a look," says Mike Boylson, Penney's chief marketing officer.

Today, teens influence up to an estimated 90% of grocery and apparel purchases, according to studies by digital marketing agency Resource Interactive. Even beyond their sway over household budgets, teen buyers, with their willingness, even eagerness, to spend, are highly sought-after consumers in their own right.

That's especially true in a shaky economy that's cut into sales at most retailers. Exhibit A: the success of Aéropostale, Urban Outfitters and some other youth-oriented specialty shops, which have been outperforming stores that cater more to older shoppers.

Penney, like other department stores, faces an uphill battle. By virtue of its size, it commands a huge share of the teen market, ranking first among mall-based stores for teens, according to market research firm TRU. But TRU trends director Rob Callender notes that those studies ask teens where they shop most often—not where they *like* to shop most often. Unless it can forge the kind of loyalty from teens enjoyed by such specialty stores as Abercrombie & Fitch and Forever 21, Penney will remain a destination that teens will follow their parents to, not one they'll seek out.

If drawing teens is crucial to gaining both the youth and adult crowds, some retailers face an institutional problem, too: Department stores can feel too physically unwieldy for teenagers, says Dan Hill of research firm Sensory Logic: "It's very hard to hug a giant."

"It's somewhat of a natural process to reject the kinds of retail environments that your parents are associated with."

— Leon Schiffman, a marketing professor at St. John's University

Some teens may even eschew department-store shopping as a way to distance themselves from their parents, says Leon Schiffman, a marketing professor at St. John's University in Queens, N.Y.

"It's somewhat of a natural process to reject the kinds of retail environments that your parents are associated with," Schiffman says.

That can frustrate parents. Wendy Queal of Hutchinson, Kan., says her 15-year-old son and 12-year-old daughter are "addicted" to American Eagle Outfitters and also favor Abercrombie & Fitch and Hollister.

"They like the stores with the loud music playing when they go in," Queal says. "They both told me to not buy them things from Dillard's anymore, which is where I have always bought a majority of their clothes. At this point in their lives, their shopping tends to be all about the name."

Well aware of this, Penney executives are stressing its brands' names—not its company name—much as Oldsmobile did years ago, when it began introducing trendier cars. Penney last month announced an exclusive new apparel line, Fabulosity, designed by reality TV star and former model Kimora Lee Simmons. In July, it will launch another brand, Decree, which Boylson says is "more updated than Abercrombie . . . with the same look, same feel, at half the price."

The clothes will be sold in departments with better lighting and more displays showing how to wear different outfits. (Penney's research found teens were seeking more fashion guidance from stores.) Apparel will be divided into different "lifestyles," ranging from wholesome active wear to hip city styles.

The Decree brand will be marketed "as if it's a national brand," Boylson says. "We don't beat them over the head with J.C. Penney."

The Teen Psyche

Youths are among the few categories of shoppers who seem comfortable spending freely these days. Other factors driving the interest in the teen market:

- Teens say they're closer with their families than the previous generation, Gen X, said at the same age, according to TRU. A recent TRU survey found that nine out of 10 teens say they're "close" to their parents; 75% agreed they "like to do things with their family"; and 59% say family dinners are "in."
- Teens are their households' de facto technology officers. They set up iPods and iPhones, troubleshoot PCs and spend hours with cellphones and social-networking sites. These 24/7 modes of rapid-fire communication allow teens—as well as brand marketers—to ignite interest in shopping trends faster than ever.

An informal *USA Today* survey of its panel of shoppers found teens are quick to name small specialty stores, such as American Eagle, as favorites. But they're habitually inconsistent.

John Crouch of Charleston, W.Va., says his 15-year-old daughter, Elizabeth, loves Delia's, American Eagle and Aéropostale. Yet, in the past two years, she's also become a fan of Penney and says it's now stylish. How about Sears? No way. Crouch says Elizabeth calls Sears' apparel "old ladies' clothing."

Schiffman says Bloomingdale's and other upscale department stores appeal to teens because their assortments and atmospheres are superior. "If you offer enough," he says, "you can get teens to go anywhere. J.C. Penney and Sears are just not pulling that."

But Adriene Solomon, like Elizabeth Crouch, disagrees, stressing the other side of the Penney story.

Seeing Penney as Hip

"My children love to shop at the 'trendy' stores: Hollister, Aéropostale, Abercrombie & Fitch, Wet Seal, Journeys, Champs (Sports) and any other tennis shoe store," says Solomon of Missouri City, Texas. "They most definitely don't like to shop at the top department stores like Macy's and Dillard's, but they will shop at J.C. Penney," because its styles seem trendy.

Roland Solomon, 15, says he'd go to Penney even if his mom weren't driving there, because he likes their jeans and shirts.

Yet, even the label "teen" is fraught with contradictions. A 13-year-old shopper bears little resemblance to a teen heading to college—at which point, says retail brand consultant Ken Nisch, high school posturing suddenly seems uncool.

"Things like resale gets to be a big trend in college, because there's more sense that it's not OK to show off what you have too much," Nisch says. "You might have needed an 'outfit' to go to high school, but when you go to college, God forbid if you have an 'outfit.' That means you're trying too hard."

LittleMissMatched, which sells brightly colored and patterned socks, loungewear and other apparel, finds that sales drop once kids head to college. They don't want to draw as much attention to clothes or to be viewed less seriously, says co-founder Arielle Eckstut.

But teen shoppers do want to look as if they know how to dress. Like Penney, the young women's apparel store Dots is redesigning stores to provide more fashion guidance. The retail design and branding firm FRCH, which is handling the redesign, is using splashy graphics and style tips. The goal, says managing creative director Steve McGowan, is to establish an "emotional connection" with shoppers.

"It's retail theater," McGowan says.

But how to reach the elusive teens in the first place?

"Newspaper and direct mail are useless against teens, and TV is not very effective," Boylson says. "Teens are much more in the digital space."

Several retailers are using social-networking sites as marketing tools. They're creating store profile pages, just the way teenagers build personal pages. H&M's boasts 60,000 "fans"—Facebook users who add a link to the H&M page on their own profile pages.

Some of the retail pages include photo albums of the store's seasonal collections and let fans upload photos of themselves wearing the store's clothing. Others provide podcasts of interviews with designers and links to virtual dressing rooms. And they send e-mails alerting fans to sales and discount codes.

American Eagle, which has nearly 30,000 fans, has a Facebook page. So do Hollister, Target, Forever 21 and Abercrombie & Fitch.

Facebook is "such a game-changer," says Dave Hendricks of Datran Media, which helps brands reach online consumers. "Facebook allows retailers to create a more viral experience. The tastemakers among youth spend all of their time in social media."

Penney is targeting teens through ads in theaters, interactive website features and mobile marketing.

"Teens know when they're being marketed to, so you have to be very careful," Boylson says.

Nor can you change their perceptions overnight.

"We understand it's about getting them to love the brands—not just J.C. Penney," says Liz Sweney, Penney's EVP for women's and girl's apparel.

Critical Thinking

1. Discuss J.C.Penney's efforts to reposition itself to the teen market.
2. With a small group of peers from your class, elaborate on the Teen Psyche based on your experiences and observations.

In Lean Times, Retailers Shop for Survival Strategies

They're cutting costs, listening to customers.

JAYNE O'DONNELL

An economic slowdown tends to spook the retail industry. When the economy sputters, people close their wallets and delay purchases, and stores suffer. Store chains, after all, can't survive very long without robust consumer spending.

But retailers don't just stand there and take a beating. They slim down, shut stores, trim inventory, slice payroll and take other strategic steps they hope will help them endure the pain. Some stores even thrive in recession even as others struggle.

With fears that the coming months could be the toughest for them since the 1991 recession, retailers are fighting to gain any edge they can over their rivals and to cushion themselves from the slide in customer spending. Many of them are redeploying staff and revising promotions; some are putting a new stress on low prices. In the end, they know, some of them will be winners, others losers.

"I see clients being more aggressive about promotion and reviewing the strategy by which they promote and how often they do it," says Madison Riley, a retail strategist with consulting firm Kurt Salmon Associates, whose clients include most major retailers.

The stores' strategies vary. So do their prospects for success. Much depends on how vulnerable they are in the first place.

Retailers that specialize in furnishing or refurbishing homes have been among the hardest hit. Specialty stores with highly discretionary products, such as the high- and low-end tchotchkes sold by Sharper Image and Lillian Vernon, respectively, may be worst off of all. Both retailers filed for Chapter 11 bankruptcy protection last week.

Retail chains know survival isn't in the bag, so they work even harder.

Specialty apparel stores are struggling, too. Even though some clothing, especially for growing kids or for career women, is regarded as essential, sales figures suggest that many of those purchases are being postponed.

Home Depot has slashed 500 jobs at its headquarters. Jewelry store chain Zales has announced plans to close 60 stores, and Ann Taylor plans to slash 180 jobs and close 117 stores within two years.

"The retailers accept that we're in a recession—smack in the middle of it," Riley says.

Among the most visible ways that stores are trying to ease their pain from the spending slowdown:

- **Merchandise.** Retailers must take care not to stock too little of the latest hot fashion or product—or showcase it too late. Many stores, Riley says, are working more closely with overseas suppliers to settle quickly on designs and shorten the development process.
- **Pricing.** Even retailers that try to avoid across-the-board price slashing are embracing the deep discounting trend, which Wal-Mart capitalized on so successfully last fall and holiday season.
- **More consumer input.** Retailers can't afford to wait until the end of a season to determine which trends will prove most popular. Riley says stores are stepping up consumer research and using their websites to gather real-time opinions from shoppers.

Thanks to luck, foresight or a bit of both, some retailers are better positioned to manage a downturn. Those with low, low prices—think Wal-Mart and off-price retailers including T.J. Maxx—and those that cater to the wealthy are tending to outperform those in the middle.

But opportunities exist for midlevel retailers, too. If shoppers are trading down to Wal-Mart, as its sales suggest, then more affluent people may be ready to cut back on their Bloomingdale's trips in favor of Kohl's. Tough economic times tend to diminish loyalty to stores across the spectrum.

"In this type of economy, the super shoppers get coupons out and check things online; they're going to be loyal to themselves first," says Phil Rist of the consumer insights firm BIGresearch. "Everyone's trying to find ways to make their money

	Target	Neiman Marcus and Saks	Macy's	J.C. Penney
Optimistic about the economy in next 6 months	33%	35%	36%	33%
Shopping closer to home	38%	26%	36%	44%
Shopping for sales more often	42%	22%	39%	45%
Spending less on clothing	39%	28%	35%	42%
Taking fewer shopping trips	39%	11%	34%	44%

How the Views of These Stores' Regular Shoppers Compare

Source: BIGresearch survey using national sample; responses are percentages of 2,434 people who said they regularly shopped at Target, 1,632 at Macy's, 2,723 at J.C. Penney and 32 at Neiman Marcus or Saks.

Here is how these retailers' shoppers compare with the U.S. population as a whole. Depending on who the store is targeting, they want to have close to or a higher composition of shoppers than the U.S. average. An index of 100 is considered average.

	Target	Neiman Marcus	Macy's	J.C. Penney
Age 18–34	104	99	92	89
Age 35–64	110	112	110	105
Age 65 and older	69	70	82	97
Education—high school	82	71	78	92
Education—college	112	115	113	105
Household size two or fewer	88	91	91	95
Income less than $40,000	63	55	56	75
Income $40,000–$99,000	121	96	116	120
Income $100,000 and more	155	240	186	122

Stores and Their Shoppers

Source: Claritas, a Nielsen company.

go as far as they can so there's something left for things they really want."

Christopher Maddox of Washington, D.C., says he's not giving up on Macy's, one of his favorite retailers, but is being far more cautious about his purchases this year.

"I'm only buying essentials due to the economy," Maddox says. "Luxury and big-ticket items are not in my budget due to increased costs of gas, food and utilities."

What follows is a look at the strategies of four retailers—Target, J.C. Penney, Macy's and Neiman Marcus—that draw from often-overlapping segments of shoppers.

As they brace for a possible recession, these stores are re-examining, in particular, four areas that will be most evident to shoppers: inventory, staffing, store openings and promotions.

Macy's

Frequent Big Sales and Discount Offers Won't Be Ending Anytime Soon

The nation's largest department store chain concedes that the economic slowdown has forced it to put off plans to scale back its sales and promotions.

"We still believe the strategy is a good one, but the timing is not necessarily good," says CEO Terry Lundgren.

In 2006, Macy's said it was trying to wean customers off frequent sales in favor of its "Every Day Value" pricing. Though Lundgren says there were slightly fewer promotions in 2007 than in 2006, he says Macy's won't reduce the timing or the number of sales until consumer spending starts to bounce back.

All the great deals now in stores are one benefit of the depressing economic news, says Marietta Landon of Cambridge, Mass. She finds sales everywhere she goes. "Especially Macy's—they make every weekend a sale with saving passes and advertising galore," Landon says.

Macy's says its plan, announced earlier this month, to eliminate 2,300 management jobs in the company's central office and create 250 new ones in its local markets wasn't necessarily driven by the economy. But saving about $100 million a year sure doesn't hurt. The plan to localize decision-making "was conceived long before there was talk of a credit crunch or mortgage crisis, but executing it now in the face of a possible recession does have its benefits," says Macy's spokesman Jim Sluzewski.

The addition of Tommy-Hilfiger-branded men's and women's apparel this fall, which will make Macy's the only place to buy the brand in the USA outside of Hilfiger stores, should further boost sales, he says.

Macy's has also announced plans to close nine poor-performing stores this year. Though struggling with some of the same issues that its rival J.C. Penney faces in catering to the middle class, Macy's holds an advantageous position, says Phil Rist of BIGresearch. That's because Macy's enjoys the image of being something of a novelty in many areas since it renamed the former May department stores in the fall of 2006.

Its clientele is generally more affluent than Penney's, notes analyst Bill Dreher. Still, in times like this, even a Macy's will likely be hurt by the tendency of customers to cut back on non-essentials.

"All the department stores are vulnerable because they are about 80% apparel and 20% home goods," Dreher says. "After years of strong apparel sales, customers have full closets, and with a weak fashion cycle, there's nothing fashionistas have to run out and buy."

Neiman Marcus

Despite the Times, Life Is Still Sweet at the High End of the Retail Spectrum

Neiman Marcus is preparing for a possible sales slowdown, recognizing that while affluent customers might not trade down to lower-quality stores, they might buy less even if they remain loyal.

The luxury retailer may adjust the amount of merchandise in stores, but otherwise is "just continuing business as usual," says spokeswoman Ginger Reeder.

Neiman "knows how to react," to economic troubles, Reeder says. That means preserving its customer service and high-quality merchandise but adjusting its inventories to concede the reality that its customers may be tightening their snakeskin belts.

"We've found our customers are very resilient," says Reeder, referring to Neiman's history during past economic slowdowns. "They're not trading down but might potentially buy less."

As at other luxury retailers with strong presences in California and Florida, Neiman's sales have suffered along with their customers' finances during the housing recession, says Craig Johnson of retail consulting and research company Customer Growth Partners. But for the "premier luxury retailer in the U.S," in Johnson's words, suffering means merely moderate sales growth—down from double-digit increases in recent years. "As the economy stabilizes and spring returns, we look for improving results," Johnson says.

Neimans focuses its promotions on two major sales a year, which Reeder says won't change.

In this economy, sales figures show, the safest demographic spot for retailers to occupy is either the low end or the very high end. "Middle-market department stores continue to bleed market share to discounters such as Wal-Mart and TJX, to high-end players like Saks and Neiman Marcus and to hot specialty stores such as Anthropologie," Johnson says.

As Reeder suggests, those who remain loyal to Neimans through economic turmoil are typically those who prize quality over price.

"I still shop at Neiman's and will continue to," says Amy Cavers, of Skillman, N.J. "If things worsen or my budget gets tighter, I may cut back on my volume if anything, but not where I shop. I still want the same quality in my purchases. . . . I would rather have fewer shoes and dresses but with the same uniqueness and flair or style that I expect."

Jennifer Stillman of Atlanta says that rather than cutting designer labels out of her apparel budget, she's buying groceries at Wal-Mart and Costco over pricier markets such as Whole Foods.

J.C. Penney

Growth Plan with Swanky Fashion Lines Calls for Full Steam Ahead

Damn the economic naysayers, J.C. Penney is designing its most ambitious five-year plan for store openings in its history and last week oversaw its largest-ever merchandise launch. Still, facing a persistent drop in consumer spending, CEO Mike Ullman says the chain is scaling back those store openings from 50 to 36 this year and will adjust its inventories to reduce the need for hefty markdowns.

Ullman hopes that Ralph Lauren's new American Living fashion, home and footwear line for men, women and kids will further invigorate the Penney brand, which has drawn more and younger customers with the addition of the Sephora makeup line and two private-label lingerie lines designed, in part, to compete with Victoria's Secret. The American Living line will be found in 600 of the chain's 1,000 stores, often with its own in-store shops.

Deutsche Bank senior retail analyst Bill Dreher questions whether now is a good time for Penney to launch a line that's about 25% higher-priced than similar merchandise already in its stores.

Under the deal, Ralph Lauren's name won't appear anywhere on the new merchandise or displays, Dreher notes. Kohl's, by contrast, was able to connect the Lauren name with its Chaps line for many years, which helped keep customers aware of the connection. The new line is "no panacea," he says.

Still, Dreher notes, Penney has successfully reinvented itself over the past decade from a chain known for "dowdy, older-lady-type fashions to one that's very much hip, on-trend and cool." More recently, Penney has recognized that its catalog business is less important now than its website, he says.

About six months ago, Penney decided to merge its store, catalog and online marketing operations; the change will result in 100 to 200 job losses. Ullman insists it's "not a cost-driven exercise," but rather one that'll give shoppers "one view of our merchandise."

"People expected us to have cost-cutting, but that's not how you grow a business," Ullman says.

Ullman says Penney benefits by serving the "middle third" of the country, where people aren't "living paycheck to paycheck." Still, all bets are off if a weak economy grows really sick.

Nick Birchfield of Garden City, Mich., is still shopping at Penney, but that could change. If the economy gets much worse and gas prices rise higher, he says, "I will not be shopping at J.C. Penney unless they are giving their merchandise away."

Target

Upscale Discounter Starts to Spotlight Low-Priced Goods in Addition to Style

"Hello goodbuy."

Couldn't that be a Wal-Mart slogan?

As the economy struggles, Target, long known as the purveyor of the well-designed product, is increasingly spotlighting its low-priced goods. "Hello goodbuy" is the tag line for ads that now focus as much on the price of its products as they do on their style. After all, in a down economy, hand-painted toilet-bowl-brush covers that cost several bucks more than the next one are seldom a major consumer priority.

That leaves Target more vulnerable in this economy than, say, Wal-Mart, says Deutsche Bank senior retail analyst Bill Dreher. It may be a discounter, but it's hard for it to compete with Wal-Mart on price, Dreher says.

"Target has historically focused more on being fashion-forward and having value-added design," Dreher says. "The problem is, consumers don't want that now. They're not redecorating or refurbishing their homes. They're looking for everyday life staples."

At the same time, Dreher says, Target is better positioned than department stores these days.

Target has been trying for years to get its low-price message across, says spokeswoman Lena Michaud. And she says its business plan will carry it through hard times: "We are very confident in our strategy going forward."

That includes trying to rein in costs in a way that customers won't notice. That may be difficult given that a key target is hourly payroll expenses. Michaud says Target is investing in technology to make sure workers are scheduled at the right times. Unlike some of its competitors, Target is sticking to its plan to open stores, about 100 of them, which Michaud says is consistent with the number it has opened in recent years.

The chain is also preparing for the departure this year of designer Isaac Mizrahi, who has a line of popular private-label apparel at Target but is leaving to join Liz Claiborne. Spokeswoman Susan Giesen says Target will still offer apparel from trendy designers, which, along with the new Converse All-Star apparel and footwear line, should fill any gaps in its clothing lines.

That might not be enough to keep clothing customers loyal. Based on BIGresearch's survey data on people who shop at Target primarily for at least one category of merchandise, these consumers are shopping around. "The folks who shop at Target for health and beauty aids—a lot of them go to Kohl's, Macy's and Penney's first for clothing," says Phil Rist of BIGresearch. "There's a lot of cross-shopping."

Critical Thinking

1. With a small group of peers from your class, conduct a comparative analysis of the four retailers discussed in the case on the dimensions of inventory, staffing, store openings, and promotion.
2. In your opinion, is it more challenging for retailers to maintain customer loyalty during tough economic times? Justify your answer.

Contributing: Erin Kutz.

Williams-Sonoma's *Secret Sauce*

The retailer's recipe for growth required two entrepreneurs. Until now, Howard Lester was the hidden ingredient.

JESSICA SHAMBORA

Professional managers like Howard Lester aren't supposed to be entrepreneurs. You know the type: the seasoned exec who takes the wheel from the founder when it's time to drive growth, layering on necessary infrastructure. He's the "suit" or the "gray-hair" whose arrival signals an end to the fun, scrappy days before people had to consult policy manuals. At San Francisco's Williams-Sonoma Inc., Lester succeeded founder Chuck Williams, who stayed on as chairman. But even Williams, 94, concedes that the home-furnishings retailer wouldn't have become a $3 billion juggernaut without Lester.

Lester, 74, who capped 32 years at the company when he retired in May, is an entrepreneur in his own right. Not only did he successfully found (and sell) a company before buying Williams-Sonoma in 1978, but his stewardship could hardly have been more entrepreneurial: He pushed for growth, took risks, made mistakes. (Laura Alber, CEO since May, is his third successor; two others flamed out.) Lester transformed Williams-Sonoma into a kitchen and home-furnishings empire, with brands like Pottery Barn and West Elm (see table). "He made a lot of bold decisions about growing this business and had real vision about the opportunity to expand a very high-taste concept in a really scaled way," says Matt Fassler, a Goldman Sachs analyst.

"He made a lot of bold decisions about growing this business and had real vision about the opportunity to expand a very high-taste concept."

—Mott Fossler, Goldman Sachs

Unlike other nonfounder entrepreneurs, Lester focused on making the brand, and not himself, a household name. Williams-Sonoma was begun in 1956, an outgrowth of its founder's passion for French culinary traditions. But Lester's zeal is what has really gotten Williams-Sonoma cooking. His passion? Business. "I had no interest in making quiches," says Lester. Here's a taste of his recipe for growth:

Opportunity Doesn't Knock, It Taps

In 1976, at age 40, Lester's only plans were to putter around. He sold Centurex, a software business he'd founded, and spent six months playing golf. He was poking around for a business to buy when a buddy suggested he look into a struggling cookware retailer and cataloguer that was for sale.

Lester ended up spending weeks "looking at every detail and talking to every employee" at Williams-Sonoma. What he saw was a financially shaky business with $4 million in revenue and $700,000 in debt. "It had no systems, no idea of inventory, and that was something I did know about," he says. Along with a partner, who never assumed an operating role, Lester bought the company for $100,000. His only previous retail experience was as a shopper.

Learn What You Don't Know

Lester found direction by hitting the road. He went on buying trips to Europe with Williams, and also traveled across the U.S. visiting kitchen stores, noting that "they were run more as a hobby than a business," he says.

Although he sniffed a big opportunity, he didn't act on it right away. Rather than jump into the capital-intensive business of building stores, he focused on growing catalogue sales by hiring a direct-marketing expert. When the company went public in 1983, catalogues represented 75% of revenue–compared with 50% five years earlier. In turn, the addresses of catalogue customers became a road map for where to locate new outlets.

Williams-Sonoma through the Years

Brand	What Do They Sell?	The Skinny
Williams-Sonoma	Fancy kitchen gadgets and appliances	From four stores to 259 in 32 years.
Pottery Barn	Home furnishings to fantasize about	PB's 199 stores produce the largest share of the company's revenue today.
Pottery Barn Kids	Furniture for little sprouts	Current CEO's pet project, launched in 1999, is now an 85-store empire.
PBteen	Furniture for teens	Catalogue-only brand started in 2003 after success of kids line.
West Elm	Modern home goods for hip urban dwellers	First catalogue mailed in 2002; today 37 stores and building momentum.
Williams-Sonoma Home	Classic, high-end home furnishings	Debuted in 2004; "future potential of this brand is limited," W-S says.
Hold Everything	Organization and storage products	Founded in 1983; closed in 2006; lost the edge to the Container Store.
Gardener's Eden	Outdoor tools and decorative doodads	Catalogue-only brand bought in 1982; sold in 1999 to Brookstone.

Lester hired experts to teach him about real estate too. Soon he was cherry-picking locations as fastidiously as a chef lines up knives. When mall owners tried to put the newfangled "kitchen" shop by the food court, he refused. Williams-Sonoma belonged with the luxury brands.

Big Bets Come from Small Insights

Williams-Sonoma pushed the boundaries of retailing, offering cooking classes, table-setting demonstrations, and tastings. A company philosophy, "Think like a shopkeeper," originated with Lester, who read every customer letter and comment card. He emphasized not inventory levels or, later, website clicks, but rather such customer metrics as this: "How many did we fail to satisfy yesterday?"

Even as the company was adding roughly five stores every year (starting in 1982), Lester could recite the revenue numbers for each store, as well as the name of its manager. That skill didn't come naturally to his successor, a 15-year veteran of the company who served as president for four years. Alber, 41, devised her own photo flash cards to replicate his total recall.

By 1986, Williams-Sonoma had grown from four shops in California when Lester had bought it eight years earlier, to 27 stores in 14 states with sales of $68 million. That year another San Francisco—based retailer, Gap, was seeking a buyer for its troubled 25-store Pottery Barn unit. Lester scooped it up for $6 million, planning to use the prime real estate to expand Williams-Sonoma.

But first he tried an experiment, applying his company's catalogue know-how to the brand by displaying the merchandise as part of a broader lifestyle. The results: double-digit same-store gains. "It was a real eye-opener for us," says Lester.

Not everything has worked. A gardening catalogue the company bought in 1982 languished and was sold in 1999. Hold Everything, which sold storage products, folded in 2006. And the company recently abandoned its high-end Williams-Sonoma Home brand.

Companies Don't Crush Innovation, CEOs Do

Alber credits Lester for attracting—and protecting—the creative minds the company needed to expand: "A feeling lives within all of us today, which is, What can we build that isn't there yet? How do you push it further?"

Alber should know: In 1997 she was among a group of women who pitched the idea for Pottery Barn Kids. After working on the project nights and weekends, they set up the store format in the garage at headquarters to show Lester. While wary, he let them test it in a catalogue. Pottery Barn Kids now operates 85 stores. And when the notion for Pottery Barn Teen came along six years later? "I didn't argue," says Lester.

It's a difficult time to be in the top spot at almost any retailer. Williams-Sonoma's revenue hit $3.1 billion in fiscal 2009, a 21% drop from its 2007 peak. But the company, which now operates 610 stores in 44 states, is showing some resilience, and the stock price has more than doubled in the past year.

Meanwhile, Lester, who was retired when he bought the business, says he's ready to go through with it this time. After all, what is it they say about the perils of having too many cooks in the kitchen? Lester, undoubtedly, knows.

Critical Thinking

1. What makes the combination of Lester and Williams such a success for Williams-Sonoma?
2. What external environmental factors pose possible opportunities or threats for Williams-Sonoma's various brands?

10 Brilliant Marketing Ideas

Everyday on TV, billboards, and other advertisements all over the place, we see some very creative advertisements. Here are 10 brilliant marketing ideas that have changed the status of businesses for the better.

JENNIFER WANG

Introduction

As every dedicated watcher of *Mad Men* knows, advertising is built on the genius of ideas. Inspiration can strike from any corner (and in every flashback). And beware: Even the greatest ideas are fleeting.

But every now and then, an idea comes along that changes the game for good. Yes, the campaign generates huge, instantaneous buzz and moves plenty of product—but it also stands the test of time, infiltrating the culture in subtle ways for decades to come.

"It doesn't happen often," says Bruce Vanden Bergh, advertising professor at Michigan State University, "because it takes a combination of the right people with the right skills, the right climate and luck."

And sometimes, it takes nothing less than a breakthrough.

Selling diamonds during the Great Depression, charging more for a spirit no one can identify blindfolded, pitching a tiny car during the era of chrome and fins—all of these campaigns made Entrepreneur's list of 10 brilliant marketing ideas. The list spans more than 70 years—from pre-TV to the YouTube era. Just don't get upset when you learn how you've been manipulated. It's the nature of the business.

In the words of Don Draper, *Mad Men's* tortured lead, "What you call love was invented by guys like me," he says. "To sell nylons."

1. 'A Diamond Is Forever'

Backstory: Diamond prices were sinking fast in 1938, so De Beers mining company enlisted ad agency N.W. Ayer & Son to help reverse the trend. A year later, it launched the "diamond is forever" campaign and brazenly promoted the idea that every marriage required the gift of bling. And plenty of it: It also invented the "two months' salary" spending rule.

Breakthrough: A slogan that transcends the campaign. "It created sentimental meaning for the product that resonated with people," says Michael Cody, communications professor at the University of Southern California, adding that the phrase is so entrenched that some people don't know its commercial origins.

Legacy: Tapping emotions. Think Nike's "Just Do It" and Mastercard's "Priceless."

2. Marlboro Man

Backstory: Incredible as it seems, Marlboro cigarettes were marketed for decades as a premium filtered cigarette for women. That all changed in 1955, when Leo Burnett's advertising firm reinvented the smokes with the most masculine of icons: an American cowboy.

Breakthrough: Image advertising. The Marlboro Man wasn't just a hugely successful trade character, Cody says, the campaign was also the first example of "image" advertising. "No attributes of the product were mentioned, but the campaign appealed to white, male individuals who perceived a connection with ruggedness and masculinity." Whatever controversy came later, the ads made Marlboro the bestselling cigarette in the world.

Legacy: If you're ever boggled by the behavior of brand-conscious youth, know that it started here. Those Abercrombie dudes could be the Marlboro man's grandsons.

3. Does She . . . or Doesn't She?

Backstory: In 1957, Foote, Cone & Belding invented the Clairol girl, a wholesome girl next door with a shocking secret: Her hair color might be fake. A series of ads for tints and dyes posed the titillating Q&A: "Does she 26 or doesn't she?" ("Only her hairdresser knows for sure.")

Breakthrough: The shock ad. Advertising Age columnist Bob Garfield calls it the birth of "shockvertising," campaigns that generated buzz by tapping into the sexual revolution. Of course it worked: Ten years later, annual sales of hair coloring rose by more than $160 million.

Legacy: Sex sells (no kidding—but someone had to figure it out). "Does she" paved the way for Brooke ("Nothing comes between me and my Calvins") Shields and Pam (naked for PETA) Anderson.

4. Think Small

Backstory: The diminutive Volkswagen Beetle wasn't an easy sell in 1960, the era of major chrome and fins. So the Doyle Dane Bernbach agency did something unheard of at the time: It paired a copywriter with an art director to create the campaign. Volkswagen's revolutionary "Think Small" ads featured a tiny image of the car surrounded by acres of white space and a few words about "our little car."

Breakthrough: Synergy—and risk taking. "It showed how breaking with the norm could also change culture," says Michael Belch, a marketing professor at San Diego State University. "Small became sexy." Adds former *Advertising Age* editor Jonah Bloom: "It's about the guts to be different and take huge risks with your message."

Legacy: Embrace the product. Honesty and risk-taking can pay off big—just ask Avis. Its "We try harder" campaign flipped a No. 2 ranking in its favor.

5. Beauty Mist Pantyhose

Backstory: To sell Hanes pantyhose, the Mullen agency famously recruited Hall of Fame quarterback (and playboy) Joe Namath. The 1974 TV commercial panned up a pair of smooth, nylon-clad legs that turned out to belong to Broadway Joe: "Now, I don't wear pantyhose, but if Beauty Mist can make my legs look good, imagine what they'll do for yours." It was just a matter of time before sales of pantyhose outran sales of stockings for the first time in the U.S.

Breakthrough: Celebrity endorsement. Namath wasn't the first celeb to hawk products, but the success (and controversy) the ad created showed the power of the right celeb.

Legacy: Cue the athlete endorsement. George Foreman and Salton. O.J. Simpson and Hertz. Michael Jordan and just about everything.

6. Absolut Vodka

Backstory: The product was clear, flavorless and more or less indistinguishable from any of its competitors. But the agency TBWA's clever use of the bottle's shape and name made Absolut the first breakout premium vodka—and inspired barloads of imitators. After nearly 30 years, Absolut Vodka is one of the longest-running campaigns in history, and still going strong.

Breakthrough: The absolute power of advertising. It's stunning, actually, that these ads moved millions of Americans to pay more for a product they couldn't identify in a taste test. "It's also proof," Bloom notes, "of advertising's ability to create value in a commodity marketplace."

Legacy: Sometimes it's all about the sizzle. With a campaign that's infinitely riffable, *Absolut* continues to innovate with the times (there's an iPhone app).

7. 1984

Backstory: *Apple's "1984"* was a single commercial, broadcast during that year's Super Bowl. But Chiat/Day's interpretation of George Orwell's post-apocalyptic novel was more effective than most large-scale campaigns. The concept: A roomful of drones stares at a large screen where an authority figure bleats propaganda. Suddenly, a strange woman bursts into the room, hurls a hammer at the screen and smashes it to bits. The scrolling text: "On January 24, Apple Computer will introduce Macintosh. And you'll see why 1984 won't be like 1984."

Breakthrough: The noncommercial commercial. It introduced Apple to the world as a rebel and game-changer, an identity that lingers despite its huge presence today. "The commercial didn't explain the product or any of its benefits," Bloom says, "but instead promised a lifestyle change, freeing you from the tyranny of your operating system." It also helped make Super Bowl ad time the most expensive on television.

Legacy: A new annual short-film festival (aka commercial breaks during the Super Bowl).

8. The Coke Geyser

Backstory: Drop Mentos mints into a 2-liter bottle of Diet Coke, step back and watch the thing blow—physics teacher Steve Spangler's hokey demo became an Internet phenomenon in 2005, spawning an unbelievable number of page views and copycat videos. A couple of guys even re-created the Bellagio fountain with Coke/Mentos eruptions. Thing was, sales of Mentos and Coke hit the roof, too.

Breakthrough: Viral marketing. "It was unexpected and unsponsored, but it opened up everyone's eyes to the potential effect of viral videos," says San Diego State University's Belch. Indeed: Saturation media coverage at almost no cost? We'll take it.

Legacy: Is it content or advertising? Come up with something cool (or crazy) enough, and customers will look for you. See Dove's "Real Beauty" campaign, or Burger King's "Subservient Chicken."

9. 'Change We Can believe In'

Backstory: Barack Obama's bid for the presidency was also a lesson in groundbreaking grassroots marketing. In addition to the instantly iconic poster and slogan, there was skillful use of the web and social media, from early discussions with Facebook founder Mark Zuckerberg to responding to negative reviews online and uploading flattering clips to YouTube.

Breakthrough: Social marketing. AdAge readers voted Obama the "2008 Marketer of the Year"—before he won the White House. "It wouldn't be an overstatement to say that the campaign underlined the advent of a new era of social marketing," Bloom says.

Legacy: Twitter, Facebook and who knows what next. Whole Foods has 1.6 million followers on Twitter. Victoria's Secret used Facebook to promote its Pink line to college students.

10. Dancing in the Tube

Backstory: In January 2009, Saatchi & Saatchi launched T-Mobile's "Life's for Sharing" campaign, which included flash mobs (that is, groups who assemble briefly in public to perform some kind of action). In this case, it was a smartly choreographed dance routine in the middle of a London Tube station. The video became a YouTube phenomenon.

Breakthrough: Too early to tell. But after tens of millions of page views on YouTube, there's no doubt that commercializing flash mobs works.

Legacy: YouTube required. But talk about knockoffs: Trident gum's flash mob did Beyoncé's "Single Ladies" dance in the middle of Piccadilly Square.

Critical Thinking

1. What common characteristics or traits feature across the 10 marketing campaigns listed in the article?
2. With a small group of peers from your class, come up with your own Top 10 list of imaginative campaigns. Justify your choices.

As Seen on TV—And Sold at Your Local Store

MATT ROBINSON

- **Infomercial goods move from late-night television to retailers' shelves**
- **The ads are "the movie trailer before the product hits stores"**

At 5 a.m. on a hot July morning, more than 45 inventors from as far away as Texas and California descended on the Fairfield (N.J.) offices of AJ Khubani, the "Infomercial King" and chief executive of **TeleBrands.** Armed with props such as air mattresses and even a kitchen sink, the would-be-Thomas Edisons prepared to pitch products, including metal-free flatware, an ultraviolet sneaker deodorizer, and a zip-lockable trash bag. The dream: that their invention will become the next PedEgg.

At a recent TeleBrands casting call more than 45 inventors showed up. Here are some of the products they pitched.

TeleBrands has used its "As Seen on TV" marketing machine to sell more than 35 million of the little gizmos used to smooth rough feet. Such products may be cheap, but they're big business; sales generated by infomercials, or direct-response TV marketing as it's formally known, are expected to rise almost 30 percent, to a record $174 billion, by 2014, according to Yoram Wurmser of Direct Marketing Assn.

One reason for the big uptick: Goods touted in infomercials are increasingly moving onto the shelves of big retailers such as **CVS Caremark** and **Target.** Rather than just enticing viewers to pick up the phone and order from a telemarketing center, the often schlocky TV ads now are used to build the brand before goods are sold at retailers or online. "They're the movie trailer before the product hits stores," Khubani says.

More than 90 percent of TeleBrands' sales now come from major retailers. Drugstore giant CVS says "As Seen on TV" products constitute one of their largest general merchandise categories, and it displays a new item each month at the end of an aisle—prime retail real estate. Those items had double-digit sales growth in the last three years, according to Erin Pensa, a CVS spokesperson. Target has expanded its assortment of infomercial-hawked products in the last two years and has logged strong growth in the past 18 months, says spokesperson Tara Schlosser.

Allstar Products Group—the maker of the ubiquitous Snuggie, basically a blanket with sleeves—has seen sales move from 50 percent at retail to more than 80 percent in the last three years. Allstar has sold more than 20 million Snuggies, which enjoy a cult-like status. Comedian Jimmy Fallon has donned one on his late-night show, and it has been featured in many **YouTube** videos. Snuggie pub crawls have been staged in San Francisco and Knoxville, Tenn.

Roger Escamilla

The **Rinse and Recycle Station** is a sink-side device that uses high-pressure water to clean used cans and bottles, making recycling easier.

Todd Fithian

The **Handle Pro** tops any broom-like handle with a rounded surface to make sweeping, shoveling, and digging easier.

Shayquita Rogers

The **Rogers Ironing Solution** is a heat-proof cover that attaches to an iron after use to protect against burns.

Dennis Rolleri

SuperSanders is a dry wall vacuum attachment that sucks up plaster as you smooth down your wall, reducing cleanup time.

Donna Crossland

Magnets connect two sides of the **Split Decision Blanket,** so a spouse who wakes up hot can easily remove his or her side with ease.

Vito Labbate and son Christopher

After sweeping up the kitchen floor, the **Snap 'n Vac** sucks up dirt, so you don't have to search for a dust pan.

Traditional advertisers "can't ignore [infomercials] anymore. Before they saw it as carnival-y," says Allstar CEO Scott Boilen. "You can't ignore the Ped Egg, and the Topsy Turvy [Tomato Planter]," which grows tomatoes upside down and has been snapped up by some 10 million customers.

Large companies are taking notice. Tim Hawthorne, founder of **Hawthorne Direct,** an infomercial ad agency, said he recently helped a Fortune 500 client increase retail sales by 100 percent after an infomercial aired for a 10-year-old product. Companies can often recoup advertising dollars even by selling a limited number of items, he says.

That's because ad rates for short infomercials are cheap—as little as $40 for a two-minute spot on a small cable station. Infomercial marketers got a boost during the recession as traditional TV advertisers pulled back, leaving some broadcasters with unsold air time. They filled it with bargain-rate infomercials that ran multiple times. The added exposure helped TeleBrands log record 2009 sales. "We just happened to be at the right place at the right time," Khubani says.

Marketers are scrambling for more products to peddle. Khubani looks for gadgets that solve common problems, sell for between $9.99 and $19.99, and make people think, "Why didn't I think of that?" He can spot a possible product "in about a minute."

At the periodic Inventor Day competitions that he's started at TeleBrands, inspired by *American Idol,* entrepreneurs whose written proposals sound intriguing get four minutes more than that for their pitches. Rather than use Madison Avenue-style focus groups, Khubani relies on his own gut and a panel of judges that includes his wife of 24 years, Poonam, and a recent addition—his son's math tutor.

Critical Thinking

1. In your opinion, why have infomercials been so effective in generating sales?
2. Evaluate the recent strategy of making "As Seen on TV" goods available in retail stores.

20 Highlights in 20 Years

Making Super Bowl Ad History Is No Easy Feat

As Ad Meter hits the two-decade mark, USA TODAY takes a look back.

Bruce Horovitz

Watching Super Bowl advertising has become a pop-culture ritual. But the ads are not just being scrutinized by about 90 million TV viewers.

For 20 years, they've also come under the magnifying glass of USA TODAY's Super Bowl Ad Meter, an exclusive, real-time consumer rating of all the game's ads. Focus groups in multiple cities use handheld devices to register their second-by-second reactions to the commercials. It's been quite a ride.

Who can forget the beer-pitching Bud Bowl ads of the late 1980s? And celebrity-laden Pepsi spots of the 1990s? And the wacky dot-com commercials that filled the 2000 game?

Through the perspective of Ad Meter, USA TODAY is spotlighting here 20 of the high points, low points and turning points in Super Bowl ads over these two decades.

Each year, Super Bowl ads mirror American culture. Most years, they aim no higher than a superficial reflection. But, once in a while, they offer a peek at something deeper.

All in 30 seconds.

This Sunday, 37 advertisers, who paid an average $2.7 million per 30 seconds, will air about 55 ads aimed at winning Super Bowl ad immortality. Odds are none will get there.

"Everyone we work with says, 'Do the next '1984'," says ad guru Jeff Goodby, a reference to Apple's famous Super Bowl spot of the woman who shatters Big Brother's image. "But that's easier said than done."

That won't stop folks such as Goodby, whose agency is a Super Bowl ad veteran, from trying. He knows the impact of Ad Meter intimately. It has forced many advertisers to work overtime trying to win the top prize—and the acclaim that comes with it. But, in the process, he only half-jokes, "It has ruined the Christmas vacations of advertising and production people worldwide."

Alex Bogusky, co-chairman of Crispin Porter + Bogusky, tries to avoid that. Because there is only one Ad Meter winner, it makes "losers" out of most Super Bowl advertisers. "I counsel clients against doing Super Bowl advertising."

In Ad Meter's history, there've been vintage years, full of highs and lows, and others best forgotten. Here are 20 indelible Super Bowl ad moments:

1 "You-Per" Bowl (2007)

Madison Avenue's biggest showcase became Main Street's newest stomping ground last year when a few cutting-edge marketers got real people—not ad agencies—to create memorable ads.

Tops among them: Doritos' consumer-generated ad contest winner in which a chip-eating driver crashes his car while ogling a Doritos-munching woman. The ad made the top five in Ad Meter alongside four pro ads from Anheuser-Busch.

Many Super Bowl ads cost upwards of $1 million to film. This one cost $12, for four bags of Doritos. That's punch for the crunch.

2 Now You See Me (2007)

Last year's Super Bowl will be best-remembered by some as the year that two ads quickly were dispatched to the commercial graveyard by special-interest groups.

A Snickers ad featured two car mechanics who pulled out chest hair to assert their manliness after sharing a Snickers bar led to an accidental smooch. Gay-advocacy groups made the ad disappear the next day.

A General Motors ad with a robot fantasizing about suicide while dreaming of losing its assembly-line job got the heave after a suicide-prevention group balked.

3 Too Tight for Comfort (2005)

How tight can a model's strappy top be before network censors squirm? That's a question for which GoDaddy.com's first Super Bowl ad got free PR galore.

In the ad, Go Daddy's buxom spokesmodel wiggles and giggles before a faux censorship committee. When an over-stretched strap snaps, one elderly committee member needs oxygen. The Fox network got so many angry calls after it aired the spot that it shelved plans to run it again later in the game.

Even then, the ad was a dud with consumers rating it for Ad Meter: They relegated it to the bottom five of all the game's ads.

But the ad got gazillions to go online to see it again. And again.

4 Tasteless Bowl (2004)

It wasn't just Janet Jackson's infamous "wardrobe malfunction" that torpedoed good taste that year. Some ads helped, particularly two for Bud Light.

In one, a romantic sleigh ride goes south after the horse passes explosive gas. In another, a guy surrenders his Bud Light only after a dog bites his crotch.

Not that Ad Meter's consumers took offense. They rated the crotch commercial best of the game.

"We hope the humor didn't offend anybody," Anheuser-Busch CEO August Busch IV said after the game. At an ad conference later, he said good taste would be a criterion for A-B ads, not just for its beer.

5 Clydesdales Bow to 9/11 (2002)

Anheuser-Busch is mostly famous for its Super Bowl commercials that make viewers laugh. This one, however, made many cry.

Airing less than five months after the Sept.11 terrorist attacks, it struck a national chord. The Budweiser Clydesdales pull the beer wagon across the country before coming to a stop with a view of the World Trade Center site. The lead horse bows in respect to the 9/11 victims, and the team follows.

"That touched a nerve in this country," says Linda Kaplan Thaler, regarded as one of Madison Avenue's top ad chiefs. "During a contest that pits one team against another, this ad showed that, ultimately, we're all on the same team." But the bow may have been too subtle. Some Ad Meter panelists didn't get it and ranked the ad just outside the top 10. But it still tugs the heart today, and A-B can take a bow for this one.

6 Dot-Com Bowl (2000)

At the height of the Internet bubble, a dozen dot-coms spent more than $40 million on Super Bowl ads to get noticed.

The hard part now is remembering many of the ads, except two:

Pets.com's singing Sock Puppet crooned *If You Leave Me Now.* The ad broke into Ad Meter's top five. And E-Trade's monkey clapped along with two men in an ad that ends with the message: "We just wasted 2 million bucks. What are you doing with your money?"

Not a total waste, however: The ad ranked just outside of Ad Meter's top 10, and the company is one of the few of those dot-coms still in business.

7 Superman Walks (2000)

Sometimes special effects make an ad memorable, like it or not. Such was the case with the eerie image of paralyzed actor Christopher Reeve walking in this commercial for Nuveen.

In the spot, Reeve gets an ovation as he leaves his wheelchair to present an award for spinal injury research. The ad took criticism because it was fakery: The late actor never walked after he was paralyzed.

Because the ad got so much pregame PR, the image did not surprise Ad Meter panelists, and it finished in the middle of the pack. After this, many advertisers kept their climax secret until game day.

8 Ego Bowl (2000)

Phil Sokolof is hardly a household name. But the retired steel industry millionaire, who had his first heart attack at age 43, wrote, starred in and bought $2 million in ad time for his cautionary health ad.

In the ad, Sokolof, who died of heart failure in 2004, waxed unpoetically on the use of cholesterol-producing drugs to prevent heart disease.

The ad bombed: next-to-last on Ad Meter. "I can't say I'm proud of that," he later conceded to USA TODAY. "It was a downer."

9 Sexy Fashion Show (1999)

Victoria's Secret was among the first to use a Super Bowl spot as a glorified promotion to lure viewers to its website.

The ad featured lingerie-clad models pitching an online fashion show. While Ad Meter men loved the ad, women mostly hated it. Perhaps that's why the ad finished in the middle of the pack.

But it worked. The live, 17-minute online fashion show later that week attracted then-record Web traffic, and the site crashed. The retailer is in the game this year for the first time since then, with supermodel Adriana Lima pitching Valentine's Day sales.

10 When I Grow Up (1999)

A Super Bowl ad full of bright-eyed, optimistic kids would surprise no one.

Which is precisely why job site Monster.com's artsy black-and-white ad showed cute kids looking ahead to career doom. One says: "I want to be forced into early retirement." Another: "I want to claw my way up to middle management."

Goodby, whose agency was named Agency of the Year by *Advertising Age* and *Adweek,* calls this the best Super Bowl spot of the past 20 years. But Ad Meter panelists ranked it right in the middle. So much for artful angst.

11 Exploding Mosquito (1999)

Why does a sweaty guy, pouring Tabasco sauce onto his pizza, just sit on his porch and watch a mosquito bite his leg?

The punch line: After biting the Tabasco eater, the mosquito explodes in midair.

This hot, hot, hot ad for McIlhenny Tabasco made Ad Meter's top five, the only outsider that year to challenge a Pepsi/Anheuser-Busch ad juggernaut.

12 Cindy's Bowl (1997)

It's rare that a celebrity appears in two ads in one Super Bowl, but Cindy Crawford did in this one.

In a Pepsi spot, she and fellow supermodel Tyra Banks blow kisses at a newborn who winks and blows back a smooch. Then, in a Cadillac Catera spot, Crawford plays a princess with a plunging neckline. It was later pulled by General Motors after complaints about its portrayal of women.

Crawford did not appear again in a Super Bowl ad until 2005. That Diet Pepsi ad, where she checks out a hot guy, was a huge hit online afterward. Say this three times fast: Cindy certainly sells soda.

13 Clydesdales Play Ball (1996)

What if horses played football? Budweiser showed just that in this classic spot pitting two teams of Clydesdales. As two cowboys watch, one horse even kicks a field goal.

The ad rated in Ad Meter's top five, and Bud updated it for the 2004 Super Bowl with a parody of the NFL's video review policy—with a real zebra checking the instant replay while the horses wait.

14 Special Effects Bowl (1995)

Great Super Bowl ads require great ideas, and sometimes great special effects. Two had both in this game.

In a Pepsi spot, the Ad Meter winner, a boy at the beach sucks himself into a Pepsi bottle.

And kicking off in this game were the famous Budweiser frogs: "Bud," "Weis" and "Er." In the swamp, the three croak their names to form "Budweiser."

They earned a long series of ads. And that led to lizards. Which led to, well, Cedric the Entertainer.

15 Hopper's Rant (1995)

This may be the Super Bowl's oddest ad. For one, it was 90 seconds. For another, it starred Dennis Hopper, in an odd bow to Gen. George Patton, as an obsessed football fan.

Hopper rants about his love for football, at one point referring to football as the "ballet of bulldozers."

Some critics charged that the ad poked fun at the mentally ill. Years later, Hopper said he regretted the campaign. "It was a career move—backwards."

16 Bud Bowl Finale (1995)

Anheuser-Busch's Bud Bowls were Super Bowl staples from the first one in 1989 that featured animated Bud Light and Budweiser bottles facing off on the gridiron.

Over the years, the formula got more complex. But the laughs kept coming up shorter, ending with this one in which Bud Light "spokescharacters" Iggy, Frank and Biff, watch the game from a desert island.

A running joke during Super Bowl blowouts was that the Bud Bowl was better than the game. For sheer endurance, score one for A-B.

17 Nothing but Net (1993)

McDonald's paired Michael Jordan and Larry Bird for a Super Bowl spot that remains an All-Star. With a Big Mac on the line, Jordan and Bird match shots in an extreme version of playing H-O-R-S-E.

What makes the ad sing isn't just the crazy shots each nails, but the stars' comic timing: Jordan's gee-whiz smirks and Bird's aw-shucks shrugs.

The spot was a slam-dunk Ad Meter winner.

18 Subaru's Meltdown (1993)

Subaru not only aired Ad Meter's last-place ad this year, it aired five of the bottom seven in the panelists' rating. No advertiser has matched that feat.

The ads were for its all-new Impreza and were just 15 seconds each. In a bid to attract women, they were narrated by an unseen Kirstie Alley.

The problem wasn't Alley or the content—it was the notion you could get a coherent Super Bowl message across in a bunch of 15-second sound bites. Call it Subaru's 15 seconds of shame.

19 McDonald's Bold Move (1991)

The chain broke new ground by addressing the issue of Down syndrome on the Super stage.

McDonald's introduced the world to Mike Sewell, who has the condition. Mike, in turn, introduces viewers to his family and friends.

The ad finished second in Ad Meter and earned McDonald's a burst of positive PR. Bravo, Ronald!

20 Coke Goes 3-D (1989)

The buildup was big. Coca-Cola distributed 20 million cardboard 3-D glasses so folks could watch its Diet Coke ad in 3-D. The ad, about a runaway Diet Coke machine, finished a laudable fifth in Ad Meter. It also was beaten by two spots for Pepsi.

Still, Coke garnered spin galore for the 3-D gimmick. Word of a run on 3-D glasses kept Coke in the news for weeks before the game. But most viewers ended up watching the overhyped ad, and related halftime show, without the special specs. After that, 3-D got the Super Bowl boot.

Critical Thinking

1. In your opinion, what is the significance of securing Super Bowl ad immortality?
2. Look over the 20 ads described in the article and develop a list of elements or features that make an ad memorable.

Best and Worst Marketing Ideas . . . Ever

Take a Cue from these 13 Killer Campaigns—and 5 Flops.

GWEN MORAN

Some marketing efforts manage to hit the ball out of the park. They resonate with the consumer, generate tremendous buzz and even permeate pop culture, becoming part of our lives and linguistics.

In a rather unscientific manner, we've gathered more than a dozen of these iconic campaigns and consulted a variety of experts to explain why they were so great. Here's a recap along with the lessons that can benefit you and your business.

Best Making the Best of a Bad Image: Las Vegas' "What Happens Here, Stays Here" Campaign

After a failed attempt to promote itself as a family destination, Las Vegas finally embraced its Sin City image with its "What happens here, stays here" advertising campaign, launched in 2003. It's still going strong: 2007 marked the city's fourth consecutive year of busting tourism records. "It resonated because it's what people already believe," says Laura Ries, president of marketing strategy firm Ries & Ries.

Lesson: Try to turn negatives into positives.

Best Product Placement: Reese's Pieces in *E.T.: The Extra-Terrestrial*

Some marketing missteps make you kick yourself. Take Mars Inc.'s failure to take the opportunity to include M&Ms in *E.T.* After Mars passed, director Steven Spielberg went to Hershey's, which took the offer. It paid off. *Time* magazine reported in 1982 that Reese's Pieces sales rose 65 percent in the months after the movie's release. Even though the movie never mentioned the name of the product, showing the distinctive orange package was enough, and the placement enjoyed heavy promotional support from the manufacturer.

Lesson: Placing your product in the right media vehicle can boost sales.

Best Video Ad: Get a Mac

Apple's "Get a Mac" campaign, which launched in 2006, puts the hip, easygoing Mac against the hapless, problem-prone PC. "The message of these ads is clear," says communications professor Stephen Marshall, author of *Television Advertising That Works*. "Every one of them says, 'Don't be this guy.' You don't want to be the PC." The TV ads also appeared online, and the company released a series of web-only ads to capitalize on consumer interest in the characters. People got the message—Mac's market share grew by 42 percent.

Lesson: Create engaging characters in your online video to help grow an audience that's receptive to your brand.

Best Contest: Nathan's Famous Hot Dog Eating Contest

Launched in 1916, this homage to gluttony plasters the Nathan's name across international media each year. Brothers George and Richard Shea launched the International Federation of Competitive Eating in 1997. The IFOCE organizes and runs more than 80 eating contests throughout the U.S. and abroad, spurring a subculture of competitive eating celebrities who receive international media attention.

Lesson: Don't be afraid to be outrageous if it suits your brand.

Best Use of YouTube: Blendtec's "Will it Blend?"

Blendtec, a maker of high-end blenders, created a series of online videos that depict founder Tom Dickson using his durable machine to smash everything from small electronics to sneakers to credit cards. The videos are on Blendtec's site as well as YouTube, where, through viral marketing, some have been viewed more than 5.5 million times. It shows people are interested—and it saves money, since Blendtec didn't pay for all that bandwidth. Says Ann Handley, chief content officer of marketing information resource MarketingProfs.com, "They created a campaign that really builds brand awareness."

Lesson: Use various tools to spread the word about how your brand is different.

Best Slogan: "Got Milk?"

What better success benchmark than having your slogan work its way into the national lexicon? It's even better when it includes your product name, says Mitzi Crall, author of *100 Smartest Marketing Ideas Ever.* The simplicity of the slogan lends itself to a wide variety of advertising interpretations, ranging from humorous TV ads to the celebrity-driven milk mustache print series. "The images of glamour and fame contrasted with the hominess of a milk mustache make the versatile tagline a hit," says Crall. A year after the campaign launched in California, the state saw an increase in milk sales for the first time in more than 10 years.

Lesson: Look for slogans that have the potential for longevity.

Best Jingle: NBC Jingle

If you can name that brand in three notes, it must be the NBC jingle. Of course, repetition over the years has reinforced the brand, but there's more to it. "It's called mnemonics, or sonic branding," says Marshall. "By adding sound to its brand identity, it adds another way for customers to experience the brand. It especially makes sense because it's a broadcast medium."

Lesson: Look for ways to add additional sensory branding elements when relevant.

Best Use of Truth in a Crisis: Tylenol

When cyanide-laced capsules of Extra Strength Tylenol were linked to seven deaths in the Chicago area in 1982, parent company Johnson & Johnson faced a full-blown crisis. While other companies might have lied or evaded the situation, then-CEO James E. Burke issued a full recall of the product and engaged in regular media updates that were shockingly honest for the time. All consumers with bottles of Tylenol capsules could swap them for Tylenol tablets at Johnson & Johnson's cost. "Telling the truth is always a good long-term strategy," says Scott Armstrong, a marketing professor at the University of Pennsylvania's Wharton School of Business. "When that's violated, it leads to a fall."

Lesson: Be truthful with your customers and you'll keep their trust.

Best Use of Social Networking to Target Tweens and Teens: *High School Musical*

After the success of the made-for-TV movies *High School Musical* and *High School Musical 2,* Disney teamed up with MySpace in what *TV Guide* called the social network's largest campaign. The promotion included a contest where fans showed school spirit by completing tasks such as uploading videos, changing profile skins and texting votes for their school.

Lesson: Find the media your audience uses and go there.

5 Worst Marketing Ideas . . . Ever

While some campaigns are notable for their brilliance, others, well, not so much. Here are five marketing efforts we could have done without.

Worst campaign to trigger a bomb scare: *Aqua Teen Hunger Force* In January 2007, Turner Broadcasting System Inc.'s promotion of its TV show *Aqua Teen Hunger Force,* which featured small electronic light boards with one of the series' characters, triggered a bomb scare in Boston.

Worst use of body parts in marketing: Logo tattoos In the 1990s, California eatery Casa Sanchez offered free lunch for life to anyone who got a tattoo of their logo. Nervous about how quickly people were getting inked, the eatery limited the offer to the first 50 people.

Worst sponsorship idea: Bidding for baby naming rights The dotcom era ushered in a (thankfully small) rash of people trying to sell off their children's names for extra dough. Poor little Widget Smith.

Worst campaign character: The Quiznos creatures Superimposed over a Quiznos sub shop were two disturbing, singing rat-like creatures. Fortunately, the shop got wise and ditched them after public outcry. But it's an image that stays with you. Go ahead, look them up on YouTube—but don't say we didn't warn you.

Worst plague-like sweep of viral marketing: Starbucks' viral marketing fiasco. A free-coffee coupon sent by baristas with no restrictions circulated the internet, causing an overwhelming rate of renewal. Ultimately the coffee purveyor stopped honoring the coupon, causing a mini controversy.

Best Celebrity Spokesman: William Shatner as the Priceline Negotiator

When William Shatner first started touting Priceline.com's cut-rate service in 1997, no one thought the relationship—or the company, for that matter—would last more than a decade. But through a savvy reinvention of itself, Priceline thrived with the campy James Bond-gone-wrong Shatner as its public persona. That long-term element is part of the relationship's success, says Ries. "You get the feeling that he's very much in tune with the brand and the company. That kind of longevity and dedication can be [very] effective."

Lesson: A little fun can go a long way.

Best Logo: Nike Swoosh

There are a number of rumors about exactly how much Nike paid Portland State University graphic design student Carolyn Davidson for the Swoosh in the early '70s (actually $35), but it's been the brand's mark since it was introduced on Nike footwear at the 1972 U.S. Track & Field Olympic Trials. The reason it works? It's an "empty vessel," says Ries. "It's so simple and visible at a distance. Another logo might have been well-known but wouldn't have done the brand as much good if it had been more complicated." Because the Swoosh has no innate meaning attached to it, Nike can use it to build any image it desires.

Lesson: Sometimes too many bells and whistles can make your logo less effective.

Best Use of Outdoor Advertising: The Goodyear Blimp

Is there anyone who doesn't recognize the blimp when it passes by? "The Goodyear Blimp is its own kind of magic," says Crall. "If we see it float by when we're going about our daily lives, we run to get our spouses and children to 'come see.' We're receptive to the brand message."

Lesson: Be unexpected in how and where you communicate with your customers.

Best Use of Promotional Items: Livestrong Wristbands

After the news broke in 1996 that champion bicyclist Lance Armstrong had cancer, he founded his Lance Armstrong Foundation the following year. Working with Nike, the foundation developed a yellow silicon wristband stamped with the Livestrong mantra to sell as a fundraiser. According to lancewins.com, more than 45 million have been sold so far. The bracelets became an immediately identifiable symbol of Armstrong, who often wore the yellow leaders jersey while cycling to seven Tour de France victories.

Lesson: Have a signature look, whether it's a giveaway or simply in how you present your brand, so people recognize you immediately.

Critical Thinking

1. Do you agree with the expert panel's choices for the 13 killer campaigns? Justify your answer.
2. With a small group of peers from your class, come up with your own Top 5 lists of Best and Worst Marketing Ideas. Justify your choices.

UNIT 4

Global Marketing

Unit Selections

36. **Emerging Lessons,** Madhubalan Viswanathan, José Antonio Rosa, and Julie A. Ruth
37. **Three Dimensional,** Masaaki Kotabe and Crystal Jiang
38. **After Early Errors, Wal-Mart Thinks Locally to Act Globally: Wall-Mart Tries to Adapt Its Methods to Local Tastes,** Miguel Bustillo
39. **Unlocking the Cranberry Mystique,** Elisabeth A. Sullivan

Learning Outcomes

- What economic, cultural, and political obstacles must an organization consider that seeks to become global in its markets?
- Do you believe that an adherence to the "marketing concept" is the right way to approach international markets? Why, or why not?
- What trends are taking place today that would suggest whether particular global markets would grow or decline? Which countries do you believe will see the most growth in the next decade? Why?
- In what ways can the Internet be used to extend a market outside the United States?

Student Website

www.mhhe.com/cls

Internet References

International Trade Administration
www.ita.doc.gov

World Chambers Network
www.worldchambers.net

World Trade Center Association OnLine
www.iserve.wtca.org

It is certain that marketing with a global perspective will continue to be a strategic element of U.S. business well into the next decade. The United States is both the world's largest exporter and largest importer. In 1987, U.S. exports totaled just over $250 billion—about 10 percent of total world exports. During the same period, U.S. imports were nearly $450 billion—just under 10 percent of total world imports. By 1995 exports had risen to $513 billion and imports to $664 billion—roughly the same percentage of total world trade.

Regardless of whether they wish to be, all marketers are now part of the international marketing system. For some, the end of the era of domestic markets may have come too soon, but that era is over. Today it is necessary to recognize the strengths and weaknesses of our own marketing practices as compared to those abroad. The multinational corporations have long recognized this need, but now all marketers must acknowledge it.

International marketing differs from domestic marketing in that the parties to its transactions live in different political units. It is the "international" element of international marketing that distinguishes it from domestic marketing—not differences in managerial techniques. The growth of global business among multinational corporations has raised new questions about the role of their headquarters. It has even caused some to speculate whether marketing operations should be performed abroad rather than in the United States.

The key to applying the marketing concept is by understanding the consumer. Increasing levels of consumer sophistication is evident in all of the world's most profitable markets. Managers are required to adopt new points of view in order to accommodate increasingly complex consumer wants and needs. The markets in the new millennium will show further integration on a worldwide scale. In these emerging markets, conventional textbook approaches can cause numerous problems. The new marketing perspective called for by the circumstances of the years ahead will require a long-range view that looks from the basics of exchange and their applications in new settings.

The selections presented here were chosen to provide an overview of world economic factors, competitive positioning, and increasing globalization of markets—issues to which each and every marketer must become sensitive. "Emerging Lessons" describes how understanding the needs of poorer consumers can be both profitable and socially responsible for multinational companies. "Three Dimensional" shows how the markets of Japan, Korea, and China are far from homogeneous. The next article discloses how Wal-Mart learned the importance of tailoring its inventories and stores to local tastes—and exporting ideas and products outside the United States.

The last article demonstrates how Ocean Spray found success in introducing its cranberry products to global consumers.

Emerging Lessons

For multinational companies, understanding the needs of poorer consumers can be profitable and socially responsible.

MADHUBALAN VISWANATHAN, JOSÉ ANTONIO ROSA, AND JULIE A. RUTH

Businesses, take note: An underserved and poorly understood consumer group is poised to become a driving force in economic and business development, by virtue of sheer numbers and rising globalization.

They are subsistence consumers—people in developing nations like India who earn just a few dollars a day and lack access to basics such as education, health care and sanitation.

As these consumers gain access to income and information over the next decade, their combined purchasing power, already in the trillions of dollars, likely will grow at higher rates than that of consumers in industrialized nations. The lesson for multinational companies: Understanding and addressing the needs of the world's poorest consumers is likely to become a profitable, as well as a socially responsible, strategy.

A characteristic associated with low-income consumers, and one that has major implications for doing business with them, is that many struggle with reading and math. Like the 14% of Americans estimated to be functionally illiterate in a U.S. government survey, subsistence consumers have difficulty reading package labels, store signs or product-use instructions, or subtracting the purchase price of an item from cash on hand—all of which hampers their ability to put their limited incomes to best use.

Our research shows that low-literacy consumers process market information and approach purchasing decisions differently than other groups of shoppers. As a result, companies may have to alter marketing practices such as packaging, advertising, pricing, store signage and the training of retail-store employees in order to communicate with them more effectively and win their business.

Here is what we learned from our studies on low-literacy, low-income consumers in the U.S. and subsistence consumers in developing markets, and our recommendations on how marketers can improve the value these groups get from product purchase and use.

Concrete Thinking

One of the key observations we made is that low-literacy consumers have difficulty with abstract thinking. These individuals tend to group objects by visualizing concrete and practical situations they have experienced.

They exhibited what science would call a low grasp of abstract categories—tools, cooking utensils or protein-rich foods, for example—which suggests low-literacy consumers may have difficulty understanding advertising and store signs that position products that way. Their natural inclination is to organize merchandise according to the ingredients needed to make a particular dish or the products needed to complete a specific task, such as doing laundry or cleaning the bathroom, and that is often what they are envisioning as they navigate store aisles, deciding what to buy.

This is reminiscent of research on low-literacy peasants in Central Asia in the early 20th century, who, when presented with a set of objects such as hammer-saw-log-hatchet and asked to select the three that could be placed in one group or be described by one word, didn't derive abstract categories such as "tools" even when prompted. Instead, they grouped the objects primarily around envisioned tasks such as chopping firewood.

Being anchored in the perceptual "here and now" also interferes with the ability of low-literacy consumers to perform mathematical computations, especially those framed in abstract terms. For example, when we asked low-literacy shoppers in the U.S. to estimate whether they had enough cash to pay for the groceries in their cart, many needed to physically handle cash and envision additional piles of currency or coins to accurately estimate the cost of goods in their cart; when the sensorial experience of counting cash was taken away, they often were at a loss.

Because handling cash while walking store aisles isn't advisable, many low-literacy consumers arrive at checkout counters not knowing whether they have enough money to cover their purchases. All too often, they hand all of their cash to the register attendant and hope for an honest transaction.

One of the most potentially detrimental results of concrete thinking, however, is the difficulty that low-literacy consumers have with performing price/volume calculations. They tend to choose products based solely on the lowest posted price or smallest package size, even when they have sufficient resources for a larger purchase, because they have difficulty estimating

For Further Reading

See these related articles from MIT Sloan Management Review.

Strategic Innovation at the Base of the Pyramid

Jamie Anderson and Costas Markides (Fall 2007)

Strategic innovation in developing markets is fundamentally different from what occurs in developed economies.

http://sloanreview.mit.edu/smr/issue/2007/fall/16/

The Great Leap: Driving Innovation From the Base of the Pyramid

Stuart L. Hart and Clayton M. Christensen (Fall 2002)

Companies can generate growth and satisfy social and environmental stakeholders through a "great leap" to the base of the economic pyramid.

http://sloanreview.mit.edu/smr/issue/2002/fall/5/

Has Strategy Changed?

Kathleen M. Eisenhardt (Winter 2002)

Globalization has quietly transformed the economic playing field.

http://sloanreview.mit.edu/smr/issue/2002/winter/10/

The Need for a Corporate Global Mind-Set

Thomas M. Begley and David P. Boyd (Winter 2003)

Many international business leaders consider a global mind-set desirable, but few know how to embed it companywide.

http://sloanreview.mit.edu/smr/issue/2003/winter/3/

The Dynamic Synchronization of Strategy and Information Technology

C.K. Prahalad and M.S. Krishnan (Summer 2002)

The authors' work with 500 executives revealed that few managers believed their information infrastructure was able to handle the pressures from deregulation, globalization, ubiquitous connectivity and the convergence of industries and technologies.

http://sloanreview.mit.edu/smr/issue/2002/summer/2/

the longevity and savings that come from buying in larger volumes. Some base purchase decisions on physical package size, instead of reported volume content, or on the quantity of a particular ingredient—such as fat, sodium or sugar—but without allowing for the fact that acceptable levels of an ingredient can vary across product categories or package size.

Misspent Energy

We found that low-literacy consumers spend so much time and mental energy on what many of us can do quickly and with little thought that they have little time to base purchase decisions on anything other than surface attributes such as size, color or weight.

They tend to think in pictures, so any change in visual cues such as sign fonts, brand logos or store layouts can leave them struggling to locate a desired product category or brand. Price displays can cause confusion because of the many numbers presented, such as original prices, discounted percentages and discounted prices. Even estimating the price of two gallons of milk if the price of one is known may require a pencil-and-paper calculation unless the price is set in whole or half-unit increments, such as $3 or $3.50.

Because so much shopping time is devoted to deciphering product labels and locating products, we found that low-literacy consumers are less able than other groups to assess the value of products based on subsurface attributes—this computer has more memory and will do what I need more effectively, for example.

When shopping in unfamiliar stores, some low-literacy consumers will choose products at random, buying the first brand they see once they locate a desired product category or aisle. Others simply walk through the store, choosing items that look attractive based on factors such as packaging colors or label illustrations, without regard to whether they even need the product.

When shopping in familiar stores, many low-literacy consumers buy only the brands they recognize by appearance or have purchased previously. While this approach reduces the incidence of product purchases for which the consumer has no use, it precludes the adoption of new and improved products as a category evolves and improves over time.

The pitfalls and uncertainty that come from choosing products at random, based on surface attributes or out of habit provoke anxiety in many low-literacy consumers, leading us to another finding: Shopping takes a heavy emotional toll on this group.

Buying the wrong items, running short of cash at the register or having to ask for help in the aisle to locate products are recurring worries, even cause for despair. The anticipation of such stressful experiences prompts some low-literacy consumers to avoid new, large or what they perceive to be threatening shopping venues or to delay shopping until family or friends can assist, even if waiting means doing without essentials. Although low-literacy consumers tend to be passive in public settings, they will remember episodes of poor treatment by service personnel and won't patronize stores or brands they associate with disrespectful treatment.

Despite the significant constraints that low-literacy consumers face, their ingenuity in coping and positive outlook are a testament to human adaptiveness. For instance, subsistence consumers overcome many of the challenges that come from not being able to read or do math problems by relying on their interpersonal networks—family and friends who may have complementary skills and knowledge. In many situations, the network includes the owners of neighborhood stores who offer very limited product assortments and high prices, but who can answer questions and offer advice to consumers unable to read the labels and determine the value of products on their own.

Subsistence consumers are resource-poor but likely to be relationship-rich, and this must be taken into account by businesses seeking to serve them.

Drawing Them In

To win and enhance customer loyalty in developing markets, manufacturers and retailers need to understand the difficulties faced by low-literacy consumers and create shopping environments that make them feel less vulnerable. Here are a few ways that companies can help customers make better purchases and avoid embarrassment:

- Display prices and price reductions graphically—a half-circle to indicate a 50% markdown, for example, or a picture of three one-dollar bills to indicate a purchase price of $3. Price products in whole and half numbers to make it easier for low-literacy consumers to calculate the price of, say, two bags of rice. These pricing practices are critically important in marketplaces where general stores and kiosks are being replaced by self-service stores, where there is less interaction between customer and store owner.
- Clearly post unit prices in common formats across stores, brands and product categories to make it easier for low-literacy consumers to perform price/volume calculations.
- Include illustrations of product categories on store signs to make it easier for low-literacy consumers to navigate new or refurbished stores. Similarly, use graphical representations of sizes, ingredients, instructions and other information to communicate product information more effectively in shelf and other in-store displays.
- Put the ingredients required for the preparation of popular local dishes in the same section of the store. This would be helpful to low-literacy consumers who often envision the sequence of activities involved in fixing specific dishes to identify the ingredients and quantities they need to purchase. The same can be done for other domestic tasks.
- Incorporate familiar visual elements—such as color schemes or font types—into new store concepts or redesigned brand logos to minimize confusion and anxiety among low-literacy shoppers and increase the likelihood that they will try new products and stores.
- Create a friendly store environment by training store personnel to be sensitive to the needs of low-literacy shoppers and by verbally disclosing and consistently applying store policies. In addition, allow employees to form relationships with consumers by learning their names and offering small amounts of individualized assistance. This is particularly important for global brands and companies entering markets where foreigners are mistrusted or have accrued a history of mistreating people.

As subsistence markets become more attractive, additional opportunities to serve low-literacy consumers will probably become available. Because literacy deficiencies are likely to be addressed at a slower pace than the pace at which poor consumers gain discretionary income and the ability to spend it on products and services, the companies that respond to this group's needs early on will have an advantage. Low-literacy consumers can be a profitable and loyal customer group if treated properly.

Critical Thinking

1. According to the articles, what are some of the challenges associated with marketing to subsistence consumers?
2. You have been assigned as a consultant for a business that is looking to target subsistence consumers. Prepare a list of DOs and DON'Ts to help it attract and retain this target market.

Dr. Viswanathan is an associate professor of marketing at the University of Illinois at Urbana-Champaign in Champaign, Ill. **Dr. Rosa** is a professor of marketing and sustainable business practices at the University of Wyoming in Laramie, Wyo. **Dr. Ruth** is an associate professor of marketing at Rutgers University in Camden, N.J. They can be reached at reports@wsj.com.

Three Dimensional

The markets of Japan, Korea, and China are far from homogeneous.

MASAAKI KOTABE AND CRYSTAL JIANG

Asia is one of the world's most dynamic regions, and offers multiple opportunities for businesses and investors. In terms of its nominal gross domestic product (GDP) in 2005, Japan has the largest economy ($4.80 trillion), followed by China ($1.84 trillion) and Korea ($.72 trillion). China's real purchasing power exceeds $7 trillion, Japan's is estimated at $4 trillion, and Korea's is estimated at $1 trillion. These giants' combined purchasing power is comparable to the $12 trillion U.S. economy.

One of the challenges faced by American and other Western multinational companies is a tendency to lump together these markets and assume that Asian consumers have similar tastes and preferences, moderated by different income levels. This is not only a very shortsighted view, but also a risky assumption when entering these markets.

Asian countries have distinct cultural, social, and economic characteristics that affect consumer behavior, with consumers in Japan, Korea, and China differing in brand orientations, attitudes toward domestic and foreign products, quality and price perceptions, and technology feature preferences. A comparative analysis of consumer behaviors can help companies identify effective marketing strategies, and enable them to successfully tackle these Asian markets (see Table 1).

Executive Briefing

Globalizing markets might not mean that markets have become similar. Although multinational companies tend to believe that all Asian markets are the same, a comparative analysis proves that consumers in Japan, Korea, and China differ in their brand orientations, attitudes toward domestic and foreign products, quality and price perceptions, and product feature preferences. To ensure success, companies must set aside narrow and risky assumptions, and tailor country-specific strategies to target these consumers.

Brand Orientation

Japan. Of all the developed countries, this is the most brand-conscious and status-conscious. It is also intensely style-conscious: Consumers love high-end luxury goods (especially from France and Italy), purchasing items such as designer handbags, shoes, and jewelry. Since 2001, Hermes, Louis Vuitton (commonly referred to as LVMH), and Coach have opened glitzy flagship stores in Tokyo and enjoyed double-digit sales growth. And the country represents 20% of Gucci's worldwide revenue, 15% of LVMH's, and 12% of Chanel's. It seems that a slumping economy has not inhibited its consumers.

Eager to "know who they are," they prefer brands that contribute to their senses of identity and self-expression. These highly group-oriented consumers are apt to select prestigious merchandise based on social class standards, and prefer products that enhance their status. Accordingly, they attach more importance to the reputation of the merchandise than to their personal social classes.

Noticeably, the country's consumer markets have expanded to China and Korea. In Shanghai or Seoul, you can see the influence of Japan's fashion trends and products. There's even a Chinese word for this phenomenon: ha-ri, which means the adoration of Japanese style.

Korea. Consumers have very sophisticated tastes, show immense passion for new experiences, and favor premium and expensive imported products. In 2004, the Korean Retail Index showed continuous growth of premium brands in certain product categories, such as whiskey, shampoo, and cosmetics. Consumers also demonstrate great interest in generational fads (expressions of their generations and cultures, not just of their economics or regions), thereby selecting products that follow their generations' judgments and preferences.

China. Roughly 10 million–13 million Chinese consumers prefer luxury goods. The majority of them are entrepreneurs or young professionals working for foreign multinational firms. Recent studies found that 24% of the population, mostly in their 20s and 30s, prefers new products and considers technology an important part of life. (Those in their 40s and 50s are price-conscious, brand loyal, and less sensitive to technology.) With higher education and purchasing power, this generation is brand- and status-conscious. It considers luxury goods to be personal achievements, bringing higher social status.

Table 1 Market Characteristics of the Three Largest Asian Economies

	Japan	Korea	China
Population (2005)	127 million	48 million	1,306 million
Nominal GDP (2005)	$4.80 trillion	$ .72 trillion	$1.84 trillion
GDP purchasing power parity (2004)	$3.7 trillion	$ .92 trillion	$7.3 trillion
GDP per capita purchasing power parity (2004)	$29,400	$19,200	$5,600
GDP real growth rate of country (2004)	2.9%	4.6%	9.1%
Degree of luxury brand consciousness	Very strong	Strong	Varied
Preference for foreign products	Strong (particularly for European products)	Weak	Very strong
Price/quality perception	Extremely quality demanding	Polarization of consumption	Very price conscious
Importance of high-tech features on new products	Very high	Very high	Varied

Sources: Central Intelligence Agency, *World Factbook*, and *Index Mundi*.

Purchasing behavior tends to vary regionally. Consumers in metropolitan areas follow fashions/trends/styles, prefer novelty items, and are aware of brand image and product quality. These consumers live on the eastern coast—in major cities such as Shanghai, Beijing, Shenzhen, and Dalian. There, luxury brands such as Armani, Prada, and LVMH are considered prominent logos for high-income clientele.

According to LVMH, this country is its fourth-largest market in terms of worldwide sales. It's no wonder that many high-end firms label these consumers "the new Japanese": a group of increasingly wealthy people hungry for brands and fanatical about spending.

Domestic vs. Foreign

Japan. Although consumers are extremely demanding and have different perceptions of products made in other countries, they are generally accepting of quality foreign products. However, Japan is mostly dominated by well-established companies such as Canon, Sony, and Toyota. Many globally successful firms experience great difficulty gaining footholds.

In this market, Häagen-Dazs Japan Inc. succeeded the exit of competitor Ben & Jerry's, dominating the premium ice cream market with a 90% market share. It successfully delivered the message of a "lifestyle-enhancement product" with word-of-mouth advertising, garnering a flood of free publicity. The company flourished by promoting high quality with local appeal.

Korea. These consumers hold negative attitudes toward foreign businesses; the majority believes that these businesses transfer local wealth to other countries, and crowd out small establishments. Consumers are very proud, and demonstrate a complicated love-hate relationship with foreign brands.

Very few consumers understand or speak English, let alone the languages of their closest trading partners: Japan and China. Often, Korean campaigns require significant rebranding—use of localized brands—to influence local perceptions. According to an official at Carrefour (the world's second-largest retailer), the company has difficulty expanding its investments into other provinces because of excessive regulations, and hasn't done enough research to keep up with Korean consumers' needs.

Nevertheless, the country is increasingly comfortable with the presence of foreign companies in previously closed industries. (In fact, the society is much too uncritical and passive in the acceptance of foreign—especially American—products.) And consumers are far less brand-conscious than before, and will embrace new products from unknown companies.

China. Attitudes toward foreign products differ, depending on consumers' age groups. Companies can no longer view this country's youth through the lens of traditional cultural values; this generation considers international taste a key factor in making decisions. Conversely, the mature generation (55 years and older) expresses a definite preference for locally made products. In general, consumers believe imported products under foreign brand names are more dependable.

Many foreign companies (e.g., Nike, Nokia, Sony, McDonald's) have replaced unknown local brands. The country retains more than 300 licensed Starbucks outlets, and chairman Howard Schultz says of this market: "In addition to the 200 million middle-to-upper-class segments of the population that are typically customers for upscale brands, there is a growing affinity from the younger, affluent consumer for Western brands."

However, some foreign companies—with an increased focus on local appeal—have lost their prominent brands' images to domestic rivals, ultimately forfeiting their market share. After all, when this country's consumers are inspired by design and function, they prefer domestic brands because of their good value for the money.

Quality and Price

Japan. These consumers are the world's strictest when it comes to demand for product quality, and they clearly articulate their needs/desires about a product or packaging operation. They view information other than price (e.g., brand, packaging, advertising) as important variables in assessing quality and making decisions. Compared with Chinese and Korean consumers, they have much higher expectations for products—and are willing to pay premium prices for them. In agricultural produce, for example, they are less tolerant of skin blemishes, small size, and nonuniformity.

Foreign companies that don't fully understand and meet consumers' needs/expectations struggle with their investments. Although Wal-Mart dwarfs the competition (with $285 billion in 2004 global sales) and owns 42% of all Japanese supermarket chains, it faces losses there. Its "everyday low prices" philosophy doesn't seem to attract Japanese consumers, because they often associate low price with low quality: yasu-karou, warukarou—cheap price, cheap product.

To cater to these consumers, manufacturers have adopted a total quality approach. To survive fierce local competition, Procter & Gamble sought the best available materials for product formulations and packaging. In the process, it learned some invaluable lessons on how to improve operations, and obtained new product ideas from consumers. (Interestingly, the company took this education on the Japanese way of interacting with consumers and applied it globally.) Today, the country serves as Procter & Gamble's major technical center in Asia, where it develops certain global technologies.

And McDonald's opened its first store in Tokyo's Ginza district, which is identified with luxury brand-name goods. It purchased expensive land—not justified by the limited profits of a hamburger establishment—to boost the quality image of its product. Today, McDonald's Japan has grown to become the country's largest fast-food chain.

In terms of cost, the younger generation prefers low-priced products—everything priced at 100 yen (similar to U.S. dollar stores). The "two extreme price markets" segmentation model explains how consumers value lower prices for their practical use while paying premium prices for self-satisfaction, social status, and the quality of products—especially those from Europe. As a result, anything that falls in the middle of the price range—such as the country's designer brands—generates petty profits.

Korea. Consumption has been sluggish since the Asian financial crisis of 1997–1999. However, the younger generation is at the forefront of a new and emerging pattern; it holds opposing expectations of/preferences for low-priced and high-priced goods. When purchasing high-tech or fashion-related items, these consumers prefer well-known brands, and tend to purchase expensive goods to attain psychological satisfaction. Yet they are willing to purchase unbranded goods with low prices, as long as the basic features are guaranteed. It has taken several decades for discount stores to surpass the retail market.

China. Most consumers are price sensitive, and try to safeguard part of their income for investment. In 2005, many global automakers readjusted their strategies in this country, based on demand predictions that most consumers would purchase cars priced less than $12,000. One popular Chinese automaker, Chery, priced its QQ model between $5,500 and $7,500; another aggressive domestic automaker, Xiali, priced its cars at similarly affordable prices.

Although this market is lucrative with growing demand, foreign brands (e.g., Honda, General Motors, Volkswagen Group) cannot compete with Chinese automakers' competitive prices. And when the younger generation worships Western and luxury brands—in eagerness to establish its social identity—it might prefer pirated versions to domestic ones, making anticounterfeiting control a major issue for companies.

Technology Features

Japan. Because of the country's harmonic convergence of the domestic market and the industrial sector, consumers have always preferred high-tech gadgets. According to an estimate by The World Bank Group, the country possesses 410,000 of the world's 720,000 working robots (which perform useful chores and provide companionship). Its electronics companies create gizmos by borrowing new concepts from the computer industry, such as personal video recorders, interactive pagers, and Internet radios.

Instead of looking for cost or value, consumers are willing to pay for better and cooler features and technological sophistication. Largely because of Japan's small living quarters, manufacturers have become experts at miniaturizing and creating multifunction devices. For instance, Sony's PlayStation Portable compacts the power of the original PlayStation into a palm-sized package. According to the company, it can deliver music and MPEG-4 video, can display photos, and even offers a Wi-Fi connection for wireless gaming and messaging. It's also no wonder that the country welcomed Baroke, the first company to successfully produce quality sparkling and still wine in a can.

Korea. The most wired country in the world is a leader in Internet usage and high-tech industries such as mobile phones, liquid crystal displays, and semiconductors. It also has widespread broadband, and high volumes of personal computer ownership. While mobile phone sales have cooled in Japan, these consumers continue to trade in phones for newer models about every six months.

Largely because of Japan's small living quarters, manufacturers have become experts at miniaturizing and creating multifunction devices.

According to a Samsung Research Institute survey, consumers prefer to express themselves without following social conventions. The Cyworld virtual community Web site, for instance, provides a subscriber with a private room, a circle of friends, and an endless range of "home" decoration possibilities and cool music. Ever-widening cyberspace reaches more than one-fourth of the population. The younger generation in particular enjoys virtual shopping malls and e-commerce.

China. It is imperative for companies to understand the major differences in consumer behavior between generations. Young Chinese consumers (typically affluent segments in the prosperous cities) are passionate about the latest developments. Recent studies found that 24% of the population—most with ages in the early 20s or 30s—prefer new products and consider technology an important part of life. Those in their 40s–50s, on the other hand, are price conscious, brand loyal, and less sensitive to technology.

Advice and Recommendations

Marketers need to tailor country-specific strategies to target consumers in Japan, Korea, and China. The existence of strategically equivalent segments (e.g., the younger generation, with its propensity to purchase high-quality, innovative, and foreign products) suggests a geocentric approach to global markets. These similarities allow for standardized strategies across national boundaries.

By aggregating such segments, companies not only preserve consumer orientation, but also reduce the number of marketing mixes they have to offer—without losing market share, marketing, advertising, research and development, and production throughout Asia.

Moreover, because product design, function, and quality determine consumers' experiences, companies must simultaneously incorporate all areas—such as product development and marketing—to establish commanding positions in mature markets. Once they create positive images in these countries, success will be forthcoming.

Japan:

- This is the most profitable market for luxury goods companies. The key to success is promotion of high quality, local appeal, and a sense of extravagance.
- As one of the most volatile markets, it requires a steady flow of new stimuli with an improved rhythm of innovations. To survive, companies must continuously develop new products and establish prestigious brand value. If they can succeed there, then they can do so anywhere.
- Picky Japanese consumers clearly articulate their requirements about products or packaging operations. As a result, companies can use the country as their technical center—to gain firsthand experience in satisfying consumers in the region.
- These consumers are willing to pay for better and cooler features and technological sophistication. Companies can win their hearts by introducing gizmos.
- Because significant differences exist among generations, and those differences will translate into diverse consumer behaviors, segmentation marketing (identifying variations based on age, region, and gender) is best. Companies must be aware of these differences, and understand what kinds of products/services can meet the market segment's needs. For example: Coca-Cola has introduced more products here than anywhere else, including coffee and green tea beverages that appeal to Japanese tastes. As a result, its net operating revenue represents more than 60% of the total Asian segment (20% of its worldwide revenue).

Korea:

- A consumer-oriented approach is crucial for identifying tastes and blending in, rather than being viewed as foreign. Careful market, brand, and advertising testing is imperative.
- It can be difficult to enter this market alone; strategic alliances with domestic companies are a practical way to understand local preferences when introducing a global brand.
- If foreign companies make greater efforts to intensify their involvements with—and long-term commitments to—the country's economic development, then consumers' perceptions of an "invasion" will dissipate over time.
- Product design directly affects a company's competitiveness. This and brand power can overcome product quality, and even product functions. To present the best product design to its consumers, Samsung Electronics hired an influential British industrial designer. According to the company's Economic Research Institute, a good design "provides a good experience for consumers"; it looks different, feels good, is easy to use, and has an identity.

China:

- Foreign companies can no longer wait; the market for consumer goods is growing rapidly, stimulated by a strong economy.
- Its diversity and the vastness of its consumer base make it critical for companies to segment consumers based on demographic, geographic, and psychographic/lifestyle variations.
- Because of the younger generation's brand orientation, promoting symbolic value is imperative for conspicuous and inconspicuous foreign products.
- Multinational companies can't assume that their first-mover advantages will be rewarded for brand recognition and established distribution channels.
- Cost-conscious consumers are quite unpredictable, so companies should avoid a too-high premium price strategy. Instead, they should research quantitatively acceptable price/value trade-offs by category.
- Because local brands are on the rise, foreign companies must work harder to localize research and development and the contents of their products. They must also better evaluate the market and the potential for long-term growth. Without competitive pricing and world-class product design/quality, companies will have a tough time surviving.

Company executives must remember that not all countries are created equally. By understanding and learning to appreciate the differences and similarities between these three Asian purchasing giants, companies from other countries can immerse their organizations seamlessly.

Critical Thinking

1. With a small group of peers from your class, conduct a comparative analysis of Japan, Korea, and China.
2. Are consumers from these three Asian nations different from American consumers? If so, describe some major differences.

Masaaki Kotabe is the Washburn Chair of International Business and Marketing and director of research at the Institute of Global Management Studies at Temple University's Fox School of Business and Management in Philadelphia. He may be reached at mkotabe@temple.edu. **Crystal Jiang** is a PhD candidate in strategy and international business at the Fox School of Business and Management. She may be reached at crystalj@temple.edu. To join the discussion on this article, please visit www.marketingpower.com/marketingmanagementblog.

After Early Errors, Wal-Mart Thinks Locally to Act Globally

Wall-Mart Tries to Adapt Its Methods to Local Tastes

MIGUEL BUSTILLO

SÃO PAULO—Having powered its way to the top in U.S. retailing, Wal-Mart Stores Inc. has struggled to extend its dominance across the globe.

But the world's largest retailer is learning in Brazil and elsewhere that the most successful ideas don't necessarily flow from its headquarters in Bentonville, Ark. That has it tailoring inventories and stores to local tastes—and exporting ideas and products pioneered outside the U.S.

Traffic-choked São Paulo, for instance, proved inhospitable to the kind of vast stores with which Wal-Mart dominates in American suburbs. At the same time, the local-market savvy of Brazilian retailers that Wal-Mart acquired has proved invaluable.

"What we have learned in the past couple of years is that one size does not fit all," says Anthony Hucker, a British retail veteran now tasked with taking winning Wal-Mart store formats and expanding them globally.

Wal-Mart's challenge abroad is to cater to local tastes for native products that are not popular elsewhere, while still making the most of the global purchasing might that lets its squeeze down its costs.

Finding new frontiers for expansion has become crucial for Wal-Mart. The company reported nearly flat second-quarter earnings Thursday, including a 1.2% decline in sales at U.S. stores open for at least a year. But Wal-Mart said it notched a significantly stronger performance abroad. The company estimated its foreign unit posted a 13% rise in profits for the quarter and a 11.5% increase in sales, if currency fluctuations are taken out of the equation.

And though Wal-Mart's stock rose smartly last year, as its low prices appealed to recession-strapped shoppers, it has slid 7% in 2009 on skepticism about how well it will prosper when the economy and consumers bounce back.

The big retailer has been gradually boosting its international spending in recent years, even as it reduces overall capital expenditures. It has estimated it will spend up to $5.3 billion on foreign expansion projects in the fiscal year that began Feb. 1. And that figure doesn't include its splashiest new move, the acquisition of a controlling stake in Chile's largest grocery chain, Distribucion y Servicio D&S SA.

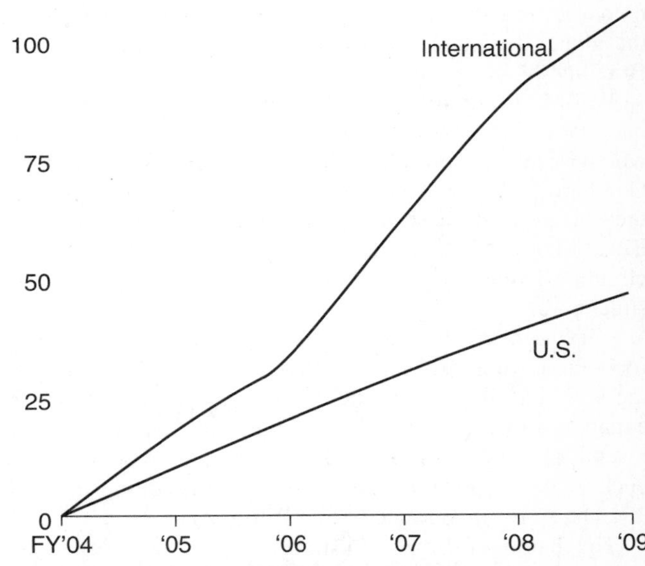

World Market Growth in Wal-Mart's sales.
Notes: Fiscal year ends Jan. 31; excludes Sam's Club
Source: The company

Wal-Mart's international division already includes some 3,700 stores and provides nearly a quarter of the company's $401 billion in annual sales. In all but one of the 14 foreign countries where Wal-Mart International does business, executives say, its sales are growing faster than that country's retail market.

Yet Wal-Mart wants its international business to be much more. It has stepped up spending in China, has struck a retail partnership in India, is exploring possibilities in the Middle East and is planning a move into Russia soon.

Though it puts the Wal-Mart name on many of its stores abroad, it also uses some 60 other names, often those of local retail chains it has acquired. In Brazil, a market Wal-Mart entered in 1995, it now is primarily building small discount stores catering to the emerging middle class, but under the name Todo Dia.

In the city of Carapicuiba on the edge of São Paulo, a gleaming new Todo Dia in a hardscrabble neighborhood pocked with graffiti offers a decidedly Brazilian take on Wal-Mart shopping. A produce section styled after a fruit stand is piled with fresh oranges. A huge display hawks the black turtle beans and salted pork ears needed to cook a *feijoada*, a traditional Brazilian stew.

Retail giant sells salted pork ears to cook feijoada, a Brazilian stew.

"This format is very close to the people," says store manager Francisco Dias, who is locked in a heated price war with five neighborhood rivals, mostly mom-and-pop businesses.

After initially failing to gain ground in Brazil with U.S.-style superstores, Wal-Mart has come on strong after acquiring two established local chains and adopting their hyper-local approach. Executives estimate the Brazil operation has been notching near-double-digit year-over-year sales gains during the global downturn, exceeding the 6% overall growth of the Brazilian retail market.

Wal-Mart remains No. 3 behind two more-established merchants: France's Carrefour SA and Pão de Açúcar Group, which is jointly controlled by a Brazilian family and Casino Guichard-Perrachon SA of France. "It's a close contest—they all have the best prices on something," said Maria-Inez Buzato-Faria, 55 years old, as she compared the three retailers' circulars while shopping at Pão de Açúcar's Extra discount superstore.

Carrefour, which pioneered the hyper-market format mixing food and general merchandise that helped Wal-Mart prosper in the U.S., has also sensed the trend toward smaller stores. It is expanding in Brazil with new outlets called Dia that closely resemble Wal-Mart's Todo Dia. "Dia enables a wider presence," says a spokeswoman for Carrefour, adding that it has 331 Dia stores in the state of São Paulo alone.

The battle of Brazil illustrates one of the biggest challenges Wal-Mart faces in trying to spread its high-volume discount retailing around the world: Established competitors have greater scale and stronger relationships with local suppliers, which sometimes allow them to buy fresh groceries and regional food brands at lower prices.

"In international discount retailing, the ability to leverage being a $400 billion company has its limits," says Anil K. Gupta, a Maryland business professor who wrote a book titled "The Quest for Global Dominance" that examined Wal-Mart's foreign missteps. "If I had to pick Wal-Mart's No. 1 weakness, it is that they have not historically factored in the fundamentally local nature of retailing, and that is surprising."

Wal-Mart executives agree that offering the regional products that locals like, while still pressing global purchasing advantages, is the balance the company must master if it is to repeat its huge U.S. success world-wide. "It's the challenge of being a global company," says Wan Ling Martello, Wal-Mart International's chief financial officer.

When Wal-Mart began an aggressive overseas expansion a decade ago, it believed that winning meant doing things the American way. Compared with veterans of global retailing such as Carrefour, which entered Brazil in 1975, Wal-Mart seemed culturally tone-deaf, peddling golf clubs and baseball gloves to Brazilians as if they were U.S. suburbanites. Wal-Mart pulled out of Germany and South Korea after heavy losses earlier this decade, in acknowledgment that its U.S. retail formula didn't work everywhere.

Now, one way Wal-Mart is having better luck is by using innovations pioneered not in the U.S. but in various countries abroad. It often takes ideas that worked in one part of its far-flung empire and transplants them to others half a world away.

In India, Wal-Mart and its local partner, Bharti Enterprises Ltd., launched a store for small merchants called Best Price Modern Wholesale. Cross-pollination is at work. The stores are based on a format Wal-Mart developed in Brazil called Maxxi. Indian store managers, rather than starting from scratch in building wholesale outlets, went to Brazil and studied Maxxi's store layout, merchandise assortment and measures used to chart success.

In China, where Wal-Mart has more than 250 stores, it is expanding with help from a discount supermarket concept called Smart Choice. This is a carbon copy of the Todo Dia convenience-store format in São Paulo—which was itself a loose translation of a Wal-Mart-owned Mexican discount store called Bodega Aurrera.

In Japan, where Wal-Mart has struggled to make inroads, the company says it now is posting a profit, thanks in part to wines, cookies and other private-label products developed by its Asda stores in the U.K. These products have become a surprise hit 6,000 miles from London. "The best-selling wine in Japan today is a private label Asda Bordeaux," says Vicente Trius, Wal-Mart's former Asia chief, who now heads its Latin American operations.

Wal-Mart is recognizing that the best ideas sometimes come from a market where it is having success, such as the U.K., where Asda is gaining ground on rival Tesco PLC amid this recession. Mr. Hucker, the executive whose job is to expand successful Wal-Mart ideas, says there was initially some resistance back at U.S. headquarters to de-emphasizing the power of Wal-Mart's Arkansas wisdom. But, noting that early big-box stores in China didn't meet expectations, he says: "There's nothing like data to win any argument."

Wal-Mart has even begun bringing some ideas back to the U.S. from abroad. It is testing two smaller store formats in the Southwestern U.S.—Mas Club and Supermercado de Walmart—that cater to Latino immigrants. The experiments piggyback on the experience of Wal-Mart de Mexico, the largest retailer south of the border, which was the company's first international triumph and remains its biggest success.

Roughly 80% of Wal-Mart International consists of acquisitions rather than new stores.

For survivors of Wal-Mart's early foreign misadventures with copies of U.S. megastores, the new spirit of collaboration and cultural diversity is striking. Jose Rafael Vasquez, Wal-Mart vice president for northeastern Brazil, says that when

Global View | Wal-Mart's international vs. U.S. store counts

Mexico	Japan	U.K	Brazil	Canada	China	Chile	Costa Rica	Others*
1,197	371	358	345	318	243	197	164	

Total international units: 3,615

U.S.: 4,258

*Others Include: Guatemala (160), El Salvador (77), Puerto Rico (56), Nicaragua (51), Honduras (50) and Argentina (28).
Notes: Data as of fiscal year end, Jan 31; Includes Sam's Clubs

Wal-Mart arrived in the country in the 1990s, U.S. executives never showed curiosity about local food tastes. He found that puzzling, knowing that catering to those yearnings was the competition's strength.

Marcelo Vienna, a São Paulo native employed by the U.S. giant, was sent to a Wal-Mart in Branson, Mo., the country-music mecca, to learn the ropes. He translated store-management manuals into Portuguese but wondered how all this would play in Brazil. "There was a lot more micromanaging from Bentonville," says Mr. Vienna, now Wal-Mart Brazil's chief merchandizing officer. Some of that was justified, he adds, because he and his colleagues were retail greenhorns.

Wal-Mart is taking the local approach further, now, by separately targeting the country's three quite-different population areas: the northeast, the south near Argentina, and the cosmopolitan southeast where São Paulo, the country's financial capital, is. This approach stems in part from Wal-Mart's acquisitions earlier this decade of two large regional retailers, Bompreco and Sonae, which were fluent in local customs.

Many poorer consumers shop at "informal" businesses, a Brazilian euphemism for merchants that sell smuggled goods or don't collect sales taxes. Wal-Mart is testing some unorthodox strategies to lure some of those shoppers to its stores in Salvador, a former Portuguese colonial capital of majestic old churches in the northeast, now home to three million people.

A Todo Dia outlet contains, in addition to merchandise aisles, a Wal-Mart-funded community center. This includes a gynecologist's office, an Internet cafe and a bank offering microloans.

The center also offers free classes for impoverished teens in basic skills such as using a computer. "My identity is created in here," says a grateful Marcos Paulo, 21, a student of the free course, which already has a waiting list. "You start to think of yourself as something more valuable than what is thrown in the trash."

So the center clearly is boosting Wal-Mart's local reputation. Whether it augments sales remains to be seen. Early results show an uptick in visits but not in purchases. Even so, the experiment is being closely watched by Wal-Mart officials in other nations.

It's easy for cultural subtleties to be lost on foreign merchants, says Mr. Vasquez, the vice president for northeastern Brazil. He believes that after Wal-Mart's early stumbles in Brazil, catering to regional differences is now becoming a Wal-Mart strength. The retailer's merchandise buyers understand, for instance, that favorite espresso brands can differ in cities two miles apart—crucial knowledge in a country where 99% of households drink coffee.

It wasn't always so. Touring a hyper-market of the Bompreco chain, Mr. Vasquez picked up a bottle of lavender perfume and observed that sales for the item spike some 2,000% before Feb. 2 each year. That was a surprise to executives of Wal-Mart when the U.S. company acquired Bompreco several years ago, but hardly to Bompreco veterans. What they knew but no one from Arkansas did: In an Afro-Brazilian religion called Candomblé, practitioners used the perfume each February in a rite honoring a sea goddess named Yemaja.

Wal-Mart Reports Flat Earnings on Cost Cutting; Sales Down 1.4%

By Ann Zimmerman

Wal-Mart Stores Inc. off-set sliding store sales with a tight squeeze on costs, enabling the giant discounter to keep profit for its fiscal second quarter essentially flat with a year earlier.

Wal-Mart said it improved profit margins with better inventory management and cost controls. But the world's largest retailer by revenue said sales at U.S. stores open at least a year fell 1.2%, excluding the effect of lower fuel prices, as consumers continued to hold back on spending. Wal-Mart had predicted its sales would be anywhere from flat to up 3%.

Wal-Mart, based in Bentonville, Ark., said a 6% reduction in its inventory helped raise gross profit margin.

Wal-Mart posted income of $3.44 billion, or 88 cents a share, for the period ende July 31, compared with $3.4 billion, or 87 cents a share, year earlier.

Net sales fell 1.4% to $100.08 billion. Excluding the impact of foreign-currency exchange, sales would have increased 2.7%.

International sales fell 5.1% as profit declined 6.2% Adjusting for currency fluctuations, international profit would have increased 13% to $1.4 billion.

The strongest-performing countries were Mexico and the U.K. although **Asda Group** Ltd., Wal-Mart's U.K. supermarket business, reported slowing sales growth in its second quarter.

Critical Thinking

1. List some major differences between American and Brazilian consumers.
2. What are some advantages and disadvantages to thinking locally and acting globally?

Unlocking the Cranberry Mystique

Ocean spray finds success in introducing the cranberry to global consumers.

ELIZABETH A. SULLIVAN

Who

Formed in 1930 and based in Lakeville-Middleboro, Mass., Ocean Spray Cranberries Inc. is a farmers' cooperative owned by more than 650 cranberry growers and grapefruit growers. With products including cranberry juice blends, grapefruit juice blends, diet juice drinks, energy juice drinks, whole cranberries and sweetened dried cranberries called Craisins—the cooperative's fastest-growing and most profitable product line—Ocean Spray's gross revenue in fiscal 2007 was nearly $1.7 billion, up from roughly $1.5 billion in 2006.

The farmer-owned business now supplies about 70% of the world's cranberries, says Garima Goel Lal, a senior analyst who covers the beverage industry at Mintel, a global market research firm. "They are the market leader," she says. "Nobody's coming close."

What

The cooperative's international division, Ocean Spray International inc., has succeeded in marketing the cranberry, which is native to North America, to an audience that is mostly unfamiliar with the fruit. For the past few years, 26 to 27% of the total U.S.-grown cranberry crop has been exported, and Ocean Spray is one of the largest contributors, says David Farrimond, executive director of the Cranberry Marketing Committee, a Wareham, Mass.-based "quasi-governmental" organization that was established in 1962 following an amendment to the Agricultural Marketing Agreement Act of 1937 and now markets U.S.-grown cranberries overseas.

Ocean Spray's international sales—in Canada, Mexico, the Caribbean, Central and South America, Africa, Asia-Pacific, Europe and the Middle East—have grown steadily year-to-year since the cooperative began its international marketing efforts in the late 1980s and now account for about one-quarter, or more than $400 million, of the cooperative's total sales.

Ocean Spray's global growth picked up pace just as the cooperative's domestic business stalled. In the late 1990s, the U.S. beverage industry's fruit juice sales hit rough straits as consumers became more concerned about sugar levels and calorie counts. At the same time, Ocean Spray encountered financial difficulties of its own, causing it to cut back on marketing and innovation, says Ken Romanzi, Ocean Spray's SVP and COO of domestic business.

The cooperative's domestic marketing team needed a fresh strategy to mount a comeback, and it found the perfect model to follow in-house: Ocean Spray International. Following the new marketing campaign's launch in 2005, Ocean Spray's domestic sales "went from 10% declines to double-digit increases," Romanzi says. Now Ocean Spray's business, both domestically and internationally, is reaping big rewards thanks to savvy marketing.

How

Traditionally, Ocean Spray's approach to international marketing has been inherently different from its domestic marketing efforts because "the starting point is that you have to explain to consumers in other countries what the heck a cranberry is," says Stewart Gallagher, president of Ocean Spray International and a 16-year company veteran.

So in international markets—such as the cooperative's biggest overseas market, the United Kingdom, or its newest: France, Japan and Mexico—Ocean Spray employees have to practice strategies learned in Marketing 101. Their mission is to explain to consumers what a cranberry is and why they should care.

"We call that [strategy] the 'cranberry mystique': the taste, the health and the heritage." Gallagher says. "We come in and we've got this red thing, which is different [and] that tastes completely different. . . . I'd say the biggest hurdle that we face in almost every market is the taste of the product, but that's our biggest benefit too." International consumers are accustomed to sweet juices, so they have to be prepared for the cranberry's tart flavor, often an acquired taste. "We have to get this product into people's mouths," he says, "and they need to have some positioning up front in terms of what to expect."

Therefore, to address the first part of the cranberry mystique strategy, the company seeks out brand ambassadors in the food service industry, lining up bakers and bartenders to promote the taste and usefulness of cranberry products. Ocean Spray also takes every opportunity to hold sampling events.

The strategy's second part, health, has become Ocean Spray's marketing trump card. Cranberries, it appears, are a veritable miracle fruit when it comes to health benefits, and the Ocean Spray cooperative tries to wring out every last drop of promotional value that that miracle status affords.

Ocean Spray has funded medical research in the United States and abroad, and several studies have shown that cranberries help prevent urinary tract infections. Various research has found that cranberries are rich in antioxidants and cranberry compounds are said to work as "anti-sticking" agents for many kinds of bacteria. Ocean Spray promotes the cranberry's power to prevent heart disease, alleviate stomach ulcers, reduce inflammation from severe gum disease and even protect against food poisoning.

Ocean Spray looks for brand ambassadors in medical communities to tout these health virtues. Definitive health claims for functional foods are hard to come by in the United States, but in some foreign markets, the medical community supports the cranberry's wonders—and in France, Gallagher says, that support is official. There, Ocean Spray earned the right to put an official French health seal on its packaging.

The unique harvest is one of the most powerful marketing ploys that cranberry growers have.

The international marketing strategy's third aspect, heritage, might seem to be simply window dressing, but Gallagher says it's pivotal. Cranberries have a long history in the United States; and Ocean Spray is a farmer-owned company that relies on men and women who plant and harvest the cranberry bogs just as their families have done for generations.

Plus, the cranberry bogs' "wet harvesting" process is a sight to behold. Gallagher says—a sight powerful enough to make consumers want to try products crafted from the little, crimson berries floating en masse in flooded bogs. At harvest time in the fall, the cooperative invites international media to visit Ocean Spray's headquarters in Massachusetts and witness the wet harvest firsthand. Tourists, too, come to take in the beauty of wet harvests in states such as Massachusetts and Wisconsin. The unique harvest is one of the most powerful marketing ploys that cranberry growers have—a notion not lost on Ocean Spray's Romanzi.

Looking to re-enliven Ocean Spray's stale domestic marketing efforts, Ramanzi took a cue from the international division's success. "We actually looked at the playbook that they were using internationally," Romanzi says. He told his domestic team, "Let's assume that nobody here knows what a cranberry is." He hoped to reenergize the cooperative's stagnant sales by putting the cranberry mystique strategy into action stateside.

To that end, the company decided to bring the beauty of a cranberry harvest to consumers. It launched a well-received advertising campaign in October 2005 called "Straight from the Bog" created by Arnold Worldwide, featuring two amiable cranberry growers immersed waist-deep in a cranberry bog discussing the merits of cranberry products. That fall, the cooperative also kicked off its "Bogs Across America" tour, a PR campaign during which Ocean Spray stages mock harvests in cities across the United States.

Both campaigns continue today. For example, last month Ocean Spray set up a cranberry harvest in Rockefeller Plaza. The company handed out free samples and recipes while cranberry farmers waded knee-deep through about 2,000 pounds of floating berries, answering consumers' questions, and explaining the harvesting process and the cranberry's heritage. The company has hosted similar events in cities such as Los Angeles, Chicago and Foxboro, Mass., many of which have been covered by local and national media outlets.

And in 2006, Ocean Spray took its bogs overseas and set up a mock harvest in a stately pond at Kew Gardens in London. The event—featuring more than 5 million cranberries tended to by cranberry farmers flown in from Massachusetts—piqued the curiosity of thousands of passersby and garnered significant media attention.

Of course, Ocean Spray can't take all the credit for the cranberry's global success. The 46-year-old Cranberry Marketing Committee has been marketing U.S.-grown cranberries overseas for nearly a decade using a three-pronged approach very similar to Ocean Spray's, based on taste, health and versatility, rather than heritage. The committee's efforts are funded by assessments paid by U.S. cranberry growers.

"We play off the industry, and Ocean Spray is obviously the biggest branded company in the industry right now," Farrimond says. "We have to maintain a neutrality," he says, but when individual companies like Ocean Spray invest heavily in international marketing programs that successfully boost global consumers' awareness of cranberries, "all boats are lifted."

Critical Thinking

1. How would you present the cranberry to a foreign nation not familiar with the product?
2. Think of another crop/product that has been produced in the United States and has not, for the most part, been marketed in countries outside the United States. Now come up with a pitch for that product to present it to buyers/importers of foreign countries.

Glossary

This glossary of marketing terms is included to provide you with a convenient and ready reference as you encounter general terms in your study of marketing that are unfamiliar or require a review. It is not intended to be comprehensive, but taken together with the many definitions included in the articles themselves, it should prove to be quite useful.

A

acceptable price range The range of prices that buyers are willing to pay for a product; prices that are above the range may be judged unfair, while prices below the range may generate concerns about quality.

adaptive selling A salesperson's adjustment of his or her behavior between and during sales calls, to respond appropriately to issues that are important to the customer.

advertising Marketing communication elements designed to stimulate sales through the use of mass media displays, direct individual appeals, public displays, give-aways, and the like.

advertorial A special advertising section in magazines that includes some editorial (nonadvertising) content.

Americans with Disabilities Act (ADA) Passed in 1990, this U.S. law prohibits discrimination against consumers with disabilities.

automatic number identification A telephone system that identifies incoming phone numbers at the beginning of the call, without the caller's knowledge.

B

bait and switch Advertising a product at an attractively low price to get customers into the store, but making the product unavailable so that the customers must trade up to a more expensive version.

bar coding A computer-coded bar pattern that identifies a product. *See also* universal product code.

barter The practice of exchanging goods and services without the use of money.

benefit segmentation Organizing the market according to the attributes or benefits consumers need or desire, such as quality, service, or unique features.

brand A name, term, sign, design, symbol, or combination used to differentiate the products of one company from those of its competition.

brand image The quality and reliability of a product as perceived by consumers on the basis of its brand reputation or familiarity.

brand name The element of a brand that can be vocalized.

break-even analysis The calculation of the number of units that must be sold at a certain price to cover costs (break even); revenues earned past the break-even point contribute to profits.

bundling Marketing two or more products in a single package at one price.

business analysis The stage of new product development where initial marketing plans are prepared (including tentative marketing strategy and estimates of sales, costs, and profitability).

business strategic plan A plan for how each business unit in a corporation intends to compete in the marketplace, based upon the vision, objectives, and growth strategies of the corporate strategic plan.

C

capital products Expensive items that are used in business operations but do not become part of any finished product (such as office buildings, copy machines).

cash-and-carry wholesaler A limited-function wholesaler that does not extend credit for or deliver the products it sells.

caveat emptor A Latin term that means "let the buyer beware." A principle of law meaning that the purchase of a product is at the buyer's risk with regard to its quality, usefulness, and the like. The laws do, however, provide certain minimum protection against fraud and other schemes.

channel of distribution *See* marketing channel.

Child Protection Act U.S. law passed in 1990 to regulate advertising on children's TV programs.

Child Safety Act Passed in 1966, this U.S. law prohibits the marketing of dangerous products to children.

Clayton Act Anticompetitive activities are prohibited by this 1914 U.S. law.

co-branding When two brand names appear on the same product (such as a credit card with a school's name).

comparative advertising Advertising that compares one brand against a competitive brand on at least one product attribute.

competitive pricing strategies Pricing strategies that are based on a organization's position in relation to its competition.

consignment An arrangement in which a seller of goods does not take title to the goods until they are sold. The seller thus has the option of returning them to the supplier or principal if unable to execute the sale.

consolidated metropolitan statistical area (CMSA) Based on census data, the largest designation of geographic areas. *See also* primary metropolitan statistical area.

consumer behavior The way in which buyers, individually or collectively, react to marketplace stimuli.

Consumer Credit Protection Act A 1968 U.S. law that requires full disclosure of the financial charges of loans.

consumer decision process This four-step process includes recognizing a need or problem, searching for information, evaluating alternative products or brands, and purchasing a product.

Consumer Product Safety Commission (CPSC) A U.S. government agency that protects consumers from unsafe products.

consumerism A social movement in which consumers demand better information about the service, prices, dependability, and quality of the products they buy.

convenience products Consumer goods that are purchased at frequent intervals with little regard for price. Such goods are relatively standard in nature and consumers tend to select the most convenient source when shopping for them.

cooperative advertising Advertising of a product by a retailer, dealer, distributor, or the like, with part of the advertising cost paid by the product's manufacturer.

corporate strategic plan A plan that addresses what a company is and wants to become, and then guides strategic planning at all organizational levels.

countersegmentation A concept that combines market segments to appeal to a broad range of consumers, assuming that there will be an increasing consumer willingness to accept fewer product and service choices for lower prices.

customer loyalty concept To focus beyond customer satisfaction toward customer retention as a way to generate sales and profit growth.

D

demand curve A relationship that shows how many units a market will purchase at a given price in a given period of time.

demographic environment The study of human population densities, distributions, and movements that relate to buying behavior.

derived demand The demand for business-to-business products that is dependent upon a demand for other products in the market.

differentiated strategy Using innovation and points of difference in product offerings, advanced technology, superior service, or higher quality in wide areas of market segments.

direct mail promotion Marketing goods to consumers by mailing unsolicited promotional material to them.

direct marketing The sale of products to carefully targeted consumers who interact with various advertising media without salesperson contact.

discount A reduction from list price that is given to a buyer as a reward for a favorable activity to the seller.

discretionary income The money that remains after taxes and necessities have been paid for.

disposable income That portion of income that remains after payment of taxes to use for food, clothing, and shelter.

dual distribution The selling of products to two or more competing distribution networks, or the selling of two brands of nearly identical products through competing distribution networks.

dumping The act of selling a product in a foreign country at a price lower than its domestic price.

durable goods Products that continue in service for an appreciable length of time.

E

economy The income, expenditures, and resources that affect business and household costs.

electronic data interchange (EDI) A computerized system that links two different firms to allow transmittal of documents; a quick-response inventory control system.

entry strategy An approach used to begin marketing products internationally.

environmental scanning Obtaining information on relevant factors and trends outside a company and interpreting their potential impact on the company's markets and marketing activities.

European Union (EU) The world's largest consumer market, consisting of 16 European nations: Austria, Belgium, Britain, Denmark, Finland, France, Germany, Greece, Italy, Ireland, Luxembourg, the Netherlands, Norway, Portugal, Spain, and Sweden.

exclusive distribution Marketing a product or service in only one retail outlet in a specific geographic marketplace.

exporting Selling goods to international markets.

F

Fair Packaging and Labeling Act of 1966 This law requires manufacturers to state ingredients, volume, and manufacturer's name on a package.

family life cycle The progress of a family through a number of distinct phases, each of which is associated with identifiable purchasing behaviors.

Federal Trade Commission (FTC) The U.S. government agency that regulates business practices; established in 1914.

five C's of pricing Five influences on pricing decisions: customers, costs, channels of distribution, competition, and compatibility.

FOB (free on board) The point at which the seller stops paying transportation costs.

four I's of service Four elements to services: intangibility, inconsistency, inseparability, and inventory.

four P's *See* marketing mix.

franchise The right to distribute a company's products or render services under its name, and to retain the resulting profit in exchange for a fee or percentage of sales.

freight absorption Payment of transportation costs by the manufacturer or seller, often resulting in a uniform pricing structure.

functional groupings Groupings in an organization in which a unit is subdivided according to different business activities, such as manufacturing, finance, and marketing.

G

General Agreement on Tariffs and Trade (GATT) An international agreement that is intended to limit trade barriers and to promote world trade through reduced tariffs; represents over 80 percent of global trade.

geodemographics A combination of geographic data and demographic characteristics; used to segment and target specific markets.

green marketing The implementation of an ecological perspective in marketing; the promotion of a product as environmentally safe.

gross domestic product (GDP) The total monetary value of all goods and services produced within a country during one year.

growth stage The second stage of a product life cycle that is characterized by a rapid increase in sales and profits.

H

hierarchy of effects The stages a prospective buyer goes through when purchasing a product, including awareness, interest, evaluation, trial, and adoption.

I

idea generation An initial stage of the new product development process; requires creativity and innovation to generate ideas for potential new products.

implied warranties Warranties that assign responsibility for a product's deficiencies to a manufacturer, even though the product was sold by a retailer.

imports Purchased goods or services that are manufactured or produced in some other country.

integrated marketing communications A strategic integration of marketing communications programs that coordinate all promotional activities—advertising, personal selling, sales promotion, and public relations.

internal reference prices The comparison price standards that consumers remember and use to judge the fairness of prices.

introduction stage The first product life cycle stage; when a new product is launched into the marketplace.

ISO 9000 International Standards Organization's standards for registration and certification of manufacturer's quality management and quality assurance systems.

J

joint venture An arrangement in which two or more organizations market products internationally.

just-in-time (JIT) inventory control system An inventory supply system that operates with very low inventories and fast, on-time delivery.

L

Lanham Trademark Act A 1946 U.S. law that was passed to protect trademarks and brand names.

late majority The fourth group to adopt a new product; representing about 34 percent of a market.

lifestyle research Research on a person's pattern of living, as displayed in activities, interests, and opinions.

limit pricing This competitive pricing strategy involves setting prices low to discourage new competition.

limited-coverage warranty The manufacturer's statement regarding the limits of coverage and noncoverage for any product deficiencies.

logistics management The planning, implementing, and moving of raw materials and products from the point of origin to the point of consumption.

loss-leader pricing The pricing of a product below its customary price in order to attract attention to it.

M

Magnuson-Moss Act Passed in 1975, this U.S. law regulates warranties.

management by exception Used by a marketing manager to identify results that deviate from plans, diagnose their cause, make appropriate new plans, and implement new actions.

manufacturers' agent A merchant wholesaler that sells related but noncompeting product lines for a number of manufacturers; also called manufacturers' representatives.

market The potential buyers for a company's product or service; or to sell a product or service to actual buyers. The place where goods and services are exchanged.

market penetration strategy The goal of achieving corporate growth objectives with existing products within existing markets by persuading current customers to purchase more of the product or by capturing new customers.

marketing channel Organizations and people that are involved in the process of making a product or service available for use by consumers or industrial users.

marketing communications planning A six-step process that includes marketing plan review; situation analysis; communications process analysis; budget development; program development integration and implementation of a plan; and monitoring, evaluating, and controlling the marketing communications program.

marketing concept The idea that a company should seek to satisfy the needs of consumers while also trying to achieve the organization's goals.

marketing mix The elements of marketing: product, brand, package, price, channels of distribution, advertising and promotion, personal selling, and the like.

marketing research The process of identifying a marketing problem and opportunity, collecting and analyzing information systematically, and recommending actions to improve an organization's marketing activities.

marketing research process A six-step sequence that includes problem definition, determination of research design, determination of data collection methods, development of data collection forms, sample design, and analysis and interpretation.

mission statement A part of the strategic planning process that expresses the company's basic values and specifies the operation boundaries within marketing, business units, and other areas.

motivation research A group of techniques developed by behavioral scientists that are used by marketing researchers to discover factors influencing marketing behavior.

N

nonprice competition Competition between brands based on factors other than price, such as quality, service, or product features.

nondurable goods Products that do not last or continue in service for any appreciable length of time.

North American Free Trade Agreement (NAFTA) A trade agreement among the United States, Canada, and Mexico that essentially removes the vast majority of trade barriers between the countries.

North American Industry Classification System (NAICS) A system used to classify organizations on the basis of major activity or the major good or service provided by the three NAFTA countries—Canada, Mexico, and the United States; replaced the Standard Industrial Classification (SIC) system in 1997.

O

observational data Market research data obtained by watching, either mechanically or in person, how people actually behave.

odd-even pricing Setting prices at just below an even number, such as $1.99 instead of $2.

opinion leaders Individuals who influence consumer behavior based on their interest in or expertise with particular products.

organizational goals The specific objectives used by a business or nonprofit unit to achieve and measure its performance.

outbound telemarketing Using the telephone rather than personal visits to contact customers.

outsourcing A company's decision to purchase products and services from other firms rather than using in-house employees.

P

parallel development In new product development, an approach that involves the development of the product and production process simultaneously.

penetration pricing Pricing a product low to discourage competition.

personal selling process The six stages of sales activities that occur before and after the sale itself: prospecting, preapproach, approach, presentation, close, and follow-up.

point-of-purchase display A sales promotion display located in high-traffic areas in retail stores.

posttesting Tests that are conducted to determine if an advertisement has accomplished its intended purpose.

predatory pricing The practice of selling products at low prices to drive competition from the market and then raising prices once a monopoly has been established.

prestige pricing Maintaining high prices to create an image of product quality and appeal to buyers who associate premium prices with high quality.

pretesting Evaluating consumer reactions to proposed advertisements through the use of focus groups and direct questions.

price elasticity of demand An economic concept that attempts to measure the sensitivity of demand for any product to changes in its price.

price fixing The illegal attempt by one or several companies to maintain the prices of their products above those that would result from open competition.

price promotion mix The basic product price plus additional components such as sales prices, temporary discounts, coupons, favorable payment and credit terms.

price skimming Setting prices high initially to appeal to consumers who are not price-sensitive and then lowering prices to appeal to the next market segments.

primary metropolitan statistical area (PMSA) Major urban area, often located within a CMSA, that has at least one million inhabitants.

PRIZM A potential rating index by ZIP code markets that divides every U.S. neighborhood into one of 40 distinct cluster types that reveal consumer data.

product An idea, good, service, or any combination that is an element of exchange to satisfy a consumer.

product differentiation The ability or tendency of manufacturers, marketers, or consumers to distinguish between seemingly similar products.

product expansion strategy A plan to market new products to the same customer base.

product life cycle (PLC) A product's advancement through the introduction, growth, maturity, and decline stages.

product line pricing Setting the prices for all product line items.

product marketing plans Business units' plans to focus on specific target markets and marketing mixes for each product, which include both strategic and execution decisions.

product mix The composite of products offered for sale by a firm or a business unit.

promotional mix Combining one or more of the promotional elements that a firm uses to communicate with consumers.

proprietary secondary data The data that is provided by commercial marketing research firms to other firms.

psychographic research Measurable characteristics of given market segments in respect to lifestyles, interests, opinions, needs, values, attitudes, personality traits, and the like.

publicity Nonpersonal presentation of a product, service, or business unit.

pull strategy A marketing strategy whose main thrust is to strongly influence the final consumer, so that the demand for a product "pulls" it through the various channels of distribution.

push strategy A marketing strategy whose main thrust is to provide sufficient economic incentives to members of the channels of distribution, so as to "push" the product through to the consumer.

Q

qualitative data The responses obtained from in-depth interviews, focus groups, and observation studies.

quality function deployment (QFD) The data collected from structured response formats that can be easily analyzed and projected to larger populations.

quotas In international marketing, they are restrictions placed on the amount of a product that is allowed to leave or enter a country; the total outcomes used to assess sales representatives' performance and effectiveness.

R

regional marketing A form of geographical division that develops marketing plans that reflect differences in taste preferences, perceived needs, or interests in other areas.

relationship marketing The development, maintenance, and enhancement of long-term, profitable customer relationships.

repositioning The development of new marketing programs that will shift consumer beliefs and opinions about an existing brand.

resale price maintenance Control by a supplier of the selling prices of his branded goods at subsequent stages of distribution, by means of contractual agreement under fair trade laws or other devices.

reservation price The highest price a consumer will pay for a product; a form of internal reference price.

restraint of trade In general, activities that interfere with competitive marketing. Restraint of trade usually refers to illegal activities.

retail strategy mix Controllable variables that include location, products and services, pricing, and marketing communications.

return on investment (ROI) A ratio of income before taxes to total operating assets associated with a product, such as inventory, plant, and equipment.

S

sales effectiveness evaluations A test of advertising efficiency to determine if it resulted in increased sales.

sales forecast An estimate of sales under controllable and uncontrollable conditions.

sales management The planning, direction, and control of the personal selling activities of a business unit.

sales promotion An element of the marketing communications mix that provides incentives or extra value to stimulate product interest.

samples A small size of a product given to prospective purchasers to demonstrate a product's value or use and to encourage future purchase; some elements that are taken from the population or universe.

scanner data Proprietary data that is derived from UPC bar codes.

scrambled merchandising Offering several unrelated product lines within a single retail store.

selected controlled markets Sites where market tests for a new product are conducted by an outside agency and retailers are paid to display that product; also referred to as forced distribution markets.

selective distribution This involves selling a product in only some of the available outlets; commonly used when after-the-sale service is necessary, such as in the case of home appliances.

seller's market A condition within any market in which the demand for an item is greater than its supply.

selling philosophy An emphasis on an organization's selling function to the exclusion of other marketing activities.

selling strategy A salesperson's overall plan of action, which is developed at three levels: sales territory, customer, and individual sales calls.

services Nonphysical products that a company provides to consumers in exchange for money or something else of value.

share points Percentage points of market share; often used as the common comparison basis to allocate marketing resources effectively.

Sherman Anti-Trust Act Passed in 1890, this U.S. law prohibits contracts, combinations, or conspiracies in restraint of trade and actual monopolies or attempts to monopolize any part of trade or commerce.

shopping products Consumer goods that are purchased only after comparisons are made concerning price, quality, style, suitability, and the like.

single-channel strategy Marketing strategy using only one means to reach customers; providing one sales source for a product.

single-zone pricing A pricing policy in which all buyers pay the same delivered product price, regardless of location; also known as uniform delivered pricing or postage stamp pricing.

slotting fees High fees manufacturers pay to place a new product on a retailer's or wholesaler's shelf.

social responsibility Reducing social costs, such as environmental damage, and increasing the positive impact of a marketing decision on society.

societal marketing concept The use of marketing strategies to increase the acceptability of an idea (smoking causes cancer); cause (environmental protection); or practice (birth control) within a target market.

specialty products Consumer goods, usually appealing only to a limited market, for which consumers will make a special purchasing effort. Such items include, for example, stereo components, fancy foods, and prestige brand clothes.

Standard Industrial Classification (SIC) system Replaced by NAICS, this federal government numerical scheme categorized businesses.

standardized marketing Enforcing similar product, price, distribution, and communications programs in all international markets.

stimulus-response presentation A selling format that assumes that a customer will buy if given the appropriate stimulus by a salesperson.

strategic business unit (SBU) A decentralized profit center of a company that operates as a separate, independent business.

strategic marketing process Marketing activities in which a firm allocates its marketing mix resources to reach a target market.

strategy mix A way for retailers to differentiate themselves from others through location, product, services, pricing, and marketing mixes.

subliminal perception When a person hears or sees messages without being aware of them.

SWOT analysis An acronym that describes a firm's appraisal of its internal strengths and weaknesses and its external opportunities and threats.

synergy An increased customer value that is achieved through more efficient organizational function performances.

systems-designer strategy A selling strategy that allows knowledgeable sales reps to determine solutions to a customer's problems or to anticipate opportunities to enhance a customer's business through new or modified business systems.

T

target market A defined group of consumers or organizations toward which a firm directs its marketing program.

team selling A sales strategy that assigns accounts to specialized sales teams according to a customers' purchase-information needs.

telemarketing An interactive direct marketing approach that uses the telephone to develop relationships with customers.

test marketing The process of testing a prototype of a new product to gain consumer reaction and to examine its commercial viability and marketing strategy.

TIGER (Topologically Integrated Geographic Encoding and Reference) A minutely detailed United States Census Bureau computerized map of the U.S. that can be combined with a company's own database to analyze customer sales.

total quality management (TQM) Programs that emphasize long-term relationships with selected suppliers instead of short-term transactions with many suppliers.

total revenue The total of sales, or unit price, multiplied by the quantity of the product sold.

trade allowance An amount a manufacturer contributes to a local dealer's or retailer's advertising expenses.

trade (functional) discounts Price reductions that are granted to wholesalers or retailers that are based on future marketing functions that they will perform for a manufacturer.

trademark The legal identification of a company's exclusive rights to use a brand name or trade name.

truck jobber A small merchant wholesaler who delivers limited assortments of fast-moving or perishable items within a small geographic area.

two-way stretch strategy Adding products at both the low and high end of a product line.

U

undifferentiated strategy Using a single promotional mix to market a single product for the entire market; frequently used early in the life of a product.

uniform delivered price The same average freight amount that is charged to all customers, no matter where they are located.

universal product code (UPC) An assigned number to identify a product, which is represented by a series of bars of varying widths for optical scanning.

usage rate The quantity consumed or patronage during a specific period, which can vary significantly among different customer groups.

utilitarian influence To comply with the expectations of others to achieve rewards or avoid punishments.

V

value added In retail strategy decisions, a dimension of the retail positioning matrix that refers to the service level and method of operation of the retailer.

vertical marketing systems Centrally coordinated and professionally managed marketing channels that are designed to achieve channel economies and maximum marketing impact.

vertical price fixing Requiring that sellers not sell products below a minimum retail price; sometimes called resale price maintenance.

W

weighted-point system The method of establishing screening criteria, assigning them weights, and using them to evaluate new product lines.

wholesaler One who makes quantity purchases from manufacturers (or other wholesalers) and sells in smaller quantities to retailers (or other wholesalers).

Z

zone pricing A form of geographical pricing whereby a seller divides its market into broad geographic zones and then sets a uniform delivered price for each zone.

Test-Your-Knowledge Form

We encourage you to photocopy and use this page as a tool to assess how the articles in *Annual Editions* expand on the information in your textbook. By reflecting on the articles you will gain enhanced text information. You can also access this useful form on a product's book support website at www.mhhe.com/cls

NAME: DATE:

TITLE AND NUMBER OF ARTICLE:

BRIEFLY STATE THE MAIN IDEA OF THIS ARTICLE:

LIST THREE IMPORTANT FACTS THAT THE AUTHOR USES TO SUPPORT THE MAIN IDEA:

WHAT INFORMATION OR IDEAS DISCUSSED IN THIS ARTICLE ARE ALSO DISCUSSED IN YOUR TEXTBOOK OR OTHER READINGS THAT YOU HAVE DONE? LIST THE TEXTBOOK CHAPTERS AND PAGE NUMBERS:

LIST ANY EXAMPLES OF BIAS OR FAULTY REASONING THAT YOU FOUND IN THE ARTICLE:

LIST ANY NEW TERMS/CONCEPTS THAT WERE DISCUSSED IN THE ARTICLE, AND WRITE A SHORT DEFINITION:

We Want Your Advice

ANNUAL EDITIONS revisions depend on two major opinion sources: one is our Advisory Board, listed in the front of this volume, which works with us in scanning the thousands of articles published in the public press each year; the other is you—the person actually using the book. Please help us and the users of the next edition by completing the prepaid article rating form on this page and returning it to us. Thank you for your help!

ANNUAL EDITIONS: Marketing 11/12

ARTICLE RATING FORM

Here is an opportunity for you to have direct input into the next revision of this volume. We would like you to rate each of the articles listed below, using the following scale:

1. **Excellent: should definitely be retained**
2. **Above average: should probably be retained**
3. **Below average: should probably be deleted**
4. **Poor: should definitely be deleted**

Your ratings will play a vital part in the next revision. Please mail this prepaid form to us as soon as possible. Thanks for your help!

RATING	ARTICLE
________	1. Hot Stuff: Make These Top Trends Part of Your Marketing Mix
________	2. Evolve
________	3. The Unmarketables
________	4. Six Strategies for Successful Niche Marketing
________	5. The Secrets of Marketing in a Web 2.0 World
________	6. The Branding Sweet Spot
________	7. Putting Customers First: Nine Surefire Ways to Increase Brand Loyalty
________	8. Making the Most of Customer Complaints
________	9. When Service Means Survival
________	10. Become the Main Attraction
________	11. Beyond Products
________	12. Imaginative Service
________	13. Service with a Style
________	14. Marketers, Come on Down!
________	15. Honest Innovation
________	16. Trust in the Marketplace
________	17. Green Fallout
________	18. What Post-Recession Behavior Means for Marketers Today: New Research Predicts How We Will Spend
________	19. Bertolli's Big Bite: How a Good Meal Fed a Brand's Fortunes

RATING	ARTICLE
________	20. Youth Marketing, Galvanized: Media & Marketers Diversify to Reach a Mercurial Market
________	21. It's Cooler than Ever to Be a Tween
________	22. Sowing the Seeds
________	23. A Shift in Meaning for 'Luxury'
________	24. The Very Model of a Modern Marketing Plan
________	25. Surveyor of the Fittest
________	26. Brand Integrity
________	27. Everybody Loves Zappos
________	28. Rocket Plan
________	29. Big Retailers Seek Teens (and Parents)
________	30. In Lean Times, Retailers Shop for Survival Strategies
________	31. Williams-Sonoma's *Secret Sauce*
________	32. 10 Brilliant Marketing Ideas
________	33. As Seen on TV—And Sold at Your Local Store
________	34. 20 Highlights in 20 Years: Making Super Bowl Ad History Is No Easy Feat
________	35. Best and Worst Marketing Ideas . . . Ever
________	36. Emerging Lessons
________	37. Three Dimensional
________	38. After Early Errors, Wal-Mart Thinks Locally to Act Globally: Wall-Mart Tries to Adapt Its Methods to Local Tastes
________	39. Unlocking the Cranberry Mystique

NO POSTAGE
NECESSARY
IF MAILED
IN THE
UNITED STATES

BUSINESS REPLY MAIL
FIRST CLASS MAIL PERMIT NO. 551 DUBUQUE IA

POSTAGE WILL BE PAID BY ADDRESSEE

McGraw-Hill Contemporary Learning Series
501 BELL STREET
DUBUQUE, IA 52001

ABOUT YOU

Name Date

Are you a teacher? ❒ A student? ❒
Your school's name

Department

Address City State Zip

School telephone #

YOUR COMMENTS ARE IMPORTANT TO US!

Please fill in the following information:
For which course did you use this book?

Did you use a text with this ANNUAL EDITION? ❒ yes ❒ no
What was the title of the text?

What are your general reactions to the Annual Editions concept?

Have you read any pertinent articles recently that you think should be included in the next edition? Explain.

Are there any articles that you feel should be replaced in the next edition? Why?

Are there any World Wide Websites that you feel should be included in the next edition? Please annotate.

May we contact you for editorial input? ❒ yes ❒ no
May we quote your comments? ❒ yes ❒ no

NOTES

NOTES

NOTES

NOTES

NOTES

NOTES

NOTES

NOTES